THE SEX OFFENDER AND THE CRIMINAL JUSTICE SYSTEM

THE SEX OFFENDER AND THE CRIMINAL JUSTICE SYSTEM

By

RONALD M. HOLMES, Ed.D.

Associate Professor
School of Justice Administration
University of Louisville
Louisville, Kentucky

CHARLES C THOMAS • PUBLISHER
Springfield • Illinois • U.S.A.

Published and Distributed Throughout the World by

CHARLES C THOMAS • PUBLISHER
2600 South First Street
Springfield, Illinois 62717

ISBN 0-398-04884-3

Library of Congress Catalog Card Number: 83-5033

With THOMAS BOOKS *careful attention is given to all details of manufacturing and design. It is the Publisher's desire to present books that are satisfactory as to their physical qualities and artistic possibilities and appropriate for their particular use.* THOMAS BOOKS *will be true to those laws of quality that assure a good name and good will.*

Printed in the United States of America
SC-R-3

Library of Congress Cataloging in Publication Data

Holmes, Ronald M.
The sex offender and the criminal justice system.

Bibliography: p.
Includes index.
1. Sex offenders—United States. 2. Sex crimes—United States. 3. Victims of crimes—United States. 4. Pornography—United States. 5. Criminal justice. Administration of—United States. I. Title.
HQ72.U53H64 1983 364.1'53 83-5033
ISBN 0-398-04884-3

To My Family

Tootie

Craig

Steve

Terry

Suzie

Katie

INTRODUCTION

The sex offender, as any violator in the criminal justice system, is an offender because he has transgressed the standards that have been legally codified in a society. The criminal justice system obviously does not concern itself with law-abiding citizens. The sex offender occupies, then, a unique status in the system because of the nature of his criminal act. The professional literature abounds with verifiable research evidence that attests to the status of the sex offender in society and within the system itself.

Because he has violated the sexual being of another and because sex is something that is highly valued and given freely by one person to another, the rapist, child molester, and other sex offenders are viewed as despicable and unclean human beings. There are some people who would not accept the label of sex offender as human.

There are many studies of sex-crazed men who have committed a multitude of heinous crimes against others. In Louisville, Kentucky, recently three young men robbed a self-service gasoline station and abducted the young female attendant. After taking her to a secluded area of the county, they raped and sodomized her. Two of the men continued their savage assault on her, tearing her nipples from her breasts, biting her buttocks, and mutilating her body until she was unrecognizable. They cut her from her anus to vagina. While she was still alive and barely conscious, they put their gun into her mouth and pulled the trigger. The oldest of the three men was sentenced to be executed in the state's electric chair at Eddyville Prison, the eighteen-year-old was sentenced to life in prison, and the youngest, age seventeen, was remanded to the custody of the juvenile court.

The story of this robbery-sexual assault-murder is unfortunately not unique. It happens all too frequently, and one needs only to consult the daily newspapers to see evidence of the ever-increasing numbers of sex-related crimes that are perpetrated. The old debate of are there really more crimes being committed or is there more publicity is really not important. The media has done its share in publicizing the sexual criminal without really seriously dealing with this very important social problem. The fact is that we know more now than ever before, and since this is the case, more should be done than ever before. It is true that many police departments have their own sex crimes units. Many universities have initiated classes on sexual-related crimes. The Southern Police Institute of the University of Louisville, for example, offers a sex crime seminar for professional law enforcement personnel from all over the nation and from various foreign countries. Experts in their fields instruct in this class, sharing their expertise with the students.

Research studies from the various academic disciplines have attempted to show relationships between one variable and other variables explaining the etiology of crime and delinquency. There have been other efforts in the total environment to help in this explanation, including lunar phases, weather conditions, and air pollution. The serious researcher, however, still appears more concerned with single-parent families, poverty, and an unresolved Oedipus complex.

Much energy has been directed toward the discovery of motives, drives, and direct causes of behavior, especially aberrant behavior. The remainder of this book is devoted to the discussion of normalcy, deviancy, theories of learning, and a detailed examination of various sex offenders and their offenses. The offenders themselves have been divided into two main categories, those whose offenses are considered to be nuisances and those whose offenses are considered to be dangerous. Also included are in-depth interviews with offenders, which lend some breath of understanding on a personal level of their own thoughts, desires, and frustrations. The combination of theoretical examination, personal interviews, and case studies are all included to give the reader a range of knowledge input that so far has not been done. The book itself has been divided into twelve chapters. The first two chapters are devoted to a broad introduction into the theory of deviancy and normalcy, with a great deal of attention devoted to historical developments regarding sexual repression and attitudinal development, standards for sexual behavior, and a treatment of sexual aberrations from a psychiatric, psychological, and sociological point of view. Chapters Three and Four are devoted to a treatment of offenders whose sex crimes are included in the nuisance category. Chapters Five, Six, and Seven are devoted to those crimes against children: incest, pedophila, and child pornography. Chapter Eight focusses on adult pornography, and Chapter Nine is dedicated to a study of dangerous sex crimes including rape, pyromania, etc. Chapters Ten, Eleven, and Twelve are devoted to the victims of sex crimes, the treatment of sex criminals, and possible community and system responses to change prospects.

Obviously the text itself is intended to be informative and educational. There is no great claim to be all-inclusive in the coverage of all sex crimes; this would require many volumes, not simply one small book. What is intended is to whet the appetite and cause some curiosity in the reader to be aroused concerning sex crimes, the sex criminals, the victims, and the role of the criminal justice system.

Only until all become sincerely interested in the problem and possible solutions can any progress be made.

ACKNOWLEDGEMENTS

No one starts such a monumental task as writing a book without a strong sense of trepidation despite an equally committed feeling of dedication toward "spreading the word." I have had both feelings, and on more than one occasion decided that the fear of the task outweighed the dedication to the subject. Finally, however, for whatever reason, a decision was made to wage the battle and accept the consequences of my actions.

The content of this book is not intended to be an all-inclusive treatment of the material. Part of the reason for this decision lies in the manifest purpose of the treatment of the topic, another because of a decision to cover a wide range of sex crimes, and a third because of the general lack of information regarding the material itself. Once the decision was made because of the combination of factors, a direction was chosen as far as material and resource persons. No one can embark on a task such as this without the assistance from a variety of persons. This endeavor proved to be no exception.

My first acknowledgement must be extended to all the sources cited in this text. Without their research, theories, and accumulation of general thought, the foundation of the book would be of sand. There are others who have offered their support and expertise. One is careful when it comes to listing a number of people because of the fear of leaving someone out. If this is the case here, I apologize. The alternative is to list no one. This is not an alternative for my value system.

First of all I would like to thank all of my early teachers: Sister Mary Sadism, Sister Mary Holy Water, and all of the other Sister Marys who taught me the values of Traditional Repressive Asceticism. Without their input, I probably would have never developed such an interest in sexual behavior. There are others, both on a personal and professional level, who were instrumental in the content and the development of this text: Doris Bard and Jim DeBurger, both of the University of Louisville, Jerry Beavers,

Louisville Division of Police, John Rabun and Detective Bob Hain of the Jefferson County Commercial Exploited Child Unit, Professor Kerry Rice of the Kent School of Social Work, Robert Baugh, Eastern Kentucky University, Claud Turpin, Mary Ann Eaglin, and Trudy North of the Sex Offenders Group at LaGrange Reformatory, and several sex offenders who were especially candid in their remarks concerning their sex crimes, John, Elzie, and Sonny. Grace Ericksen of the Rape Relief Center in Louisville, Kentucky, also deserves acknowledgement since she and the Center provided this author with a wealth of information regarding rape, and much of the information included in this text on rape was provided by Ms. Ericksen.

A final acknowledgement is extended to my wife, Tootie. Her partial understanding of my interest in aberrant sex is admirable. I am sure she is sometimes concerned about my interests, but seldom does she voice an objection to my research. Her attitude toward my work is composed of patience, compassion, and a faint hope that someday I will move on to other academic interests.

CONTENTS

THE SEX OFFENDER AND THE CRIMINAL JUSTICE SYSTEM

Chapter 1

SOCIETY, MORALITY, AND SEX

Within every society there must exist some form of culture. This culture can be seen as a normative system of behavior, a behavioral system that instructs each person who desires to live within that society as to what is the proper way to behave. Obviously, there are standards that are needed that preserve the society and other norms that are merely "nice" to have. These imperative standards allow all to live and grow as a people and a society. These norms of behavior are called rules, regulations, and laws. In sociological terms, these standards are termed folkways and mores.

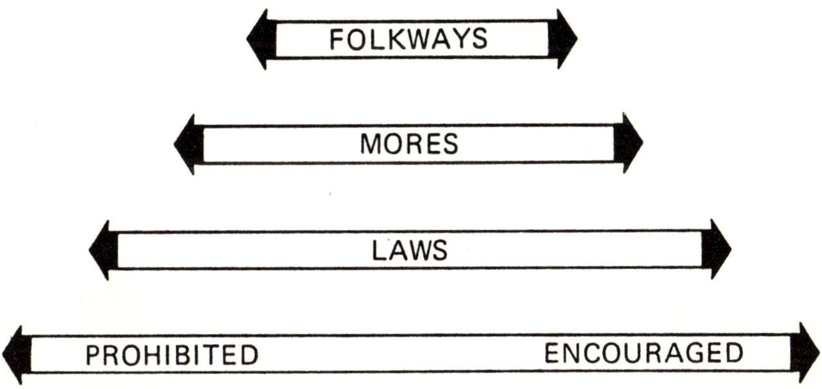

Folkways are those normal, habitual ways of doing things. It is proper to chew one's food with one's mouth closed. It is proper in American society for the male to behave in one fashion and the female to behave in yet another. It certainly makes little difference in walking down the street for the female to walk next to the curb. The original reason for the male to walk next to the street and the female to walk away from the curbing has been lost over time and technological advances. In the Middle Ages, garbage was thrown from many second-story dwellings, and in the age of chivalry it was the male who was the recipient of the thrown debris. In our time, garbage is collected by sanitation workers, placed in compactors, or otherwise properly disposed. Therefore, if the female is walking in the "male's" position, she may become a target for a runaway car but not for last night's leftovers. Parents take great care in the raising of their children to instill proper manners. Little children are "to be seen and not heard." These societal values are inculcated into the mindset of the child from his earliest recollections, and these inculcations are taught by both formal and informal methods. The educational system is also involved in teaching proper modes of behavior. Politeness, courtesy, thoughtfulness, neatness, punctuality, and a multitude of other approved modes of behavior are instructed. This is the manner of approved behavior for parents, improving the social behavior of their offspring so that their children will fit in well with others who are interacting with them in society. These folkways are desired patterns of behavior that if violated will not result in any serious social difficulty. They (the violations) may cause some inconveniences and may result in some lack of socially approved behavior, but society will not crumble and die because a person does not eat with his mouth closed, walks on the wrong side of the street, or performs some other function that violates a custom.

There are, however, another set of folkways that are termed "*mores*." The mores are certainly more serious in the repercussions of violations. The mores are those behaviors that if violated would result in the destruction of society. The violations (either actual or perceived) are thought to be so serious that society has created laws and taboos that forbid the performance of behavior that would destroy society. We do not, for example, allow people in our society to kill one another. Of course, there are social circumstances when we do allow one person to take the life of another, e.g. in the time of war, in self-defense, and during the execution of a person by the state. If we (the society) would permit to allow our citizens to indiscriminately kill on whim or fancy, life in our villages, towns, and cities would be precarious to say the least.

In the area of sexual behavior, there are certain acts that are surrounded by social definitions as encouraged or discouraged. In a wedding recently, the minister went to great lengths to tell the newly married couple of their responsibility to procreate the species. It was their right to copulate and their responsibility to procreate. It was their hope to recreate. As Kinsley Davis once stated in his discourse on human behavior, "... it is not the quality of the act which accounts for its deviancy, but the application of sanctions by those in power." Is it not true that the act of intercourse is the same in the procreation of the species between two married people who truly love each other and are using the sex act as a sign of their love and commitment and the sex act between two people who are complete strangers and one is paying the other for the privilege of vaginal masturbation? The act is the same (intercourse), but the circumstances surrounding the act are certainly defined socially different. When the husband and wife share one another in an intimate and physical manner, we in our society view the act in a positive fashion. When the rapist commits (and this word is used intentionally) sexual intercourse against another human using the same, the society defines the act as a perversion. Is it not in reality the same act? Of course it is. The only difference is the social setting—the social setting defines one set of circumstances as good and the other set of circumstances as bad.

It appears, upon some scrutiny, that the act of sex is the same, but the norms that surround the act are important because it is a norm that is applied by those in power that really accounts for the label of deviant or perverted.

WHAT IS NORMAL?

We are, then, left with a question concerning human actions. What is normal? This is a simple question, but the answer to this question is not at all simple. It is very complex, indeed. When one asks "what?", there is a demand to the receiver of the question to respond in a very direct and simple fashion. But there is no manner in which a short answer in simple terms can be exchanged, especially in the area of "normal" sexual behavior. Sex is a topic loaded with psychological weights and personal restrictions that disable many people in discussing it openly and with candor. Married couples and others who share intimate feelings can talk about a wide variety of topics with no feelings of inhibitions, but when it comes to talking about this very important item in their lives, often there is little but silence. Does one wish to be left with the concept that one is not normal? Do we not always try to be within the normal range of "average?" But what does society really mean when we say "normal?" Naturally, we all know what is normal and what is proper. But whatever we judge normal behavior to be, it is always judged by some standard or norm that has some relevancy to the person who is the judge. What are the standards utilized in judging behavior, including sexual behavior? They, these standards, can be broken down into various categories, and the importance of the category will, of course, vary from one person to the next.

STATISTICAL NORMALCY

This is a very simple norm to use to develop a standard for what is normal behavior. If more than 50 percent of the people do something, then it is necessarily normal behavior. This is easy to judge but dangerous in its application; for example, if 95 percent of the male population perform a certain task, is it normal behavior? It would appear so from a casual point of observation. But let us take a closer look. If we agree with the findings of Kinsey et al. that 95 percent of males masturbate, then is it normal to masturbate? If the divorce rate among all once-married couples is more than 50 percent, then it would be normal to be divorced. Many parents are caught into the web of their teenage child saying to them that Billy, Bobby, Mary, and Jane are all allowed to do something—say, stay out until 2:00 AM, then little Elmo and Naomi should be allowed to do the same. The "all the other kids are doing it, why can't I?" argument is basically predicated upon assuming that the majority is doing the "right" or "normal" thing. How can we ignore this logic? There is no way we can if we blatantly accept the argument that the majority is right, the majority is normal.

We see the statistical norm being used continually in the media. The announcer says that 75 percent of the people use this product to wash their clothing and their detergent gets clothes 85 percent cleaner than Product X. A certain toothpaste results, when used as directed, in less cavities. The advertising industry is attempting to get our business by resorting to numbers so we will purchase their product. After all, if more than half the people buy toothpaste Y and we don't, there must be something wrong with us. Therefore, we find ourselves manipulated by the media, and also we manipulate others in an attempt to legitimize our behavior and the behavior of others.

The numbers game is a dangerous game to play because there is no morality to it. In this instance, the word morality is used not in a religious sense but in a sense of functionalism and social good. Numbers are numbers, and when one places values on the results of the numbers, social functioning and social good can be circumvented or otherwise destroyed.

CULTURAL NORMALCY

In any society there are existent structures that instruct each member of that society what is the normal form of acceptable behavior. The society, the people who live in the culture, must abide by the extant rules and regulations or some form of punishment will be enacted upon them. The punishment itself will, of course, vary from one act to another and from one person to the next. However, as was stated earlier, it is not the quality of the act that accounts for the deviancy but the application of sanctions by those in power. If the act is committed by a person in power in the society, the social sanctions can be expected to be not as severe. The behavior is controlled by folkways, mores, laws, and institutions. Folkways and mores have already been discussed. Laws are those legally sanctioned folkways and mores. As codified folkways and mores, some laws are more serious in their nature than others because some laws are reflected in their base as folkways while others are reflected in the base as mores; for example, in many cities it is against the law for a person to jaywalk. Simple assault is also against the law. However, society will not crumble and die if we permit all citizens to jaywalk, although a few persons may be killed at an intersection. Simple assault also may be hazardous to the victim, but again, society will not be a terminal victim as a consequence of this behavior. But we will not permit people to arbitrarily kill one another. There are laws that prohibit the voluntary killing of another person. First-degree murder is punishable in many states by execution (at the time of this writing, 36 states have the death penalty in force). The murder offense is reflected in the mores base. If we permit people to take another person's life without a just cause, the society might certainly be in danger. This same argument is used in the case of suicide. We will not allow a person to attempt to take his own life. The person, if successful, is obviously beyond the law, but the person who is not successful for one reason or another is often placed in a mental hospital for observation. We will, as a society, permit a person to take his own life if he is truly offering it for an altruistic cause. Roger Young in WWII in New Georgia in the Solomon Islands offered his life for his buddies in a foxhole. He was decorated by the U.S. government and pronounced a hero. The kamikaze pilots in the same war were viewed by the Americans as fanatics. Did they not commit the same form of suicide? It appears that it depends on which side of the cultural fence one is standing on to make that definition. Fatalistic, anomic, and egoistic suicide are all violations of the mores of our society. Regardless of the reason, even if one has cancer and has one day to live, he must suffer the pain until he can die in a natural fashion. Most of us had little patience when George Saunders left his suicide note stating that he was bored with life and had seen all there was to see and done all there was to do. Apparently, after marrying one of the Gabor sisters, one has seen all there is to see and done all there is to do. But this is not a valid reason in our society to commit suicide. This violates the mores of a society that has placed a high value on human life.

Almost everyone in American society is expected to marry. This is a cultural norm. The sole form of marriage is monogamy (which is often confused with monotony). As Robert Rimmer has pointed out in his several works, monogamy is probably the most fragile form of marriage existing today. Successful arguments can be made for other forms such as polyandry, polygyny, and group marriages, but we cling to monogamy as the desired form. We demand the man and woman to be faithful until death "do us part." Why is this the sole practiced form? Jealousy, unfaithfulness, lying, and other forms of human reactions come from the social value of placing everyone in the same marital avenue of one husband and one wife in their white frame cottage with a picket fence surrounding it. Our laws require that if one chooses to marry, there are restrictions: one may marry only one person at a time, he must marry someone of the opposite sex (with few states excepting), and other restrictions that vary from one jurisdiction to another. But this is the norm, and many strive toward this goal with tremendous psychological and personal cost demanded and paid.

The laws surrounding the behavior of societal members often

arise from the needs of the culture. Our contemporary way of life does not have a great need for children. They have turned from being an asset to being a deficit. They are not needed to plow the fields, and to get a young person to carry out the family's garbage is quite a feat.

Nonetheless, it still appears that American culture demands that married couples have children, but the number of desired offspring has diminished. The normative structure of the society (the culture) instructs the inhabitants of the society in the proper ways of behaving. If we behave in the ways the society tells us, we are considered to be normal. More importantly, we consider ourselves to be normal. The words, ideas, customs, and beliefs of a society are openly and clandestinely transmitted to each and every member of the society. This element becomes part of the personality, and we all judge the person according to the standards that become part of the society via the culture. The whole concept of proper behavior and deviancy is relative, and in a culture, what may be considered to be normal one day may very well be defined as abnormal the next.

The concept of deviancy—and it is a concept, not a reality—will then depend on the needs of the society. In ancient Greece when the adult male had a sexual relationship with a young boy who had not reached adolescence, it was done in the open and was not seen as a perversion. Today pedophilia is viewed as an aberration and one of the most putrid forms of behavior. The act is the same; the time and needs have changed. The Oneida Community of America in the mid-1800s endorsed group marriage as their form of marriage; the Mormons around the same time predicated their marital form on the principle, polygyny. Both forms were endorsed by their founders as commanded by God. The law of the culture, however, condemned both forms, and the U.S. Supreme Court ruled in 1899 that the practice of polygyny was not indigenous to the practice of the Mormon faith. Thus, there is often a conflict between the norms that are in existence, and in this case the conflict was in the areas of a cultural norm and a religious norm.

RELIGIOUS NORMALCY

Thus far, two norms have been discussed that influence the process of judging normalcy. The third standard is the religious norm. With many people, this can be thought of as the most important because their religious beliefs play a paramount role in their lives. Religious beliefs have historically been very dogmatic and have neatly placed behavior into one of two dimensions: right or wrong, sinful or not. This leaves the religious person with a comfortable position because, very often, behavior is in the area of black or white, good or bad. Up until the last few years, some young people dating were taught that to hold a kiss longer than five seconds at a time would place them in an occasion of sin. So they would keep one eye closed and the other on their wristwatch. Today, this can be considered a farce and would have little impact on the dating habits of young people. There are many other items that interact on the restrictive behavior of today's people in the area of their sexual behavior and misbehavior. Even the term of misbehavior is viewed as sinful, and the perpetrator is desiring of punishment in the everlasting fires of hell.

Where did we get this traditional repressive attitude regarding sexual behavior? Certainly as a student of history and religion, one gets the idea that early family types were not as restrictive in their sex and sexuality as we are today. The ancient Mesopatamians, circa 3200 BC, were a civilized group of people. Their religion was concerned with fertility, food, and family, and it provided them with the assurance for survival. The gods, Baal and Ishtar, the male and female fertility gods, were worshiped as gods who would provide fertility in all areas.

The religious ceremonies were culminated in the Akita festival, when the high priest and high priestess would celebrate the religious experience in sexual intercourse. The act would be a public affair in front of the congregation. This act does make sense when one keeps in mind that the religion appeared to be preoccupied with fertility. If one is interested in survival, then fertility is in essence to the central thought.

The ancient Egyptians were, like the Babylonians, also concerned with survival, and fertility was a central theme. Atum, the high god, created the world through masturbation, and one drop of his sperm became the earth. Osiris and Isis were the counterparts of Baal and Ishtar, and the holy act was sex. The student in sex history is certainly aware of the Grecian housewife inserting the oiled phallus of Hermes that rested near the entrance of the family's home. The gods Hermes, Cupid, and Aphrodite were central to the worship process, and sex was a vital element.

When the Roman family became an important figure to be considered, Jupiter became the god of the citizens. Venus replaced Aphrodite, and the philosophy of the time was hedonism. All males were expected to be married; if this did not occur within a reasonable time, a severe tax was placed on the young man. Divorce was approved; females were granted almost equal status and sex was viewed as natural and *necessary*.

The Hebrew family, unlike the contemporary families of the Greeks and Romans prior to the time of Christ, were patriarchal, patrilocal, patrilineal, and polygynous. The Jewish father was monarch, and his word was law. Since the female's status was only slightly higher than the sheep they herded, it did not matter where the married daughter lived. The married male child, especially the eldest son, was expected to live near or in the home of the father. The lineage was important only to trace the male's side of the family. However, the Jewish family also institutionalized the practice of polygyny. This also makes sense from a sociological perspective. If you have a small society and you wish it to grow rapidly, this is the form of marital family one would choose. Not only did the Jewish family practice polygyny, they also allowed the father to have concubines. The concubines were provided for sexual release and procreation (for a full treatment of this arrangement, see the story of Abraham and Hegar).

The many attitudes and values that were held dear and true by the various family types as described above were reversed by the early Christian family. The erotic feelings that were thought to be so natural and so fun-filled were now defined as being evil. The whole process of living was now to be devil-like, and sin was under each rock. Many values were reversed; for example, in the Roman family there was no room for the single person and in the Christian family there was no room for the married person. Everyone should be single and preferably virginal. St. Paul in his various writings extolled his followers to follow the example of Christ (as he saw it), and many have called Paul the founder of the repressive asceticism philosophy. Christ Himself was erotic-phobic. He refused to be born of a natural sexual union of a man and a woman. In addition, Christ never married, at least in his public life.

The early Christians followed with fanatical dedication their fierce attack on bodily pleasures. St. Simon the Stylite, a hermit, never bothered to bathe. As a rope that he used as a belt gradually ate its way into his side, the ugly sores became infested with maggots. As the maggots dropped from his side, he carefully picked them up, one by one, and said, "Eat little children what God has given to you."

Jerome advised women, especially virgins, never to bathe because to see oneself nude would be an occasion of sin. In his letter to Laeta, he did advise this mother of a fourteen-year-old daughter not to allow her to bathe for this very reason. Silvia, a virgin, in her sixty years of life never took a bath. Is it any wonder there were so many virgins? Surely the stench of sanctity must have been stupefying (Murstein). The dogma of the virgin birth emerged several years after the time of Christ as well as various other laws of the Church, e.g. the celibacy of the clergy.

The total feeling of repressive asceticism apparently permeated the sexual value structure of the early Christians. These feelings, with all of the positive and negative values and attitudes attached have certainly stayed with us to this present time. Sex is something to be done with someone to whom you are married and with whom you are in love. In some strict Christian religions and sects, procreation must still be a possibility. The violations that occur during daily transactions in our sexual lives are violations only because somewhere someone somehow designed arbitrary norms to establish normalcy and deviancy. The feelings of violation must somehow be negated. It is no wonder that a person feels somewhat helpless because of "normal" transgressions of standards devised by statistics, culture, and religion. How does one attempt to rationalize these transgressions? It is believed that the fourth standard is probably the most important.

SUBJECTIVE NORMALCY

No one wishes to believe that he is truly weird or perverted. Ted Bundy, John Wayne Gacy, or Wayne Williams and all the other famous offenders of contemporary criminal justice all consider themselves normal. Certainly, they are the extreme examples. We, in our everyday sex lives, do not rape, sodomize, commit acts of necrophilia, or otherwise violate "civilized" norms of sexual conduct. A young person may be quite adept at onanism but still suffer great guilt feelings arising from subtle inculcations from the institutions of the family and religion. He may justify his actions by saying to himself that he is really a fairly nice person and cannot be too weird or perverted, and after all . . . " everyone is doing the same thing."

The subjective norm is the most important standard. It defines for oneself the important rules and regulations for behavior. While the aforementioned standards define *for* the person appropriate sex behavior, this standard sets the norm for the individual. It justifies his "deviancy" and legitimizes his actions. He is normal and average. The standard is the *rationalizing* factor in the process of judgment, and as behavior increases in scope, the standard becomes an ongoing process of legitimization. So, consequently, as the behavior merges in antisocial areas, the more important is the role of the subjective norm. When Ted Bundy talked with Ken Katsaris, the former sheriff of Leon County, Florida, about his involvement in the sexual mutilations and killing of more than two hundred women, the twinkle in his eye did not convey a self-assessment of a sexual criminal but only of a person quite caught up in his accomplishment.

NORMAL BEHAVIOR?

So what is normal sexual behavior? This is a question that should be addressed out of society's need for survival, since we personally have much at stake. Those who violate the outer limits of public morality must be effectively deterred and somehow rehabilitated. There may be a better way to address this issue. When one speaks of normal behavior, the norms used (and violated when one speaks of deviancy) are essential in judging normalcy. After all, there can be only deviancy if there are violated rules. The norms change with the times and the needs of the society. When there are specific needs to be satisfied, the norms will change; for example, abortion has not always been against the rules of the Catholic Church. Less than three hundred years ago, the Church allowed abortions if the fetus was less than forty days old if a male and eighty days old if the fetus were a female. Apparently it took twice as long for a female to become a human being as it did for a male. The needs were different at the time and the values were reflected in the needs of the society. These needs of the society become reflected in the attitudes surrounding acceptable behavior. Rather than speaking about normal and abnormal behavior, with all of the connotations surrounding the violation of normalcy, maybe a better approach would be to speak from a perspective of acceptable and unacceptable behavior. This latter terminology, in some manner, removes some of the feeling of negativeness from an attitudinal and value point of view and leads some inference to merely, at one time or another, allowing one to discern appropriate or inappropriate, acceptable or unacceptable. The acceptability will then be judged more on the basis of the needs of a society than on a set of norms that may be out of date and no longer suitable. If a certain social need is manifested, appropriate behavior can be formulated and accepted. Of course, acceptable behavior necessarily must be accompanied by appropriate values and attitudes. The social definition of "acceptable behavior" would then rely on the social demands and the necessity of the functional relationship between the behavior and the values concerning the behavior. Regardless of the type of behavior perpetrated by a member of the society, there would be no longer an artificial criteria of "sin" or theological morality but rather a sense of public morality that has been violated.

Chapter 2

THEORETICAL MODELS OF SEXUAL DEVIANCY

THE PSYCHIATRIC MODEL

The psychiatrist will testify in court whether or not the defendant is sane (depending on who is paying him). While insanity is a legal term and not used in professional psychiatric jargon outside the courtroom, the psychiatrist has evolved as the legal medical "expert" in the field of deviancy. He occupies the highest seat in the professional mental health arena, and he is the father-figure, all-knowing and all-powerful. His theories of deviancy and sexual aberrations have evolved in a continual fashion over the last half-century and will probably continue to evolve as psychiatry becomes more successful in its search for truth in etiology and effectiveness in treatment.

The psychiatric model for deviancy is not simple. It is ladened with terminology that is strange to the person not familiar with the argot of Freud. It appears that we all have within us an entity that wants what it wants when it wants it. This is called the id. The id holds savage impulses centered around immediate gratification. Most of these savage impulses are in the area of sex and aggression. A containing shell that surrounds the id is termed the ego. The ego is the internalized id and is now able to say "I want" or "I need." Still, the ego-dominated person will want satisfaction and has some difficulty in delaying gratification. "I want sex now!" is what an ego-centered person would say. However, it is one thing to say this and quite another to place oneself into the high gear of action. Societal norms exist that restrict sex activity and allow only appropriate sexual behavior. This is where the superego interacts with the id and the ego. The superego, the third-shell surrounding the id and ego, acts as society's censor and tells the ego what it should or should not do. It is permissible, for example, to engage in sex as the ego wants, but there are appropriate times and circumstances for this activity. In our society, the appropriate times are when one is married, when one is in love, or other times when a value will permit. These restrictions levied on the personality by the superego will obviously vary since the restrictions will change as the values of the society change. There is an interaction exchange occurring between the society's needs and the superego. This may not be the traditional point of view of the psychiatric model, but it deserves some serious, professional, theoretical examination. Crime results, then, when the superego is not able to contain the savage impulses of the id.

Since in Freudian psychiatry there is tremendous influence placed on the unconscious (without adequate empirical evidence to substantiate the theory), some mention must be made of the role of the unconscious as far as criminality is concerned. The founder of psychoanalysis had little to say regarding crime specifically. His main theory in regard to the etiology of the criminal was that,

> . . . it was a surprise to find that an increase in this unconscious sense of guilt can turn people into criminals. But it is undoubtedly a fact. In many criminals, especially youthful ones, it is possible to detect a very powerful sense of guilt which existed before the crime, and is therefore not its results but its motive. It is as if it was a relief to be able to fasten this unconscious sense of guilt on to something real and immediate. (Freud)

Many attach themselves to this particular theory.

In the psychoanalytic model, man is basically dominated by instincts, biological drives, unconscious drives, and motives. The eros (the repository of sexual capacity) and the phanatos (the source of aggression) tend to be irrational since they are punitive. The ego, then, is the psychic mechanism designed to control and rationalize the drives so the individual can function in a social matrix. The superego is the combination of the social rules and values. The best the society can hope for in one of its citizens is a compromise. This compromise is an agreement between what the person desires and how much input he allows from his culture as far as social restrictions are concerned. This "social contract" is the restraining force on man.

This psychoanalytic model provides us with a negative, detrimental, and deterministic nature of man. The early experiences in learning will determine later behavior and choice because of limited and unique social experiences. In the psychodynamic view of man, crime is symptomatic. The difference, then, between a law-abiding person and a criminal is the latter's inability to control his aggressive impulses and channel sex and aggression into socially approved avenues of performance.

Alexander and Straub argued that since all people have antisocial tendencies, the relative strength of the id, ego, and superego are the critical factors (Yochelson & Samenow). So crime results when the ego is unable to contain the savage, primitive impulse of the id. The reason for committing a crime is really not known to the criminal. The reason for this is that the motivations for behavior all lie on the unconscious level. Psychotherapy, the basic treatment form in psychoanalysis, is directed at uncovering problems and making the person aware of problematic causes. Of course, merely to understand the problem is not enough. As David Abrahamsen stated, "... the criminal very rarely knows completely the reasons for his conduct." He must be helped to deal with the problem.

The therapist must be interested in dealing with the offender and offering to the patient a hope for change. There must be not only a change away from the problem but also a substitute for dealing with his problem. Therapy itself is directed toward uncovering stresses that are in the unconscious regions of the mind.

The criminal, then, is "said to be 'sick' and can only be restored to 'health' by treating the underlying disorder" (O'Leary & Wilson). The psychotherapist needs to restore the person to healthy standards using traditional psychotherapeutic techniques.

SYMBOLIC INTERACTIONISM

Up to this time, the discussion of personal deviancy has centered around the role of the unconscious and its impact in the etiology of the sex deviant. This philosophy has ignored, generally, feelings of anxiety, frustrations, and deviant behavior. There has been a movement away from the psychodynamic model into several other philosophies. One of the viable models for examination to be included is the social psychological school of thought, in particular the school of symbolic interactionism. In this model, the self is no longer considered to be simply an identity. While it is important for the person to recognize himself as a person with integrity and worth, this self now becomes more than an identity, it becomes "... a process profoundly involved in our coming to know and understand the world" (Lillyquist).

The role of "me" as an understander and integrator of the social world becomes very important. It is important because the self now becomes an evaluator of the social world. Thus it is now essential to consider two components of a developmental process of learning, the self (with the consideration of it being a process) and the external, physical world. The symbolic interaction between the self as process and the world with all of the environmental influences it contains becomes the theater for the molding of the personality.

As an emerging field within the psychological field of personality, Carl Rogers became an early leader in 1951 when he stated, that

1. Each person is unique, with inborn capabilities and a life history like no other person.
2. A person's behavior depends on his or her perception of external events.
3. Since it is the person's perceptions and definitions of reality that underlie the behavior, any long-lasting change in behavior will be the result of a change in those perceptions and definitions.
4. When a person perceives a threat, perception is defensively narrowed and desired change in behavior will be blocked.
5. Out of a person's entire perceptual and psychological field, a portion becomes differentiated and stands out. This is the self-concept, the attitudes that the person holds toward himself or herself.

It is with ease that a concept of "me" or "self" comes into being. The identity process of "me" gradually emerges out of a continual range of experiences with the external world. Bruno Bettleheim, probably not at all identified with symbolic interactionism, nonetheless, has offered an interesting argument for this connection. In his book, *The Empty Fortress*, his theory of crying was discussed. He suggested that females cry and males do not because females are "supposed" to cry and "big boys" are not. Bettleheim stated that very early in their lives males and females are treated differently, even in the hospital nursery. Infants cry because they have made the connection between them crying and the consequences in their external, real world of relief to their discomfort (wet diaper, hunger, etc.). As one grows older, crying becomes inappropriate in these circumstances. As a matter of fact, crying is considered very inappropriate for boys and men in almost every social occasion. "Big boys" do not cry. Men, therefore; do not cry and consequently suffer higher rates of heart attacks, ulcers, and other illness because they are not allowed to vent their feelings. What becomes very interesting for the female is now that even though they are permitted to cry they cry not because they are in the midst of some psychological or emotional trauma but they are crying because it is a learned response to receive attention and manipulate others (this may not be a popular point of view among many advocates of the sexual equality movement). Moreover, there are one of two requirements necessary for the female to cry. Either there has to be someone there to watch her cry or she has to imagine there is someone there to watch her cry. Regardless of how the reader views and values his theory of crying, it is important to remember the role of the social world and its response to the self. Because crying was rewarded by a kind word from the parent, a dry diaper, or a warm bottle, this connection of "self" activity and positive reward by the world is made and becomes stronger when the more positive connectors are engaged between the behavior and the consequences of the behavior.

In the interactionist approach, as differentiated from the psychodynamic model, the person is born with a blank tablet, a value system devoid of judgment. What he holds in his value system is not based on innate feelings of goodness or badness. Upon this blank tablet, the person will imprint the experiences of the social world. The symbolic interactionist no longer has to contend with inborn instincts or aggression or sex and no innate ability to judge the goodness or badness of an act. The self emerges as ongoing and, therefore, continually changes. Actually, it is from this change process that the hope for rehabilitation rests.

The self then emerges out of the interaction of the self and the environment, and behavior is a function of both person and situation (Lillyquist). The input of the total environment, the family, the school, peers, etc., will all have impact on his behavior and personality. He is no longer controlled by instincts, but now he is an acting agent dependent on the significant interaction between the self and the total environment. Each person will interpret his experiences differently, because the world is defined by the person in a phenomenological manner.

If one accepts the statement of Becker that it was not the quality of the acts that accounted for deviancy but the application of sanctions by those in power, then we have an important element in the interactionist theory. The criminal act, be it a property offense, a violent personal offense, or a sexual offense, has to be judged by someone as "bad." The act perpetrated by someone is not totally incidental, obviously, but the definition of criminal will depend on another party or group to account for its criminal attachment. There appears to be a reciprocal relationship existing between the person who commits the criminal act and the person(s) who judges the act to be deviant. The act is judged in the social context of the world.

The behavior of the human, then, rests on the interaction between the personality and the symbolic meaning. The meanings have symbolic attachments, and the self emerges out of the interaction with others. The theories of Cooley (the Looking Glass Self) and Mead (the Generalized Other) are fundamental building blocks for symbolic interactionism. The self-concept is an evaluative process in which the person is able to step outside his own body and judge himself in light of how others see him. The person becomes the object of his own thoughts.

Concerning the theory of social psychology and symbolic interactionism and its explanation of sexual deviancy, it is readily apparent that the etiology of the deviant is not unconscious motives and drives. The role of the environment plays an important role in the development of the personality. The symbols that are attached to everyday sexual behavior are overtly and covertly inculcated into the sexual value system of the person. The sexual socialization of the child is obviously an ongoing process. To the adherent of symbolic interactionism, the learning of sexual behavior is complicated by tremendous input of values that are transmitted by significant others, peers, and the media. Since personality as a concept is an ongoing process, the values attached to specific forms of behavior will change in importance and significance as time, needs, and values change. Some studies in pedophilia (see Cohen et al., 1969) suggest that changes in familiar relationships may account for some incidences of child molestation, especially among the "regressed child offender" category. Sexual difficulties many times can be traced to faulty information processing from those significant others. By the very operational definition of significant, the values inculcated by parents, siblings, and peers certainly have great positive impact on sexual attitudes and later behavior.

It would be a mistake, however, according to a symbolic interactionist, to believe that all sexual behavioral patterns are set by a certain age. There may arise circumstances in adult life that may lead into a self-identification that in turn results in adoption of some specific sexual role pattern (Gibbons).

To briefly summarize the position of symbolic interactionism, the behavior of a person is predicated upon his interpretation of the symbolic world around him. An individual acts toward things on the meanings things have for him. Those meanings are learned in the interaction with others in a continual check and recheck of the interpretation of the meanings (Blumer, 1969). Deviancy is not viewed as a mind-set by a certain age but rather as a behavior that may develop because of societal pressure, family circumstances, or other environmental incidences. Human action, deviant or not, is something that develops in stages, sometimes positive and sometimes negative (Cohen).

In several studies, it was found that there is no great personality differences in the sex offender and other criminal offenders (Gibbons; Ellis & Brancale; Gebhard et al.). From these sources, as well as others, it is the general theoretical feeling that sexual deviants are more alike in their personalities than they are different. The basic reason for their sexual crimes lies not in unresolved unconscious psychological problems but rather in the attachments to meanings and pressures/alternatives in daily life. Little stock is placed also in the medical model of deviancy of inborn criminality.

CONSTITUTIONAL CRIMINOLOGY

Despite the laughter that arises out of the monologue of a well-known comedian who said, "The devil made me do it," there are many people who do believe in factors outside the environmental in crime causation. This belief is reinforced daily in many people's lives regarding the "born criminal," with his high forehead and his shifty, beady eyes. The criminal is a person who is a biological throwback, a reject. But by his being so, society shares no culpability in his antisocial behavior. And, by the same token, there is little that can be done in the rehabilitation of the offender. If he is born to be an offender, then outside of surgery or execution, there is little that can be left for society to offer.

Few theorists in the field of criminology believe that it is totally the environment or totally the heredity of a person that causes someone to be a criminal. For that matter, it would appear to many that it is the interaction of the two elements that accounts for the personality, a personality that may be prosocial or antisocial.

The relatively new field of sociobiology attempts to consider the social environment as well as the biological inheritence of the person to explain his behavior. The interaction of the two in a social context and social contract would result in behavior. This explanation has not always been the case.

CRIMINALITY AS BIOLOGICALLY INHERITED

Two major researchers in the area of constitutional factors in crime causation were Cesare Lombroso and William H. Sheldon. As members of the Positive School of Criminology, both were greatly instrumental in the rapid rise and maintenance of a body of thought that would explain criminality from simply a physical viewpoint and almost completely ignore the environment as an input area.

Lombroso identified himself as an anthropoligical criminologist and attempted to prove to his interested public the relationship between the physical characteristics of a person and criminality. His interest in the biological foundation of crime causation was sparked by an autopsy he performed on an Italian criminal:

> At the sight of that skull, I seemed to see all of a sudden, lighted up as a vast plain under a flaming sky, the problem of the nature of the criminal—an atavistic being who reproduces in his person the ferocious instincts of primitive humanity and the inferior animals. Thus were explained anatomically the enormous jaws, huge cheekbones, prominent superciliary arches, solitary lines in the palms, extreme size of the orbits, handle-shaped or sessile ears found in criminals, savages, and apes, insensibility to pain, extremely acute sight, tatooing, excessive idleness, love of orgies, and the irresistible craving for evil for its own sake, the desire not only to extinguish life in the victim, but to mutilate the corpse, tear its flesh, and drink its blood (Ferrero-Lombroso).

It appears from his writings that Lombroso was greatly influenced by the writings of Charles Darwin and adopted his theory of biological throwbacks, atavism, from the survival of the fittest. In his book, *L'Uomo Delinquente*, he stated that some people are born criminals, and his statistical judgment was predicted upon his study of Italian prisoners with a control group of Italian soldiers.

In his later studies, he relaxed his earlier blanket discourse and estimated that only 35 percent fell into the category of criminal (Lillyquist). He described the "homo delinquents" as possessing "asymmetrical skull, flattened nose, large ears, fat lips, enormous jaws, high cheekbones and mongolian eye characteristics" (Savitz, 1972).

The "bad seed" train of thought has been prevalent throughout the years. The constitutional factor involved has been translated into several forms in addition to Lombroso's theory. So in the early 1900s, Goring replicated the earlier study by Lombroso, using firemen and policemen as his sample. The general findings of Goring indicated no such relationship between physical factors and criminality (Goring). But the old debate has never died. In 1949, Sheldon developed a rather sophisticated system of somatotyping, placing persons into three main body types. His three body builds were endomorphic, ectomorphic, and mesomorphic.

The endomorph is a person who is fat and soft. In his relationships with others, he is gregarious, likes to be around others, is jolly, and easy to get along with. He will seldom get in trouble with authorities because of his temperament and disposition. His temperament and disposition are determined by the body build. The ectomorphs are the Don Knotts types. He is thin and fragile, easily excitable, afraid of people, and introverted. He does not usually get into trouble because of his lack of self-confidence and his inability to become involved with people. The mesomorph, however, is an entirely different person. He is the athletic, muscular person who, because of his physique, is competitive and full of adventure. Lombroso spoke of the criminal type having an "... irresistible craving for evil for its own sake ..." and having an "... insensibility to pain ..." (Ferrero-Lombroso) and Sheldon describes his mesomorph as being ruthless, psychopathic, and indifferent to pain.

Some studies do indeed show some relationships between physical characteristics and criminality. Sheldon's studies of delinquent youth did indicate more than a casual relationship between juvenile delinquency and body types (Sheldon).

The famous researchers, Glueck and Glueck, alluded to their findings on delinquency and body types when they reported that delinquent boys were larger and stronger than nondelinquent boys (Glueck & Glueck, 1950). In the early 1970s, Cortes and Gatti reported that the male delinquent sample in their study were significantly more mesophorphic than their control, nondelinquent sample (Cortes & Gatti).

Over the years, the physical attributes of a person as a primary contributor to his criminality has not been dismissed. In a publication by Halleck, it was suggested that people with abnormal electroencephalograms (EEGs) were more likely to be criminals.

So the sex offender in this particular model would be a person who, because of physical characteristics, would run afoul of the sexual laws of a society. It simply would not be a conscious choice for him to commit a sex offense. Moreover, it would not be only those constitutional factors with which one is born. He may in his later years be a victim of some form of chemical inbalance in his system. Homosexuality, for example, may not be born, but may actually be affected by a lack of equilibrium between male and female hormones (Portillo).

The treatment program for the sex offender would lie in the professional realm of the physician and other members of the medical team. The patient is to be quantified in every detail, and rehabilitation would be realized not usually through psychotherapy or environmental engineering in its broadest sense, but rather through medical care and perhaps an operation. Lobotomies may be a treatment procedure for violent sexual offenders and injection of male hormone(s) for some sexual offenders may be the best suitable treatment plan.

SUMMARY

From an examination of these three models of the etiology of behavior, specifically criminal behavior, it can readily be seen that all three have a different focus on etiology and a different implication for treatment. The role of the unconscious is paramount as far as the psychodynamic model is concerned. The positive model certainly views criminality in a different perspective, and treatment is more predicated on traditional medical theory since criminals are thought to possess constitutional factors that predestine them to be violators. The social psychological model views deviancy as a learned set of behavioral adaptations, with special attention being directed to significant others and the importance of symbols in the interaction with others. The change from criminal to noncriminal does not lie in many hours of psychotherapy, probing the unconscious or receiving injections or operations, but rather through a process of resocialization, relearning the predominant prosocial societal attitudes for positive functioning within the society.

These points of view, as well as others not covered here, are not considered to be all-inclusive. There are theoretical gaps in all the models. Perhaps, then, it is best to say that deviancy, while it is still considered an "artificial" label, has a base that lies not in any one school of thought but has a range of causes that vary from one individual to the next. The author could have very well covered in some detail other theoretical models of deviancy. The deviancy of the sexual act will obviously depend on the definition of the situation. The roles to be learned with the value attachments are all learned in symbolic interactionism. Perhaps the total concept of deviancy could be better understood if the social context of the act itself could be determined. The pathology of the offender in its social context is what is to be evaluated. This dead system of reciprocity between the act and the social system is the theater for deviancy. All the symbolic meanings from whatever theoretical point of view are to be considered and weighed regarding input and validity of input for a final judgment of the deviancy and sexual affront.

Volumes upon volumes could be written concerning theories of deviancy. It is not, however, the general purpose of this book to be definitive regarding sex crime causation. The etiology must be considered to be in multiple causes and the "cures" for behaviors that have been termed criminal must lie somewhere in the social world. What follows in this book is a general listing of sex crimes and a plan for societal action in the area of dealing with the offender and the issue of individual and societal responsibility.

Chapter 3

NUISANCE SEX CRIMES

Among any group of people, there are ones who violate certain folkways. These offenders do not endanger the very existence of society, but they do cause some discomfort and a general level of alarm and suspicion. This same behavioral and value reaction can be seen among citizens when it comes to the nuisance sex offender. By its very operational definition, this person does not cause a life-threatening situation to his victim(s). He may be guilty of only invading the privacy of another, as in the voyeur-victim situation, or he may be an active actor in invading the visual field of another, the exhibitionist. Regardless of the social setting, the nuisance sex offender does not endanger society's survival. What he is doing is a bother, and his actions cause some discomfort. He is viewed in a different manner from the child molester, rapist, or piquerist. He is often treated with some humor and a flippant remark because of the lack of danger he portrays. Nonetheless, he is still in violation of the sexual norms, and society feels some responsibility for his actions and his "rehabilitation."

What are these nuisance sex crimes? This chapter will list and discuss in some detail these sex acts. Much general discussion of etiology has been deliberately omitted. Because of the treatment of the causative factors in the previous chapter, it is believed it would not only be repetitive but also very boring. What the reader should keep in mind is that, while these acts are not significant in their danger to others, they do occur in great numbers, and there is some evidence that some nuisance sex offenders do gravitate to more serious sex crimes.

FETISHISM

It has been said that many people are affected in an erotic manner by certain inanimate objects. Thus, the operational definition of a fetish object is that it has attached to it some sexual overtones. This, obviously, would differ from partialism. The fetish object, then, means different things to different people. It would appear that fetishism is on a continuum and occurs in degrees. In its mildest form, a fetish exists for all and elicits a pleasurable response. The mind boggles when the range of fetishes are examined. The objects can be anything: bras, panties, garter belts, spiked heel shoes, raincoats, and a variety of other objects. It is with some certainty that there must be someone who has a fetish for exhaust pipes.

Fetishes play a great role in pornography. Black garter belts, high heel shoes, and other popular objects are all prevalent. The girl in the fold-out in *Hustler* is often depicted with garter belt, black hose, and high heel shoes. Men, because they are more visually stimulated than women, are obviously more involved in the fetish mode. By being on a continuum, it is believed that a fetish is at least statistically normal. It does not become an obstacle to "normal" sexual functioning. But, when the male can only achieve sexual gratification when his partner wears boots, a fur coat, or some other object, the fetish itself becomes a hindrance to sexual functioning.

Fetishes are almost never found in females. This is male "domain." The exact figures are unknown because of the lack of accurate data. Much such data as collected do not reflect the true pictures. If we say that a certain percentage of males are "leather freaks," then we cannot truly substantiate the statement because much of the data is hidden by the lack of data by "closet" cases. What can be said with some degree of accuracy is that more males than females are involved in fetishism.

PARTIALISM

This particular type of fetish is an erotic attachment to bodily parts. In American society there is a great deal of attention paid to women's breasts as a bodily fetish, or more properly defined, as partialism. Erotic feelings are attached to body parts, be they breasts, legs, ankles, blond hair, or whatever physical characteristic the person possesses. Ted Bundy, the self-admitted killer of scores of women in several states, killed only women with long brown hair, hair that was parted in the middle (Rule). Dolly Parton, a pop-country music singer, is often described as a person with a great deal of talent in her field, but her greatest known attribute is the size of her bosom.

As in the case of fetishism, most Americans are involved in partialism. Partialism is alluded to in our advertising campaigns when the viewer is bombarded by body bits to sell a product. Obviously, it is when the dedication to a partialism interferes with normal sexual functioning, when one can only reach sexual gratification with a blond female with large hips, then partialism can be termed as a perversion. It is clear to many that we all prefer certain physical attributes. Moreover, it can be said that the person we *choose* to become sexually involved with is an ideal failure. Regardless of the beauty possessed by the partner, this human does not possess all of the qualities and possess them so perfectly as to satisfy the pursuer. The striving for the perfect without a realization of the imperfect is the plight of the person with a partialism for the perfect body, the never-ending search for the "10."

The partialist, be he wherever on the continuum of normal to abnormal, requires certain physical characteristic(s) to be present in the sexual partner for sexual satisfaction to be experienced.

VOYEURISM

As in the case of many aspects of sexual behavior, the behavior of the voyeur is shared by many. The obsession of the voyeur is to view the acts of another without the permission of the victim. Despite the popular point-of-view that the voyeur only derives sexual satisfaction from viewing another in the act of dressing or undressing, bathing, or in some alternative private situation, there is some indication that the mere invasion of another person's privacy is enough to erotically arouse the perpetrator (Bartol).

The practice of voyeurism, also known as scoptophilia or inspectionism, is on a continuum. The average man on the street receives some form of erotic satisfaction by viewing an attractive female. To some, a completely nude female is very sexually appealing. To others, females wearing leather boots or high heels or females with large bosoms are sexually arousing. The voyeur, or the inspectiontist, has a tendency to gain sexual excitement and gratification from the observation of others in usually some form of sexual act(s). From various sources of research, it appears that the voyeurist is almost always male and most of their satisfaction is received from watching females undressing or couples engaged in some form of sexual relationships. In some instances, there may be a victim-doer-victim relationship between the voyeur and his victim. There have been some cases where a female exhibitionist will leave her blinds up so a voyeur may invade her "privacy." However, this in no way detracts from the culpability of the voyeur. He is invading the privacy of another person, and this may be enough to construe it as a nuisance type of sex offense.

It must be, though, that the act of voyeurism is not any more harmful than any other form of nuisance sex crimes, since there is no strong research to show that the voyeur progresses on to more serious sex crimes. The Queen's Bench study, for example, showed that less than 10 percent of the voyeurs involved themselves in serious sex crimes later in their careers, such as rape (Savitz & Johnson), and "Contrary to rumor, the typical peeper is not criminally inclined and seldom attacks women" (Goldenson).

The usual voyeur receives his sexual high from watching and invading the privacy of another person. He may then duck behind some shrubs or into another private area, masturbate, and fantasize about his immediate past experience.

The chief explanation regarding the etiology of the voyeur is that he tends to be a person who is very shy, typically an isolated individual who is introverted and may doubt his sexual adequacy. The act of invading the privacy of another gives him satisfaction without risk of rejection or failure (Goldenson). The male as a voyeur deviates from normalcy because of his obsession with viewing sexual acts by others. It is thought that voyeurism as a continuum type of behavior is prevalent in most people, especially males. An attractive female walking down the street is certainly viewed by most males in various degrees of approval or evaluation. What separates this "normal" method of observation is that the voyeur has a need for a persistent search for opportunity to spy on others, deriving most or all of his sexual satisfaction from observing them.

The treatment approaches toward the voyeur usually can be centered around two models, the psychodynamic and the behavioristic. The former views the voyeur as being one who is shy, timid, and reserved. He is trying to regain some of his self-image and sexual identity reinforced by this behavior. The treatment in this instance would be of the interview variety and would center around relationships and the need to experience this form of sexual behavior in order to have an orgasm. Other data seem to suggest that voyeurism is a deviation from normal sexual behavior, but it is not a crime in and of itself. Treatment should emphasize the control (rather than the elimination) of voyeuristic sexual impulses (Smith, 1976). In the first treatment model, the etiology of the problem would be examined, and in the latter, it may be necessary only for the voyeurist to gain some insight into the control of his behavior, not necessarily the need to eliminate it.

EXHIBITIONISM

Exhibitionism refers to the intentional exposure of sex organs under inappropriate conditions (Ullmann & Krasner). There are some indications that exhibitionism is one of the most frequent sex offenses known to the criminal justice system. However, the exhibitionist is not, in all cases of persons charged with exhibitionism, the true exhibitionist at all. In the case of a skid row alcoholic relieving himself in an alley or a door stoop, the act may be more a matter of poor judgment than a deliberate exposure of one's genitals.

The incidences of exhibitionism among females are extremely rare, so it is quite logical to believe that exhibitionism tends to be a male sexual deviation. There is another side to this argument. Males make the laws, and since this is the case, the laws against women appearing in the nude, or at least exposed, do not carry the same penalities doing the same thing. The exhibitionist will expose his genitals usually to the members of the opposite sex and sometimes to children of either sex. As far as the situational characteristics of the exhibitionist, it seems that the most favorite and frequent places of exposure are public, such as streets, parks, movies, and other places where people gather. If the exhibitionist has children for a target, it would be assumed, therefore, that most of his acts of exposure would be in the area of schools and playgrounds. The automobile also tends to be a favorite method of use for the exhibitionist, as he may pull up to a truck stop or street corner and expose himself to the person standing there.

What is so interesting about the typical exhibitionist who has been termed as being quite shy and passive is that the act of exhibiting himself is not a prelude to heterosexual relations but is in and of itself the man's sexual act, which usually culminates in masturbation. The "street flasher" normally stereotyped by the grandfatherly type will open his raincoat, make his impression, and then run or walk away. The typical exhibitionist prefers strangers and usually, if the victim is an adult, a single female or, if the victims are children, to a group of children.

There is some evidence that exhibitionists are involved in some form of partialism because many of their victims share the same physical characteristics: a girl with shapely legs, females with hair parted in the middle, or other such characteristics. What is so unusual regarding the behavior of the exhibitionist is that there appears to be almost a neurotic need to be caught. The act is usually performed very routinely as far as the time of the day and the location, and the behavior of the exhibitionist is so predictable that arrests are usually easily made.

As far as the criminal justice system is concerned, the exhibitionist composes probably the largest single group apprehended for sexual offenses. As was stated earlier, rarely are they placed in jail or prison. In the preponderance of the cases, these men tend to have come from homes that can be typified as possessing a philosophy of traditional repressive asceticism. A dominant mother is usually present, and the sexual feelings and overtones are restrictive, to say the least. The exhibitionists according to some theories are thought to be strongly inhibited and too emotionally immature to have relationships with the opposite sex; moreover, masturbation is not an effective outlet unless it is under the special excitement of exposing themselves.

In regard to the characteristics of the offender, it appears that in many cases the peak period of exhibitionism is usually between the age of fifteen to thirty years of age. If exhibitionism commences after that, often it is accompanied by the onset of senility. Not an abundance of statements can be made regarding any abnormal incidences of higher or lower level of intelligence. Exhibitionists tend to have an average intellectual ability, but because of their relationships within their home, they tend to be underachievers both educationally and occupationally. Even though the data tend to show this underachievement, they seem to have stable and reliable work histories. Severe emotional problems, possession of mental illness, or other bizarre emotional components of the exhibitionist are not found in any more frequency than in the normal population. The main reason for the exposure of the genitals may lie in the need to observe the reaction of the victims' eyes of fright and shock. By observing the reactions of the victims, he then will become sexually excited and will probably masturbate after the act. What is so surprising between the victim and the doer is that if the victim fails to show fear or fright, the exhibitionist will usually suffer disappointment and a lowered self-esteem.

In regard to marital life, it appears that many of the exhibitionists are married, but their relationships with their spouses are not what they feel they should be. The marriages are often a result of family pressure, and in practically all cases they have failed to achieve satisfactory sexual relations with their wives (Goldenson). Many men who are exhibitionists will expose themselves to others after they have received a negative stroke to their ego. So it does appear that the urge to involve themselves in this act of sexual behavior stems in part from their feelings of inadequacy.

Each time the exhibitionist performs his act of exposure and is positively rewarded, the more he is entrenched in exposing himself. What is all the more difficult, as far as the criminal justice system is concerned, is that adults seldom report to the police about a flasher. Most of the complaints come from parents whose children have been victimized.

There appears to be a great deal of literature involved when it pertains to exhibitionism. The review of the literature of exhibitionism reveals no empirical support for any particular etiological theory, although the behavioral approach is potentially the most useful. It seems, however, as was stated earlier, that there is a varied composite of social factors involved in the etiology of the exhibitionist.

One study suggested that the phallus serves to catch the eye and the attention of the victim, so that the exhibitionist acquires the "power" he needs. It was suggested that exhibitionism can be therapeutically understood and treated in the context of the privacy of the "eye" (Bodenheimer). This is obviously a psychodynamic assumption concerning the etiology of the exhibitionist, where power is manifested symbolically in the projection of the penis. However, other treatment approaches tend to be more practical such as exhibitionism being seen as a symptom. Treating current significant relationships as the focus of concern may provide strong opportunities for inducing satisfactory changes (Johnson).

Regardless of the frivolity with which most people view exhibitionism, this tends to be a sex crime that on one hand is not particularly dangerous and on the other hand does become quite a nuisance, especially when children are involved. The key to change appears to lie more in the area of looking at present relationships and trying to amend, change, or restructure them.

TRIOLISM

A variation on the voyeuristic theme is triolism. The triolist is one who receives some sexual satisfaction by seeing others, along with himself, in sexual scenes. This particular type of perversion appears more frequently in men than women and is a common type of behavioral pattern among swingers. Swinging in the United States has been with us for many years. However, only within the last few years has swinging reached the popularity that it has today. There are numerous publications devoted to swinging: *The American Swinger, The Kindred Spirit*, and *Select*. The latter two are probably the slickest of the publications. These magazines invite their subscribers to list in their personal ads sexual preferences as well as prohibitions.

With the advent of the instamatic cameras, video-tape camera equipment, and the lax enforcement of laws regarding the commercial handling of photographic material, the triolist may take a picture or film a scene of himself and/or others in their various sexual activities.

It is obvious that not all involved are swingers. It seems that this particular type of nuisance sex activity is one of which we will never know the full extent, since most of it is done behind closed doors, undoubtedly including mostly husbands and wives. In adult book stores, it is not uncommon to see triolism in advertisements. The mirror that can be attached to ceilings with suction cups, rented video-tapes, and cameras all lend themselves to the desires of the triolist.

In some cases of triolism, men force their wives to have adulterous relationships with other men so they can watch; some other cases have been reported where fathers watch their daughters in sexual relations with boyfriends, siblings, and cousins (Smith, 1976). This particular type of behavior in swinging is explained by one theorist as being a subculturally approved latent homo-

sexuality practice (Rosengard, 1971). The writer believes that it is not the sexual excitement of the wife that arouses him, because she is available at all times, but the thrill is the excitement of the friend. It is clearly the friend, not the wife, whom he desires, but this would be too painful for him to admit.

Such treatment for people who involve themselves in triolism would be similar to those who are involved in voyeurism. With the added component, at least in some people's minds, of homosexuality, it seems that triolism, while indeed a nuisance at least from the point of view of one of the partners who is being forced into this behavior, still remains in the area of nuisance and, at least at this point in time, is not in the area of dangerous sex crimes.

KLEPTOMANIA

Kleptomania can be defined as a compulsive urge to steal. While historically it has been found that most kleptomaniacs are females, and it does appear from the review of the literature that approximately 90 percent of them are women, there is growing evidence that kleptomania may be especially prevalent among young males.

What separates the kleptomaniac from the ordinary thief is that often the article stolen has some form of sexual overtones. It can be said, therefore, that there is a fetish involved, with the kleptomaniac and his theft. Men may utilize the fetish object for masturbatory activities or at least have it within their psychological field of vision. Women may steal an object from a store and experience some form of sexual rush from the anticipation and the realization of their theft.

Kleptomaniacs are found in many instances to come from families where stealing is not a necessity as far as obtaining the material objects they wish. It appears that their families certainly are economically able to purchase those objects that have been stolen. The danger and excitement, not only the symbolism involved, is believed to contribute to the sexual stimulation. One convicted murderer told this writer about one of his fellow convicts who reached a sexual rush and orgasm whenever he burglarized a home. The moment he entered a window and took an article of clothing, he experienced an orgasm.

The treatment of kleptomania tends to fall into categories around psychotherapy or behavioristic therapy. Warman reported of a fifteen-year-old female who was treated for her kleptomania using aversion therapy, and it appeared quite successful. Behavioristic treatment with a great deal of success has been reported by Keutzer and Marzagao. Despite the use of the behavioristic model in treating kleptomania, it appears in much of the literature that kleptomania is still viewed as a sexual nuisance crime as a result of the influence of the psychosexual model. The stealing is interpreted as an act of revenge against parental authority. It also may be an expression of more general hostility against society in its ethical standards and conventions. Any of these motives operate apparently on an unconscious level and may explain why so many kleptomaniacs continue to steal until they are caught (Goldenson).

Kleptomaniacs engage in antisocial behavior because of poor impulse control rather than a deeply motivated compulsion to steal. In recent years, it appears that aversion therapy has provided promising results (Barker, 1968), and tranquilizing and antidepressant drugs have proved successful (Barker, 1967).

FROTTAGE

Frottage is a nuisance sex crime in which sexual satisfaction is reached by touching, rubbing, or hugging a person of another sex. What is so interesting about frottage is that so many times the females victims are not aware that they have been victims at all. In crowded places such as elevators, subways, busses, etc., while people are closely packed together in a normal fashion, the person who is into this particular type of deviation may rub the body part of another and receive sexual pleasure.

Frottage (French for rubbing) often passes unnoticed and probably is more common than is recognized. Frottage has many characteristics involved in ordinary sex foreplay and is considered only a perversion when the frotteur does not or is unable to realize sexual gratification through normal sexual coitus. The exact reason for frottage is unknown. The psychodynamic explanation may be that there is some form of instinctual biological basis for the need to rub against another person and receive some form of gratification from this. However, the frotteur who adopts this particular form of sexual stimulation may involve himself more and more because of his feelings of inferiority, insecurity, and inadequacy.

The basic explanation for frottage is probably not too different from the explanations of the other nuisance sex crimes. In the very famous *Psychopathia Sexualis*, the author explained in a very simplistic manner that frottage is a masturbatorial activity of a bisexùal individual who is uncertain about his virility. What separates frottage from the dangerous sex crimes is that it appears that frottage is used as a tool for masturbation and is quite prevalent in conjunction with fantasies (Kraft-Ebbing).

It is in some ways amazing that more information is unknown about this particular form of sexual behavior. Perhaps because of its hidden nature and its lack of scientific inquiry, there is no direct empirical evidence that the frottuers may involve themselves more frequently as time progresses and then move on to more dangerous sex crimes such as rape and lust murders.

BESTIALITY

Domesticated animals have always held a special place in the minds and the homes of civilized man. There has been research concerning domesticated animals that has evidenced facts about territoriality, dependence, and aggression. The personality of the pet owner has been researched with particular attention to the reasons for acquiring a pet, the choice of a pet type, the role the pet plays in its master's life, and the master's reaction to the pet's death. There seems to be some evidence that regardless of the role of the pet in man's existence bestiality has never been practiced by the majority of humans. A review of the literature reveals this belief. Bestiality as a behavior pattern appears to be a result of a wide range of psychopathological conditions (Bauer, Friedel, & Hagenbuchner).

Regardless of the moral values that appear in American culture, bestiality appears not to play a major danger to American society. It seems that in some circles this form of sexual behavior was, among all sex crimes, the least frequently reported (Kinsey, 1948, 1953). Kinsey's studies reported that man's sexual contact with animals accompanied by orgasm was reported by 17 percent of males residing in rural areas and only 3 percent among women from the same geographical areas.

Bestiality as a form of sexual behavior is a very prevalent theme in pornography. A woman having sex with snakes, dogs, horses, and others is prevalent in many men's fantasies. The literature also contains many fables and myths about sexual relationships between humans and animals. The Old Testament contains in very explicit fashion prohibitions against bestiality for men, but it was not prohibited for women. Later, however, Jewish women were prohibited from bestiality, and Leviticus 18:22–23 says, "And you shall not be with any beast and defile yourself with it." The ancient Romans conducted special festivals in which many women were captured and exposed to animals who were specially trained to have sex with them, eventually killing the women for the sport of the spectators.

It rarely appears that bestiality assumes any form of important type of sexual behavior in human life among the majority of any population. Most contact is coitus with animals who have rather even temperaments and less frequently with oral stimulation experience.

An accompanying sexual perversion to bestiality is that of zoophilia. Zoophilia is an unnatural fondness of animals. There are cases brought almost daily to the attention of the civil courts of a person who dies and leaves her estate to her pet animals. A case recently was discovered where an elderly lady was reported by neighbors because of the stench that was caused by her collection of more than sixty cats. Some of the cats had already died, and she had placed these animals in her freezer. The police officers, as a result of their exposure to this scene, had to have their clothes, the police car, and even their own homes deloused because of ticks, fleas, and other parasites. The woman was cited for health violations.

It appears that zoophilia is more prevalent among older people than younger persons. It may be that in our society the elderly are more lonely and turn to animals for comfort and support. It is true that animals, especially dogs, are very supportive and demand little from their owners other than some attention. However, zoophilia can be hazardous to one's health. In another case recently, an elderly couple had been reported to the health department by neighbors because of their large collection of dogs. The police stated that there was so much dog dung in the home they were unable to stand up and walk through a doorway because it had piled up so high. Apparently, the two had never cleaned up after their pets had urinated and defecated.

Zoophilia does not involve sex with animals, and mistreatment of the animals would be unheard of.

There appears to be a prevalent theme in witchcraft, however, concerning the extreme form of bestiality, which is accompanied by sadism. The excitement is not merely copulating with the animal but in killing the beast at the moment of orgasm. It should be obvious that bestiality can be seen only as a perversion when it interferes with normal sex relationships between humans. As was the case in the other forms of sexual perversions, bestiality may reflect a fear of inadequacy and rejection in approaching other human beings for the purpose of sex.

COPROLAGNIA

Coprolagnia is a sexual variation in which the sexual gratification is gained and associated with fecal matter. The coprophiliac has a desire to eat, smell, or handle human excrement. The accompanying sexual variation in this particular type of perversion is urolagnia, which is associated with the handling, smelling, or drinking of urine.

Probably one of the more renowned coprophilists was Adolph Hitler, who supposedely never had sexual intercourse with women. "Several of his intimate female friends reported that he required them to degrade him, kick him, and especially to squat over him and defecate and urinate on him" (Smith, 1976).

The coprophiliac and the urophiliac have a particular type of perversion that lends them to little involvement as far as damage to others, but the health hazard associated with these deviations is the bacteria located in the fecal matter. For this particular reason, it has been noted that the life span of the true coprophiliac is relatively short. In the book *Pauline*, the Oatmeal Cookie Man is a shining example of the taste of the coprophiliac. In the most extreme case, the coprophiliac can only obtain sexual satisfaction when he is feeling, handling, or smelling excrement. There once was a case in Kentucky where a man had been missing from a party located in a large horse farm estate. This particular estate still had several outhouses in operational condition. The man had been missing for several days, and the last persons to have seen him were guests at the party. His body was found by investigators at the bottom of a pit in an outhouse. He had lowered himself into the pit, and his rope had broken. He fell, hit his head against the side of the wall, and drowned in the excrement and urine.

Little of the professional literature has been devoted to the coprophiliac and the urophiliac. Both the gay and straight communities have their share of "golden shower" devotees, those people who have a preference for being urinated upon. The particular action of being urinated or defecated upon serves as a psychological aphrodisiac and allows them to become sexually aroused. The true coprophiliac is manifested not only in the fecal matter and urine but also in the objects or dirty words being used. Coprophiliac tendencies can be shown in many ways: constant talk and jokes about excretory functions, special interests in animal dung, etc. In psychoanalytic theory, this form of sexual variation represents a fixation at the anal stage of psychosexual development. The collection or holding of any objects can be later explained as a return to the anal state of development. In some cases, the particular interest in mud, mire, finger painting, and other such activities are claimed to be a very valuable psychiatric technique because this enables the child to gratify his urge to handle and smear fecal material. This is, however, a type of psychodynamic explanation without benefit of empirical scientific validation. Furthermore, among some psychoanalytic theorists, it is believed that the fecal material equates the male sex organ in some minds, and the castration anxiety plays a major role in the coprophilist's need to see fecal matter leave his body. Again, this particular type of explanation is reported but not substantiated.

As has been stated, the coprophiliac and the urophiliac pose no great danger to others, only to themselves. There has been some evidence of coprophiliacs hoarding their fecal material and raiding public restrooms and other public places.

The story of a young nurse recently came from the news media. This young woman had been rushed to the local emergency room at a large metropolitan hospital. She was "cured" of her mysterious illness, but within a short period of time, she was again in the hospital for the same illness. Again she was "cured." The third time she came for emergency treatment, she died. Upon investigation, it was ascertained that the nurse was dissolving fecal matter of her pet parrot and injecting it directly into her blood stream.

The coprophiliac and the urophiliac appear to be more of a health problem than a danger to the criminal justice system. It is included in this section because of the fact that it is seen by many people as a sex deviation that comes to the forefront as a public form of sexual activity very infrequently and usually is uncovered by the medical profession and not the law enforcement profession.

PYGMALIONISM

Pygmalionism is a sexual desire for a statue, a doll, or mannequin. This particular type of sexual deviancy has been manifested in the last several years by an increase in the sale of inflatable dolls that have all of the "necessary" human orifices for sexual penetration. These inflatable dolls are used as instruments for sexual gratification and may have by this time a cassette tape mounted within the doll that may utter "dirty words" (coprophilia) or may simply moan and/or groan if the correct button is depressed.

The use of statues, dolls, or mannequins almost necessitates in most instances a solitary type of activity between the pygmalionist and his object. Again, the extent of this particular type of deviation is unknown, and the wide range of objects used edifies the imagination. The inflatable dolls may have human hair attached to the outer texture around the head and pubic hair around the genital area. There are openings that would simulate a vagina as well as a mouth for the insertion of the male sex organ. It can be only theoretically assumed that one who would resort to a statue, doll, or mannequin as a source for sexual gratification has a fear of relating sexually or even personally with others. By relating to an object, there is no fear of rejection or any type of retaliation. This problematic area would result in a nuisance in the situation where a mannequin in a store display or statues in churches, museums, and other public places were defaced and used for the purpose of the pygmalionist. The criminal justice system, therefore, may play a part in attempting to locate the pygmalionist and offering some type of reaction to this form of sexual deviation.

The treatment of the pygmalionist would obviously be centered around the need for him to relate to an object rather than to a person for sexual gratification and personal involvements. The feelings of inadequacy and insecurity and the basic desire for companionship would all be involved in the therapeutic situation and may be resolved in some form of in-depth counselling. In some cases, aversion therapy may be the treatment plan.

Chapter 4

TRANSVESTISM, TRANSSEXUALISM, AND HOMOSEXUALITY

The decision to include a separate chapter devoted entirely to the particular topics of transvestism, transsexualism, and homosexuality arose from two major considerations. In the first place, there is a great deal of misunderstanding regarding these three forms of sexual behavior. Obviously, all three choices are involved in the criminal justice system, not uniquely because of the practice of any of these three behavioral patterns but rather because of the fact that the activities are on the fringe of acceptable behavior. In the case of the transsexual and homosexual, for example, these persons are often seen in the gay bar situation, and both are viewed as one. The transsexual may find it easier to find a sex partner with a person who is biologically the same sex as himself, the homosexual, than in the straight bars. A man who dons female clothing, excluding the drag queen, because of the sexual excitation that accompanies wearing the female clothing, is often confused with the homosexual. This is not the case at all. The transvestite, the transsexual, and the homosexual are treated many times as being one.

Considering the second reason for the inclusion of these three forms of sexual behavior and preferences, it is apparent that there is some interaction of the three among the components of the criminal justice system. The police officer on the street, the person in the correctional institution, as well as those who are engaged in the professional practice of the law are often in contact with these people, all at different stages within their environment of the system itself. In discussing these three sexual practices, it is the objective of this chapter to succinctly and scientifically discuss the various components of the activities of each of the three practices as well as attempting to differentiate among the three and lend to the educational process the differing elements and behavioral patterns.

TRANSVESTISM

Transvestism, or eonism, is a behavior in which a male derives sexual pleasure from dressing in the clothes of the female (Gotwald). This particular type of sexual variation is often confused with the gay drag queen. What appears to be very important about this definition are two things. First of all, over a time span of the last thirty years, there has been a movement away from thinking the transvestite is actually a homosexual. In the *Sexual Offender and His Offenses*, it was stated, " . . . what we find in transvestism is essentially a combination of homosexuality and fetishism, castration anxiety if the transvestite be a man, and penis envy if the transvestite be a woman, are the psychologically controlling factors. The male transvestite is seeking a woman with a penis while the female transvestite tries to convince herself that she possesses a penis, i.e., that she is a man. Both of them make a fetish of the clothes of the opposite sex in which they repeatedly attire themselves" (Karpman).

Extent of Transvestism

In the early forties, it was reported that among a sample of transvestites 35 percent were found to be homosexual, 35 percent were found to be heterosexual, 15 percent were bisexual, and 15 percent were autoerotic or asexual (Hirschfeld). Other research of the late fifties and early sixties alluded to the fact that many transvestites are either homosexuals or bisexuals, but at least one admitted that it would be a mistake to assume that the majority of homosexuals are transvestites. Recent studies show that most homosexuals dress and look like members of their own sex (Goldenson).

Most of the recent data and research done in the area of transvestism seems to paint a picture of the transvestite who is not the blatant homosexual or the disparate homosexual who is a drag queen parading through the bars or the streets of the city. The drag queens, who will be discussed in a later part of this chapter, are dressing in the clothes of the opposite sex for a particular reason. The transvestite may be a businessman who comes home after a long and difficult day, changes in his wife's clothing, nightgown, and slippers, and appears to find some comfort and calmness in this form of behavior that he is not able to do otherwise. The average transvestite is a married man, a father who works in a male occupation. In American society, it appears true that we allow women to dress in the clothes of the male, blue jeans, flannel shirts, etc., without being concerned about their reason to do so. She may wear her husband's pajamas to bed, wear his dress shirts around the house, and don a variety of masculine apparel without much thought given. The same behavior on the behalf of the male is rarely tolerated.

Psychological Profile of Transvestites

Recent studies in the area of transvestism have shown a variety of different findings. Gosselin and Eysenck reported that transvestites while functioning as males and also while crossdressing scored lower on neuroticism and to a lesser extent on extraversion. It was the suggestion of the authors that when the transvestite is expressing a female personality he is able to reduce anxiety and shyness seemingly common to him (Gosselin & Eysenck).

Other research has indicated that there may be discrete types of transvestites: a nuclear transvestite group, which may be satisfied merely with crossdressing, and a marginal transvestite group, which in addition to crossdressing may desire feminization by hormones or surgical intervention. Both groups had shown fetishistic arousal to crossdressing (Buhrich & McConaghy).

Etiology of Transvestism

Explaining the etiology of the transvestite obviously depends in which school of thought one places more credence. In yet another study, a report assessed the nature of the relationships of homosexuals, transsexuals, and transvestites with their parents during childhood. Regarding the transvestites, it was found that significantly more mothers hoped for a girl prior to the birth of the subject. The fathers lacked interest in them as children or were absent from home. But there was no evidence to support the view that the transvestite had pathological relationships with his mother. Intrafamiliar childhood environmental factors reported by the subjects appeared to be nonspecific (Buhrich & McConaghy).

In an attempt to reappraise transvestism in light of new concepts in the psychoanalytical theory, the mechanism of projective and introjective identification and disorders in self-representations can be demonstrated not only in sexual disorders other than perversions but in nonsexual disorders as well. Perversions are especially susceptible to analysis in terms of self and object relationships theory. In articulating psychodynamic interrelationships between gender identity and sex psychopathology in transvestism, there are some dramatic illustrations that show the interconnections between gender development, sexual development, development of self, and object relations (Person & Ovesey).

Regardless of the possible causes of transvestism, and there appears to be no single reason for a person becoming a transvestite, it is clear that the majority of transvestites never come into contact with the criminal justice system. The increase in sexual behavior, as one who is involved in transvestism reports, is that because of the fetish involved in dressing in the clothes of the opposite sex, there does appear to be an increase in masturbatory activity. The masturbatory activity of the transvestite appears to be well developed by the age of twenty, and there is some thought that the transvestite, by clothing himself in the apparel of the female, is able at least for the moment to escape the pressures and the demanding role of the male and to retreat to his perception of the passive and undemanding role of the female. By dressing in the clothes of the female, he is able to escape momentarily these problems of everyday living.

The transvestite, as differentiated from the transsexual and the homosexual, is a person who is very much heterosexual, very happy to be a male, and one who wishes to maintain a social, sexual, and emotional commitment with a person of the opposite sex. The true transvestite has no desire for a homosexual relationship, nor does he desire to have a sex change. These two elements differentiate him from the transsexual and the homosexual in a discrete manner. There are, however, some other transvestites who are transsexuals and may desire a sex change operation.

In the course of the description of human life-styles, it would be foolhardy to state that all people behave in one fashion and have one set of needs and one set of values. What is called for in this section is an overall description to give the reader a clear description of a type of sex variant who is no particular hazard to the criminal justice system but may become peripherally involved because of his need to crossdress.

The experience of a former student related her surprise when she found in her husband's dresser drawer some women's underwear that was not her own. This couple had been married for over twenty years, and she had not been aware of his propensity for crossdressing. After a period of confrontation, he admitted that he had been involved in transvestism since he was a teenager and procured female clothing by stealing it from the clotheslines and back porches in his neighborhood. He would not purchase any type of underclothing, since he felt he could only be sexually aroused when the clothing had been worn.

So, it appears that many transvestites keep their behavior hidden from the criminal justice system and significant others for many years, or if successful, forever. When this activity is shared with the spouse, the wife may accept the situation or she may reject her transvestite-husband. One study related that some of the wives were reported to be moral maschochistic and tolerated the self-centered, obsessive-compulsive behavior of the transvestite. Many had experienced multiple losses and poor parenting. The transvestite husband fulfilled their dependency needs (Wise, Dupkin, & Meyer). It should not be assumed that all wives are moral masochists and are tolerant of "obsessive-compulsive behavior" of their transvestite husbands. As in the case of any behavior, some people are more acceptive of others and some are more understanding of others.

Treatment of the Transvestites

In treatment of the transvestite, by addressing purely the physiological factors of transvestism, at least one study investigated the testosterone level of twenty-six members of a club for transvestites and found that plasma testosterone serum follicules and hormones levels were not significantly different from the normal population. This particular point of view was strengthened by a further study that argued that a person's hormonal level and condition plays no part in sexual activity and sexual preference in any of its forms, including transvestism (Ross, Rogers, & McCollough). It may be that the father apparently plays more of a role in the etiology of the transvestite than had been formally considered. The father as a role performer in symptom and modelling is important, and the father-figure should be more intensively examined in future studies (Krueger).

Figures 3a, 3b, 3c, & 3d. Homosexual female impersonators. They are not transvestites; they cross-dress for entertainment and to attract men. Photos by the author.

TRANSSEXUALISM

The transsexualist is a person who is biologically one sex and psychologically the other. The usual case is a male who believes that he is truly a female; that is, he considers himself a female trapped inside a male's body. Transsexualism, however, also occurs in females, but the majority of cases, and the estimate is as high as 90 percent, is the male into the female model. D. O. Cauldwell was the first to use the term "transsexual" in his article "Psychopathia Transsexualist."

Transsexualists We Have Known

Probably the most famous transsexualist is George Jorgenson who went to Denmark for surgery in 1952. Jorgenson, a soldier, believed that he had been confined to a male body when he was in fact a female. After the operation, Jorgenson emerged as a famous, or infamous, character named Christine Jorgenson. She captured the media and became an international celebrity. There was some word that Christine had married in the last few years and was leading a quiet life in New England.

Within the last few years another celebrated case has emerged as far as the transsexual is concerned, Dr. Richard Raskin. Dr. Raskin, a California ophthalmologist, underwent the sex change operation and became Dr. Renee Richards. Dr. Richards is a professional tennis player on tour throughout the world. At the time of the sex change operation, however, considerable furor was voiced by the female tennis players as well as the U.S. Tennis Association, which instituted a sex chromosome test as a basic qualification for the tennis matches.

Transsexualism may occur in either sex. The desire for the sex change may arise as a result of early upbringing in which the individual has been dressed and treated as a member of the opposite sex. In most cases, transsexualism is not viewed as a mental illness nor should it be confused with a form of transvestism or homosexuality.

In the course of this author's research into the area of homosexuality and deviant sexual behavior in general, he has become acquainted with several transsexuals who frequent gay bars. Jake, a transsexual who calls himself Pat, is a frequent customer at a local gay bar. Jake, in his relationships both personal and sexual with other men, is indeed, from an outward appearance, having a homosexual relationship. The activity is certainly viewed as being between two males. But sexuality is more dependent upon the emotional and mental values and attitudes held than by the expression of genital contact. In giving lectures in universities, medical schools, learned societies, and national conferences, this author often states that, "... sexuality is 99 percent between your ears and 1 percent wherever else you want to place it."

What Jake is actually doing while having a sexual relationship with another man is very much being involved in a heterosexual relationship. Jake really views himself as a female upon whom nature has played a dirty trick by trapping him in the body of a man. He preceives himself as female even though he has a male's body. By having sex with another male, this is not at all participating in a homosexual relationship.

Peck, a highway engineer, is a female who believes that she is truly a man. Both Peck and Jake have plans to undergo the sex change operation and are presently involved in counselling. Peck dresses in men's clothing, not for the purpose of erotic arousal but because in assuming the role of the opposite sex, which is part of her therapy, she feels more comfortable and more at ease with herself.

The exposure of transsexuals to the criminal justice system has been relatively limited. Transsexuals often have been confused by the law enforcement profession as being homosexuals, and it has been noted quite often that psychiatrists, psychologists, and others in the helping professions still do not understand the differences among these three sex variants.

In recent years there has been a recent increase in the number of operations performed for transsexual purposes. The Janus Information Facility is an educational organization that helps men and women and their families find resources to solve their particular psychological and physical dilemmas.

Etiology of Transsexualism

The exact etiology of transsexualism is unknown. Some theorize that the cause may lie in the self's failure to adequately identify with the person of the same sex. Others may feel that the cause may lie with the failure of produced hormones to normalize the person, and others may hypothesize that the androgen has failed in its relationship with the hypothalmus. As far as early history of the transsexual is concerned, it appears that most signs of transsexualism usually occur in the early stages of psychosexual development. There is some evidence that by the age of three identification with the opposite sex has begun (Stoller).

It is supposed, by the lack of information otherwise, that most transsexuals do not become actively involved with the criminal justice system. It appears, therefore, that most live within the parameters of the mores and folkways of society and lead productive lives, both on a personal and professional status.

As one moves along within the development stages, it appears that the older one grows, as far as the involvement in transsexualism, the more socially introverted one becomes and the more involved is the transsexual commitment. An important finding is that the older males who are transsexuals as compared to younger gender disordered males have a more predominately strong heterosexual orientation. The older transsexuals appear to be more typical of normal heterosexual males, and there is some evidence to suggest that males who receive surgical reassignment surgery during their middle years use their desire to "become a woman" as a defense mechanism against underlying depression (Steiner, Statterberg, & Muir). A fifty-one-year-old man, after nearly thirty years of marriage, went to the point of castration in order to fulfill a longstanding fantasy of being a woman (Van Kammen & Money). Obviously, this particular case is one that is not at all unusual as far as transsexualism is concerned.

The Sex Change Operation

Those who are involved in the sex change operation obviously should be made aware that the operation is irreversible. The surgery performed is cosmetic and a functioning penis is at this point in time not a reality.

The female-to-male-change hormones are administered usually after a period of counselling. These hormones affect the voice, develop the muscles, facial and body hair, as well as thickening the skin. The breasts are reduced in size, and the uterus and ovaries are removed. In some cases artificial penises may be worn during intercourse, and in other cases the surgeons may construct a semi-erect penis using skin grafts from the patients. Orgasms can still occur since the clitoris is left intact and can be stimulated during coitus.

When a male is surgically transformed into a female, the main problems as outlined are not present. Through the use of hormones prior to surgery, breast development will have occurred as well as rounding out of the body, which is considered to be feminine. Beard growth as well as other hair growth is arrested, and female voice is developed not only through the use of hormones but also with training. The Adam's apple is reduced in size and some patients have their breasts enlarged with the help of silicone implants. The tissue inside of the penis is removed, leaving the outer skin intact so it can be used to line the inside of the vagina, which is formed just above the rectum. The urethra from the penis is shortened and placed in a position that is usual for female anatomy just above the vagina. The scrotal sac is fashioned into labia (Gottwald & Golden).

There are some feelings among many in our society that the transsexual should be content to live the life as he has in the past. However, "If their minds cannot be changed to fit their bodies, then perhaps we should consider changing the body to fit the mind" (Goldenson).

HOMOSEXUALITY

Homosexuality comes from the Greek derivative "homo," which means the same. It is not from the latin "homo" meaning man. A homosexual is a person who desires a sexual, personal, and emotional commitment with another person of the same sex. Homosexuality applies to either a male or a female, although the term lesbian pertains to females only.

The Isle of Lesbos in ancient Greece was the home of a very famous school for girls. The headmistress, Sappho, wrote lurid and erotic poems to some of her students, and these poems were all but for a few destroyed (Roche, 1966).

> Your magical laughter—this I swear—
> Batters my heart—my breast astir
> My voice when I see you suddenly near
> Refuses to come.
>
> My tongue breaks up and a delicate fire
> Runs through my flesh; I see not a thing
> With my eyes, and all that I hear
> In my ears is a hum.

The sweat runs down, a shuddering takes
Me in every part and pale as the drying
Grasses, then, I think I am near
The moment of dying.

In the ancient world, homosexuality, especially among men, was widely practiced and accepted. In the ancient Greek and Roman upper class, especially among the former, the homosexual love affair between an adult male and an adolescent boy was not a clandestine arrangement. This arrangement was consummated in the home of the man with the wife fully aware of the homosexual relationship developing between the husband and the young male. In all fairness, however, the relationship between the adult and the child was not strictly a sexual relationship. The older man was viewed as a tutor, and in many instances this was the only formal education that the young man received.

The relationship between the two many times terminated when hair appeared on the adolescent on the chest, under the arms, and in the pubic area. On this occasion, the young man moved out of the home, and the Greek adult found a new boy for another relationship. This particular love affair was viewed as the highest form of love. This is very clear if one understands the role and status of the female in the Greek household. Her status was low, and the husband would not be seen in public alone with his wife.

This is not meant to convey that all citizens of ancient Greece practiced homosexuality. It is probably more safe to say that the upper class and elite were more prone to this form of sexual behavior than the middle and lower classes.

The Bible and Homosexuality

Bearing in mind the need of children, the ancient Hebrews actively condemned the practice of homosexuality. In Leviticus 18 it is written, "You shall not lie with a male as with a woman; it is an abomination . . . Do not defile yourself by any of these things, for by all these the nations I am casting out before you defiled themselves."

In Leviticus 20, it is further commanded, "If a man lies with a man as with a woman, both of them shall be put to death, their blood is upon them."

It is certainly evident that, if you have a small group of people who are persecuted and their population needs to grow, the practice of homosexuality, a form of population control, would certainly be condemned.

As the early Christian church moved into a period of social statements, St. Paul in his writings to the Corinthians stated, "Do you not know that the unrighteous will not inherit the kingdom of God? Do not be deceived: neither do the immoral, the idolaters, nor adulterers, nor homosexuals . . . will inherit the kingdom of God."

In the Middle Ages, homosexuals were tortured and executed for the practice of homosexuality. A variety of different methods of executions were available such as plouncing, burning at the stake, and hanging. It is needless to remark on the negative feelings held by the Christians regarding homosexuality. Even today, most religious institutions still believe that the person who practices homosexuality commits a very grievous sin and his chances of everlasting salvation are slim to none.

Extent of Homosexuality

Probably the most famous of all studies concerning homosexuality was performed by Alfred Kinsey in his *Sexual Behavior of the Human Male* (1948) and the *Sexual Behavior of the Human Female* (1953). Kinsey devised a schematic representation that labelled heterosexual/homosexual behavior from a scale point of 0 to a scale point of 6.

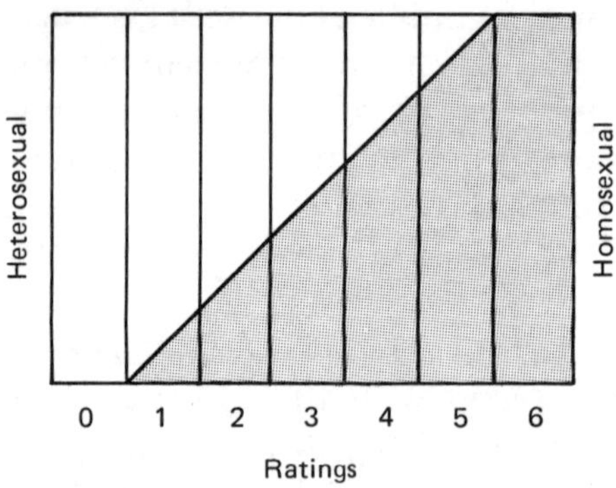

Heterosexual-homosexual rating scale of Kinsey et al. (1953). The ratings are defined as follows:
"0 = entirely heterosexual
1 = largely heterosexual, but with incidental homosexual history
2 = largely heterosexual, but with a distinct homosexual history
3 = equally heterosexual and homosexual
4 = largely homosexual, but with distinct heterosexual history
5 = largely homosexual, but with incidental heterosexual history
6 = entirely homosexual"

On this particular scale, a person who rated himself as a 0 would be one who has never had any type of homosexual activity. The scale point 0 would be one, male or female, who would rate themselves regarding their own overt activities as well as any type of psychological response to heterosexuality/homosexuality. On the other end of the continuum, scale point 6 would be a person who rates himself as being completely homosexual, a person who has never had any heterosexual physical or psychological feelings or activity.

In his research more than forty years ago, Kinsey found that among his white male population of his sample (and one has to consider the social climate of the times), he reported that 37 percent of the white male population had experienced a homosexual experience to the point of orgasm. In the female sample, it was related that 13 percent of this group had also experienced a lesbian activity to the point of orgasm.

The Blantant Homosexual

The homosexuals who are more apt to come into contact with the criminal justice system are those who are more blatant in their display of their homosexuality. Unfortunately, these are the stereotypical gays, the males who swish from one side of the street to the other, talk with a lisp, and gesture with a limp wrist. The female, the so-called bull dyke, may wear a leather jacket, don chains, and wear traditionally male attire. It would certainly be a gross mistake to assume that all gays are of this particular type.

Larry is a heterosexually married homosexual with five children. The youngest child is in elementary school and the oldest is a student in a state university. Larry has been involved with homosexuality for many years. His father was an alcoholic and played a minor role in the development while the mother was very dominating and was the ruler of the home. Larry slept with the mother until the night before he married, at the age of twenty-five. Larry said there was never sex involved with the mother, but he felt that the mother used him as a "birth control method." Larry married a particularly homely woman after a love affair with a parish priest turned out badly. This woman is aware that Larry participates in homosexual affairs several times a month and she tries to be understanding of his "problem." Her only request is that Larry not tell her when he is going to a rendezvous with one of his lovers. The children are not aware of his homosexual tendencies.

Not all married homosexuals tell their spouses of their tendencies. Ray, a man in his late fifties, has been involved in a variety of homosexual affairs for the last thirty years. He is self-defined as being one who is passive and likes to be dominated. He has one "master" who whips him, leaving some welts on his body, and on occasion orders Ray to have oral sex with the master's dog. Ray said that his wife would never understand his needs and preferences and for that purpose the wife is not aware of his activities. Ray says that he is very happy with his life-style and plans no changes in either his life with his family or his clandestine relationships with other gays.

The Adjusted Homosexual

Neither Larry nor Ray could be classified as blatant homosexuals. Both hold responsible jobs in the community, appear "masculine," and while being very adjusted with themselves, neither one desires that his employer know of his homosexuality. The difference between the blatant and the so-called adjusted homosexual is basically that the blatant stands out by his behavior and in some instances his attire. There can be no doubt regarding what the former category is. There is another group of homosexuals who will not only be quite adjusted to their homosexuality but also tend to be very adept to place themselves where other homosexuals gather, e.g. gay bars, public parks, tea rooms, and a variety of other places. By placing themselves in these situations, these homosexuals run the risk of being identified as being homosexual and open to extortion and blackmail. In some large cities there are certain sections of town where homosexuals can be picked up and paid for serving other gays. This can lead to a particularly dangerous situation for the soliciter, and there are many instances of johns being injured and even killed by gay prostitutes who prey upon men driving through these areas of the city for the purpose of impersonal sex for money.

The Homosexual Prostitute

It appears that there is a group of homosexuals, the homosexual prostitutes, who are coming more and more into the limelight. These homosexual prostitutes are usually young men, ages nine through sixteen, who are engaging themselves in sex for the pure monetary reward. These young men usually have no self-identification as far as being homosexual. They view themselves as being very heterosexual and will be very upset if one would call them gay. These fellows will work in a particular part of town, stand on a corner, and wait to be picked up. In large cities, there are well-known street corners where young men can be picked up for sexual purposes. There is an 800 long-distance toll-free number that one can dial, and a young man will appear at the door within the hour for a homosexual prostitution purpose.

The homosexual prostitute, although not self-identifying himself as a homosexual, is becoming more and more a problem to the criminal justice system. The commercially exploited units of various police and social service departments are becoming more active than reactive in their dealings with the young prostitute and the homosexual pedophile.

The Homosexual Pedophile

The homosexual pedophile, another category of the homosexual population, is a child lover. He involves himself with children sexually, and many times he will pay the homosexual prostitute for their sexual favors. This particular type of homosexual will be dealt with in a later chapter.

What is so very interesting about homosexuals, as it is also with heterosexuals, is that all homosexuals are different as all heterosexuals are different. The likes and dislikes and the fashions and fetishes vary from one homosexual to another. It is not known how many homosexuals there are. The estimates vary from 3 percent of the population to a high of 10 percent. Probably 3 percent may be a little low, especially if we include those people who have had at least one experience to the point of orgasm, and 10 percent may be too high. There are many closet gays, those people who have successfully kept hidden their homosexuality.

Etiology of Homosexuality

The origin of homosexuality is, of course, unknown. There are a variety of different theoretical etiologies involved in homosexuality that run from the chromosome issue to hormones to the domineering mother and passive father to flouride in the water. The medical model never seems to die. In a recent report, a statement was made that homosexuals are not born, but they are actually affected by a lack of equilibrium between male and female hormones, or hermaphroditism, which under the influence of social and environmental factors evolves into homosexuality. The more famous explanation of the etiology has to do with psychodynamic model. In this particular theoretical framework, the homosexual is formed by his inability to properly resolve the Oedipus

Complex. In this thought, the mother of the young boy is a woman who is sensual and seductive. The young boy, on an unconscious level, has certain sexual feelings toward his mother and, if these feelings are not properly resolved, he will later search for the love of the father in adult homosexual affairs. The same type of arrangement for the young girl in her attempt to resolve the Electra Complex is essentially the same. She attempts to resolve her sexual feelings for her father and, if successful, will develop into a mature, heterosexual female. If not, she will develop into a lesbian.

For the purposes of this particular section, it is really not important to theoretically design any one model for the etiology of homosexuality or any of the sex offenders. It is important for the reader to understand that in this particular form of deviant behavior not all homosexuals will come into contact with the criminal justice system. Those who will are probably more in the category of disparate, blatant, or the homosexual pedophile. With the advent of the social movement of the sexual equality movement, children are no longer viewed as chattel, and those who use or exploit children are held as accountable as those who misuse women.

Chapter 5

PEDOPHILIA

Pedophilia, more commonly known as child molesting, refers to an older individual whose conscious sexual desires and responses are directed either partially or wholly toward prepubertal children, those normally under the age of thirteen. There appears to be, moreover, an ongoing number of pedophiles whose interest lie in the area of sexual activity with children once they have reached adolescence. These pedophiles are called hebephiles. The hebephile is a person who desires a sexual relationship either partially or exclusively with children who are between the ages of thirteen and fifteen. Unlike the relationship in incest, the case of the pedophile usually does not occur in cases where there is a close family relationship.

Pedophilia and the pedophile have been with mankind throughout the ages. There is sufficient documentation to show that some very famous people have been involved in pedophilia, people such as Plato, Aristotle, Benjamin Franklin, and others. Consequently, sex with children is nothing new to modern man. The use of a child as a sexual object is seen by some as someone to be used, abused, and then discarded. This type of behavior can only be termed as abominable. As *Screw Magazine* very aptly brings out in a review of *The Best Kept Secret: The Sexual Abuse of Children*,

> In one sense, *The Best Kept Secret* is part of the general backlash of sexual liberation. But in the decade of the Moral Majority, our best defense against backlash is to pay sympathetic attention to books like this one and to remember that physical coercion—as opposed to the fantasy exploitation found in most pornography—is the opposite of liberation (Perkins).

The extent of pedophilia is not well known. There are only estimates, and these range from one to two million youngsters who are involved in being sexually exploited and molested. These types of arrangements may be very informal where a child is picked up in a public place, offered a piece of candy, and then carried away to a secluded place and sexually molested. Or it may be a very formal circumstance where one can call a toll-free telephone number and have a child at your doorstep within the hour. Regardless of the extent of this particular social problem, there seems to be uniform agreement among policymakers, religious leaders, and the society at large that this form of activity cannot be tolerated. On the other hand, the average citizen knows little about pedophilia, the extent of the problem, and the dangers involved to the child. The child offenders, as in the cases of the nuisance and the dangerous sex criminals, are not all alike. For this very reason, it was decided to devote a complete chapter dealing with pedophilia, another with incest, and yet another chapter concerning child pornography.

The persons dealing in pedophilia, the relative in incest, and all those interested in kiddie porn are certainly not those people who always are viewed on the bottom rung of society's ladder. The exploitation of children can never be condoned regardless of the amount of the material goods that have been given, the amount of affection displayed, or any other monetary or emotional exchange.

TYPES OF PEDOPHILES

As early as the 1960s, there appeared a movement in the professional literature to differentiate among the different types of pedophiles. Cohen attempted to label different levels of pedophilia. The pedophile in his first category was termed the immature child offender. This lover of children only desires to fondle, touch, or caress the child. This person has never been able to establish a positive relationship with his peers and only feels comfortable when with children. As a teenager, the offender tended to avoid the usual pattern of socialization with teenagers and showed little interest in dating and competitive sports. As an adult, he generally did not initiate or actively pursue sexual relationships. If this did occur, it usually occurred because of the initiative of his partner. For instance, a young man, age twenty, accused of sexual assault on an eleven-year-old boy, earned a living by being a male prostitute. In this capacity, he had sexual relations with adults, both males and females, but his own sexual preference was for preadolescent boys. These involvements (his prostitutional contacts) were only situational in nature and never replaced the primary sexual attraction toward underage males.

> Sexual thoughts and fantasies about children or adolescents preoccupy the offender, and interest in them often reaches the level of an obsession. The offender appears sexually addicted to children. Conversely, sexual relationships with adults would be avoided out of fear and/or punishment; feelings of inadequacy or inferiority; experiences of shyness, guilt, anxiety, or embarrassment; or simply because he does not find adults to be sexually desirable—they do not turn him on (Burgess).

The second group of child offenders, the regressed child offender, experienced a fairly normal childhood with good relationships with his peers. He also had a positive sexual experience with others. Feelings of self-doubt and inadequacy later developed in his life, causing poor social and sexual performances and resulted in some cases of alcoholism and poor working performance. The sexual act against the child is usually precipitated by some substantial jolt to the offender's sense of sexual adequacy. The offense is impulsive and is an attempt to deal with certain life stresses. The regressed offender does not exhibit any major sexual attraction to children through his sexual development, and if this did occur it was merely situational or experimental. "Typically, this offender is married, and a situation develops which threatened their relationship. Feelings overwhelmed by the resulting stresses, the man becomes involved sexually with a child" (Burgess). The offender becomes distressed by his offense and behavior, exhibiting feelings of remorse, guilt, or shame.

The final type of molester, the aggressive child offender, is by far the most dangerous and the most antisocial. He is often sadistic and violent in his need for stimulation and sexual excitement. The attacks are vicious and aggressive in nature, consisting of anal and oral sex, often resulting in harm, extreme pain, and in many cases even death. The sadistic child offender inflicts pain on the child, and this physical aggression is eroticized. Consequently the abuse and the degradation of the child is necessary for the sexual gratification of the molester. This is not necessarily an impulsive act on the part of the molester because the child symbolizes everything that the offender hates about himself, and therefore the child becomes the object for punishment. The connection is somehow made between aggression (sadism) and eroticism. "The complete domination, subjugation and humiliation of the victim is desired and typically a weapon such as a gun, knife, pipe or belt is used for the purpose of offense" (Burgess).

A further delineation of the type of pedophilia can be made using the following five categories (Mohr et al.):

1. Heterosexual Hebephilia—sexual activity of any type where the female partner is pubescent.
2. Heterosexual Pedophilia—sexual activity of an type when the female partner has not shown any pubertal changes.
3. Homosexual Hebephilia—sexual activity of any type when the male partner is pubescent.
4. Homosexual Pedophilia—sexual activity of any type when the partner of the same sex has not shown any pubertal changes
5. Undifferentiated Pedophilia—sexual activity of any type when the partner's sex is not differentiated.

A further categorization was made by Rossman in his article entitled "The Pederasts." The pederast is a pedophile who is a lover of young boys. In this article, the first type of pederast was labelled the "temporary" or "substitute" pederast. This was a person who has sex with a boy when women are not available. This type was common in the past when men were involved in occupations that necessitated travel and when time apart from their family was a common occurrence. The famous "peg" houses in San Francisco of the late 1800s were houses of prostitution catering to sailors and others of the travelling professions. The young males were forced to lower themselves onto wooden pegs that were of different sizes in length and diameter. The customer would pick out a boy whose anus had been dilated to the size of the wood peg that approximated the size of the male customer's penis.

From the reports of service personnel serving in Viet Nam, it was related that there was a great deal of pederasty during this conflict, not because of the lack of women but because the new "thrill" of sex with a young boy was accepted.

A second category of pederasts was termed as the "criminal" or "exploited" pederast. These were pimps for young boys, criminals who ran pederasts hangouts, blackmailers, and others on the fringe of society. Some of the pederasts limited their sexual activity almost exclusively with young boys and did not consider themselves to be pederasts. Many of these types are in the pure sense of the word pederasts because they seem to have a true passion for affection with young boys.

A third category is that of the "promiscuous" pederasts. This category includes men who cruise the areas where young boys ply their prostitutional trade. Most of these pedophiles consider themselves to be exclusively pederasts, and many have been arrested for having sex with children. They are not apt to use force or coercion, which may be a common theme of some of the other categories. Many of them, however, are exploitive of the children.

Yet another category of pederasts are the "careful" pederasts. These men generally do not limit themselves solely to young boys but are quite aware of their pederasty. Their station in life permits them to have sexual relationships with boys, and their personal and legal risks are kept to a minimum. Some may make their contacts with children in different cities and countries. There are even some cases where fathers trade their sons for sexual encounters of the "worst" kind, so-called "sporting groups." These children, as well as the adult men and their parents, usually do not fall into the hands of the criminal justice system because of their care in their clandestine dealings and relationships.

The "responsible" pederasts is another form of pedophilia, and in this group are men who are often wealthy with good positions in the social and business world. They will avoid any kind of sexual contact with children but may have at one time or another some form of sexual relationship with a child. Aware of their problems and possible consequences, they will go the "extra mile" to avoid any further problem. They appear to be reacting to their previous activity in such a manner that negates the possibility they will ever become involved in pedophilia again (Rossman).

Within each of the categories, there lies a continuum and a gray area for which one cannot easily determine a neat label and therefore fit a person within that particular group.

THE CHILD AND THE PEDOPHILE

Not all children who are involved with child molestation as victims are forever stamped with a negative self-image, and very few are eternally damaged either psychologicaly, emotionally, or physically. This is not to say, however, that the sadistic child offender and his offenses should be minimized or ignored. He is a real and present danger. As was stated earlier, the aggressive child offender is one who is a great danger to children and to the society.

He is harmful, dangerous, and antisocial. He has made that connection between violence and sexual satisfaction.

Despite Arthur Frederick Goode III's statement that he was not a violent person, this twenty-seven-year-old was found guilty of killing two preteen boys, one in Florida and the other in Virginia. In March, 1976, in Cape Coral, Florida, Goode abducted a nine-year-old youngster who was waiting for his school bus. The young child was savagely beaten, molested, and later killed. Later that same month, Goode kidnapped an eleven-year-old boy from a Falls Church, Virginia, bus stop, took him to a wooded area behind a shopping center, and molested, mutilated, and killed the youth as another boy looked on. At his trial in Virginia, Goode told the presiding judge, "If I ever get my hands on another boy, especially a sexy little boy, he will never make it home." Goode was sentenced to life in prison for his crimes.

The famous case of Wayne Williams in Atlanta certainly points out the dangers of the aggressive child offender as does John Wayne Gacy in Chicago. Ted Bundy, presently on death row in Florida, admits to killing scores of women throughout the United States. He was also found guilty of killing a pretty twelve-year-old girl in central Florida after he sexually molested her. The age range of the victims of these killers is wide, but what is clear is the underlying tone of violence and aggression that provides the perpetrator with erotic satisfaction.

Some pedophiles are interested only in having a sexual encounter with the child. Others add another dimension to taking pictures of the instamatic variety, video taping, and other methods that do not necessitate commercial handling. Often, these movies are exchanged or sold to others who share this common interest. A case in Kentucky recently featured a local wealthy businessman who pleaded innocent to charges that he took pictures of boys once he lured them into his exclusive highrise condominium with drugs and alcohol. This person was charged with fifteen counts of using a minor under sixteen in sexual performance, a punishment that carries with it a fifteen-year prison sentence, twenty-one counts of using minors older than sixteen in sexual performance, one count of bribing a witness, three counts of promoting sexual performance by a minor, two counts of distributing material portraying a sexual performance by a minor, eleven counts of unlawful transactions with a minor, and one count of possession of marihuana. All of these crimes occurred within a two-year period. This pedophile's arrest followed an intensive investigation by the local exploited child unit, which is composed of police, social workers, academicians, and other professionals in the field of criminal justice. The man picked up his boys by waiting outside churches and in public parks where young boys congregate. He also solicted other boys in the porno area as well as the public housing areas of the city. The arresting officers stated that the man's wealth apparently was the bait that lured the young boys, many of whom were impoverished. He never actually paid the young fellows in money, always in terms of clothes, gifts, and travel. Materials seized from his home included pictures taken of boys from all over the United States as well as Mexico, Spain, England, Canada, Germany, Japan, Barbados, and many other foreign lands. His victims, all black young men (he is white), ranged in ages from thirteen to twenty-six. This case has not been tried at the time of this writing.

PEDOPHILE ORGANIZATIONS

There are several organizations that have recently emerged that are propedophile. In a speech by Roger Young, Special Agent, FBI, addressing a National Organization of Victim Assistance Conference in Las Vegas only recently, it was reported that only about 10 percent of all cases of child exploitation are reported. If this statistic is to be believed, and there is actually no way to validate this estimate, then the risk to society's youth and functioning is indeed in peril.

A pedophile's survival code published in the *Child Lover's Handbook Guide to Better Child Loving* states the following pedophile code:

Child Lover's Code

In order to survive whether in jail, prison, mental hospitals or free in the street, the child lover must do these things:

1. He must accept himself as he is. Unless he does have sadistic tendencies to hurt children, then he must get psychiatric help from a competent doctor to change his ways of loving a child, not hurting them (sic).
2. He must communicate with others who are suffering as he has learned from the experience of others so that you can survive in this anti-child society.
3. He must support all child loving groups or societies such as the Rene Guyon Society or the Childhood Sexuality Circle.

4. He must try to help to change the laws rather than break the law regarding child sex, although most child lovers feel that loving a child sexually is like going 65 in a 55 MPH zone. It is so easy to break an unjust law.
5. He must be patient for the law regarding child sex will change. (sic).
6. He must learn to tolerate extreme frustration.
7. He must teach his children to love sexually and to participate with them (sic) if possible. Children must be taught that sex is not filthy or dirty.

The particular goals of these organizations are centered around their belief that by the year 2000, children will be permitted to love sexually and the child lover will be able to legally engage in sex with children with no legal repercussions. It is their belief that as long as no child is being hurt psychologically or physically, there is no harm to the child. The organizations are also desirous that child sex laws be changed within the next twenty years to the point that fines or probation would be the ultimate punishment

for any adult who would have sex with a child when there is no injury. Of course, the man who would hurt a child would receive a prison sentence or even capital punishment. A mental hospital commitment would also be a treatment option for the sadistic child offender. A final goal would be that incest between an adult male and a juvenile female, regardless of their relationship, e.g. daughter, stepdaughter, niece, etc., would be legalized or at least tolerated.

Certain organizations are very active in the fight to legalize pedophilia. The Rene Guyon Society (Sex After Eight is Too Late), Pedophile Information Exchange (PIE), the Childhood Sexuality Circle (with more than 10,000 members), and the North American Man Boy Love Association (NAMBLA) are all well-known formal organizations that are in positions to lobby for lax laws regarding sex with children.

There are media representations of organizations that advertise for sex relationships between the adult and young boys. An example of this would be the *Broadstreet Journal*, a pulp publication that has been printed since 1972.

Inside this newsletter are ads as well as pictures of men who are looking for boys for sexual encounters (see opposite):

> White male, 35, seeks brother, 12–18, am very generous and clean, discreet, distance not important. Please write with full confidence of discretion to ________.
>
> White male, 32, 6 ft, 165, good looking, very masculine, wants a son under 16 who is slim, for a good home. Write to ________.

The subscriber to this magazine is then encouraged to write directly to the *Broadstreet Journal*, which will in turn forward his letter to the original subscriber. Also included in this publication is an ad from the Rene Guyon Society that seeks the reader to avoid juvenile delinquency by having sex with children.

"Where the Young Ones Are" is yet another publication that lists ads according to cities and states where young boys are readily available for sex. The publication contains a disclaimer and stated that some places change in character, and at the time of the writing the places were verified by their "field agent" and were true gathering places of young males. However, the pedophile should be careful, the publication warned, because possible police entrapment was noticed in some locales. The pedophile was notified that what he was doing was "morally right" but "legally wrong." The careful pedophile should be aware of the numerous local statutes and ordinances regarding sex with children was one last admonition.

ETIOLOGY OF THE PEDOPHILE

The precise identification of the pedophile's etiological factors of behavioral symptoms depends on the theory to which one subscribes. "Immaturity, for instance, which is the problem most consistently raised with pedophiles, can be seen as an organic malfunction, as a deficient learning process, as a lack of proper conditioning, or as a psychodynamic fixation or regression" (Mohr et al.). The theoretical contributions on pedophilia have related the etiology of the sexual desires for underage children either to psychological concepts of arrested psychosexual development, intellectual deficiency, mental illness (psychosis), or physiological conditions of functional disturbances, such as impotency, degenerative diseases (alcoholism and senility), or cerebral trauma.

In the examination of pedophilia, it was shown that older clinical studies linked pedophilia etiologically with such severe mental disorders as mental retardation. This can be explained by the fact that the cases examined in these studies were referred to a psychiatrist, not so much because the patients were pedophiliacs but because they had shown obvious signs of mental disturbances. The proportion of actually psychotic or severely retarded pedophiles is quite small.

Since there is not one specific etiology in pedophilia, psychosocial factors are especially important as an influence on the balance of impulse control. The fact that many offenses are promoted by specific conditions and situations and that treatment is primarily by way of increase in controls rather than by eradication of impulses gives an emphasis to the examination of social stresses.

The adolescent pedophile often shows a retarded maturation level and impaired functioning and judgment. Offenders tend to have difficulties in school and go through a period of drifting in their attempts to establish themselves in a job. Parents and other persons are seen in many cases as gratifying the pedophile's strong dependency needs. The relationship with his parents has to be therefore assessed in regard to these distortions and their potential for correction.

The middle-aged pedophile tends to be married, and it is important if this is the case that an assessment of the total family situation be made. Often, family relationships have deteriorated, and severe disturbances in the family are common. Additional family problems resulting from alcoholism and dissatisfaction with work are often present (Mohr et al.). The wife will often exhibit personality and behavioral characteristics that tend to reinforce the pedophile's impulses. His whole range of relationships should be examined because of the potential problems resulting from those relationships.

TREATMENT OF THE PEDOPHILE

In order to deal effectively with the pedophile, the primary task should be to determine what the risks are allowing the pedophile to remain in the community. After all, the protection of the community would and should be the primary concern to those in the criminal justice profession. The safeguards for the society should be addressed and structured for the benefit of the community as well as for the benefit of the offender.

In order to estimate the possibility of repetition of the sexual offender, the sexual contact with the child must be viewed in the context of the pedophile's life history. His history of development, the social history, current life situation, etc. should all be considered. When predicting repetition, two items must be considered: what are the external factors versus the internal factors, and second, under what conditions is the offense likely to occur (Burgess).

To answer these questions, assessments must be made of such internal personality factors as well as a needs assessment. External factors such as stress, child availability, and personal management must also be considered.

In assessing the danger of the offender, many factors must be considered. For instance, the type of sexual activity occurring during the sexual molestation must be of concern. If there was simple fondling versus a vicious attack, this would be a determining factor in the evaluation. The relationship with the child should also be a paramount factor to be considered. Whether the child was a relative or picked up at the bus stop would have impact also on the decision. The closer the emotional relationship, the greater the risk (Burgess).

The psychological factors as well as the psychiatric factors must be considered. The manner in which he is able to control his stress and impulse control management system is vital. If he has a low tolerance in these management systems, his ability to stay away from the child-lover behavioral pattern will be reduced. The historical data of religion, job, family, work, court record, etc. must all be known in order to assess a successful rehabilitation.

It should be obvious that if children and society are to be protected, some form of treatment should be mandatory. Some offenders may seek treatment because of family pressures. Others may seek treatment because it is the mandate of the court. A few others will seek out professional help because they sincerely believe that they wish to change. Unfortunately, the rate of success among child molesters is less than 5 percent.

There appears to be a real backlog in the treatment profession for sex offenders, not only the pedophiles but also for the wide range of sex offenders. Behavioral modification, aversion therapy, sociodrama, peer group sessions, and psychotherapy are all available alternatives. Prisons, hospitals, halfway houses, and outpatient programs are all institutional alternatives. It would be a great mistake to expect that the sex offender, in this case the pedophile, will change overnight. It is believed that the ones who admit their problem would stand the better chance of rehabilitation. For successful rehabilitation, it appears that several things are essential. First of all, as already mentioned, the person must admit his guilt. This is not an easy thing to do for many pedophiles. John B., an incarcerated pedophile in a prison in Kentucky, for example, refuses to do so:

> When I was in jail, both a psychiatrist and a psychologist came up to see me, to talk to me. The psychiatrist said to me, Well, how would you describe your condition? What condition? I am not sick. I don't have a cold. I don't have cancer. I am different. I have always been different.
>
> I am the black sheep of the family. Never have I been totally accepted by my family. My mother had twins, and I was the last one. My twin brother was two and a half hours older than I was. So he was the first one and they were expecting him. Theoretically they knew he was coming, but they didn't know I was coming. If I was born first, then they might not have expected him. But all my life it was, 'well, we didn't expect you; you almost killed your mother when you were born. Your mother had a hard time and never was able to get back on her feet for a long time.' When my father died, I was thirteen. The statement sticks in my mind since that time was when my

> mother said, 'It's your fault.' When you're thirteen and your mother says that it's your fault that your father died, well, it's something that I have never forgotten. My mother never had the time, or maybe even the ability, to show that she cared. My father was sick a lot and we never had the time to go hunting with him and do things that most kids do with their father. I never knew or cannot remember having a childhood. I can remember being five and ten and thirteen, but I can't remember having a childhood.

Regarding his involvement with children as a pedophile, John again denies any moral or personal culpability:

> It's the parents' responsibility to teach them right from wrong. I'm not saying they've been victimized. The question is,'Who is being victimized?' Seriously, who is being victimized? The kid who is going to come up to me and say, 'John, give me ten dollars, I want to do this or that? We can do something about it, we can go to bed.'
>
> I have needs too. I have a need to be wanted, I have a need to be accepted. I have a need to have sexual gratification. These kids have needs also. I am not saying that what I did was right, but I will not say I was 100 percent wrong.

It is imperative that the pedophile be held accountable for his actions. Third, the offender must be made aware of the possible circumstances that lead to his deviant sexual behavior so he can detect early warning signs. The offender must also be willing to develop other ways of relating to children in a nonsexual manner.

It is important to remember that there is not one treatment program for all sex offenders, much less all child offenders. As there must be a myriad of factors that produce pedophiles, there must be a variety of different treatment modes to undo what has been done. This is especially important because of the nature of the crime itself and also because there now appears to be an extremely high rate of recidivism among pedophiles, as high as 98 percent.

Chapter 6

INCEST

When speaking of incest, it is important to remember that incest is not all physical contacts between an adult and a child that are expressions of love. Physical contacts between a father and a daughter, or a mother and her son, may run a gamut of acts that should not be arbitrarily termed as incestuous. Sexual child abuse is involved with the exploitation of the child by an adult. Incest is sexual involvement with a relative of the child where law prohibits marriage. It is easy to see, then, that incest and pedophilia are not synonymous.

PHYSICAL AND NONPHYSICAL TYPES

Not all sexual contacts between the adult and the child may involve physical contact. There may also be contacts of a non-touching nature. Touching offenses are those that are normally thought of when one thinks of sexual activity: kissing, fondling, touching of the genitals, rape, and so on. Nontouching sexual activity includes those acts such as saying things that arouse the interest of the child, exhibitionism, voyuerism, and patterns of sex play where the child is a viewer of the sex act.

THE MALE AS PERPETRATOR

The most frequent offender in the incest relationship is the father of the daughter. There are other offenders, such as grandfathers, uncles, cousins, and brothers. It is important to bear in mind that the victim can be either male or female. It appears to be a myth that only little girls are involved in incest with fathers. This is simply not true. Small sons may also be involved with anal and oral sex. Sonny, presently an inmate of a local prison, stated that he was regularly sodomized by his father until he was old enough to reject the sexual advances of his father. Sonny is now in prison because he raped and sodomized over twenty-two young people. The father is often seen as immature with little self-confidence and low self-esteem.

There is some evidence that suggests that the younger the person the more apt he is to use violence in his sexual dealing with the victim. This is especially true of the sadistic incest perpetrator. However, in the majority of the cases, it appears that rather than violent attacks sexual contact in incest cases commonly takes the form of gentle variations of adult lovemaking. When gestures become too seductive, too lingering, centered on sex organs, or continued into adolescence, they turn into sexual abuse. The father is often immature with little self-confidence and a low self-esteem, and he expects too much from his offspring. Parents who are unsure of their own sexual needs and feelings may seek their children as partners, thus expressing their own frustrations of love. Sometimes it may be a form of self-punishment, viewing the child as an extension of self. It may also be an expression of uncontrollable anger directed toward a spouse, viewing the child as an extension of the spouse. Sometimes, unfortunately, the intent may be to defile, humiliate, and degrade the child.

THE FEMALE AS PERPETRATOR

Mother-child incest seems to be rarely reported and may well be rare. However, with the attitude of the male culture, this form of sexual relationship may be underreported because of the view in which sex is held. The son engaged in sex with the mother may not view the same act in the negative way in which the daughter involved in sex with the father would. The social repercussions on the mother may be more severe, or less believable, than of the same situation as far as the father is concerned. Brother-sister relationships appear to be more likely reported when the brother is a great deal older than the sister.

FAMILY RELATIONSHIPS AND INCEST

Evaluations of family situations where father-child incest has developed has demonstrated that the marital relationship between husband and wife may not show equal participation by both: the husband and wife are not seen as equal partners in the marriage relationship, and in the case of the father having an incest relationship with his daughter, there may be some signs of marital castration in social, sexual, and personal relationships by the wife/mother. Often, one partner is more dependent than the other parent, and frustration and immaturity have rendered the relationship unsatisfactory and/or ineffective. From a psychodynamic model approach, the husband may be looking for a mother image instead of a wife in a marriage. He may provide financial support for the family but is not able to give the needed emotional support to the wife. He may relate to her more as a dependent child than a partner. When she finds the independence and self-sufficiency she needs elsewhere, the husband may turn to his daughter as a surrogate wife-mother. Often, when a daughter has responsibilities (for any number of reasons) of preparing meals, doing laundry, and spending leisure time with the father, a sexual relationship may evolve. In such circumstances, his attitude toward a teenage daughter dating is predicated upon his fears of her abandoning him for another male.

Incest, like pedophilia, has many causes. One common motivational factor may be the retaliation on the part of the husband against the wife for actual or imagined unfaithfulness. Also, there is among many cases a feeling of "entitlement" to one's own children, that they are "sexual property." Among other parents who are involved in incest, two general characteristics are a general lack of impulse control and a confusion of roles, where the child becomes an object for the needs of the adult without the adult recognizing the inappropriateness of the behavior or the inability to meet these needs. These two dynamics are common not only to instances of sexual abuse but also to child abuse cases in general. Additionally, the practice of incest may cross from one generation to another. This point is well documented in the cases of incest found in the rural part of eastern Kentucky, where incest is a common fact in many families.

If there is more than one female child in the home, the father many times may abuse all of his children, sometimes concurrently, but more often consecutively. Often, the incest becomes public when the older abused daughter wishes to protect her siblings from similar abuse and is determined to use any means to prevent this abuse, including reporting. Other times, when the daughter determines that all of the daughters in the family are victimized, although the father told her that she was an especially chosen person, her sense of protectiveness for the others is lost and the trauma of her situation drives her to report the pattern of incest. In some other cases, the incest reporting is prompted because the father refuses to permit his daughters to have friends outside the home. He often has a rigid, uncompromising attitude when his teenage daughter starts to show interest in boys of her own age.

Incestuous relationships usually endure from one to six years and start at varying ages. There was some thought that teenagers were more often the victims of incest than younger children. According to some more recent studies, this was found not to be the case, and it appears that the onset of incest commences very early in the child's life. It appears that girls are more often the victim of incest, but the number of boy victims appears to be on the increase. There are some data that suggest that there is an increase in the percentage of mothers who are becoming involved in incestuous relationships with their sons as compared with the percentage of boys who are having homosexual incestuous relationships with their fathers.

A mother usually has a reason to suspect that her husband is involved in an incest relationship with the daughter. However, when forced to admit the fact, the wife many times may blame her own daughter. Often, the message transmitted to the daughter by the mother is that father is first and the child is second. The mother does not want to fight the father over this incest because she may fear that if she loses him, everything is lost. For the mother's survival, then, the daughter must be left to her own devices because the mother cannot defend her, and if the necessity develops, she will even sacrifice the daughter for the father.

The mother's initial reaction may be both shock and horror. If the marriage is poor, she may be angry enough to leave the father. If this is not the fact and the marriage is "not that bad," she needs help to evaluate her situation. If she reports, there is a likelihood that the husband will be arrested, the daughter may be removed from the home, and/or the community will know. The mother really has four choices, four considerations: her loyalty to her daughter; to threaten the husband but not press charges; to tell significant others, thereby not keeping it a family secret; and to seek crisis counselling. In the fourth instance, hopefully she will demand as a consequence of the disclosure that the husband also become involved in counselling.

In some other instances, the wife may become very dependent on the husband emotionally and sometimes financially. She may be insecure and not able to face the possibility of having to take care of herself and the children. She may have a previous marriage that ended in divorce or abandonment and feels that this reflects on her worth as a wife. In all of these instances, the wife, upon discovery of incestuous behavior of the husband, may be reluctant to take any decisive action that would threaten her marriage.

A father who normally behaves in an acceptable manner may try to rape his daughter when he is intoxicated. The daughter may rebuff these assualts if the mother is supportive. Otherwise, she may eventually submit. Incestuous fathers may be very respected members of the community, who in the privacy of their own home seek gratification through deviant sexual activity. Some core variables of fathers who practice incest may have the personality characteristics of being a loner and feelings of insecurity, inadequacy, and depressions. The sexual relationship between the father and the mother may also play an important role in the etiology of the father involved in incest. If the sex relationship is poor, lacking in some quality of enrichment (a subjective evaluation), then this also may be a contributing factor.

Many other men who are involved in incest seem to share common background characteristics. Their childhood appears to have been disorganized with family members; often they were victims of incest themselves. Their living conditions were many times termed as deteriorated, and the relationship with the father was termed as poor. As an adult, the incestuous male tends to show problems in masculinity, identity, and sexual potency. Some other fathers involved in incest may come from the best living conditions, educated in the best institutions of higher education, and be socially prominent.

Certainly, in not all cases where the sex relationship between the husband and the wife is lacking in pleasure and fulfillment does the husband turn to his children for sexual activity. Besides being the pillar of the community, he may be a good provider and in a professional field, such as a physician, lawyer, college professor, etc. He may possess a poor self-image, have a possessive attitude toward his children—not seeing them as individual persons, and not think of his activity as incest. When he does discipline, it is at a childlike level, not relating the discipline as an adult to a child, but as one child to another, using threats rather than discipline.

Most parents who are involved in the incestuous relationships are not oversexed or fixated with children as sex objects. They rather have normal sex drives, fairly normal sexual development, and most are not criminal types. A number of situations may develop when a mother is pregnant and a father initiates sexual activity with a child in the family, as well as other instances where alcohol is a significant factor may well be underestimated. Often, the daughter will not report her parent because she may fear that the parents may become separated or divorced, that she may be removed from home, that she would not be believed, or that the father might be sent to prison. Sometimes the abuse is followed by an outpouring of love and remorse. Unlike rape, this type of behavior develops slowly. Usually the child victim is confused; she loves her parents and tries to understand the behavior. She is faced with a dependency for her needs in life upon the person who is performing this act. She may not know that all parents do not act in this manner, and this may be the only attention and affection shown this child, thereby lending pleasure accompanied with guilt and revulsion.

In the final analysis, the family unit may be broken up with the termination of the marriage, the removal of the child, or the parent imprisoned. The entire family suffers from community repulsion. These, and other reasons, are facts behind why many cases of incest go unreported. Much public education is necessary in the dynamics of incest, including the education of the child to convince the youngster that he/she has not done anything wrong to precipitate this form of sexual abuse.

Incest can be less detrimental to the child if intervention takes place with goals set and followed to successful completion. Intervention should include therapy, both individual and family, with a goal toward prevention of the child from future assaults and another goal of trying to keep the family together but not endangering the welfare of the child in the process. Factors for consideration include the age of the child, which affects the child-parent reactions; dependency level of the child; emotional and competency level of the child; and which kind of molestation occurred. It is a multiproblem situation with one component being incest. Family conflict, alcoholism, financial reverses, birth control, drugs, and many other problems may be involved. In any circumstance, incest is always an act of violence obliterated by professions of love and mutual fulfillment, and it is imposed against a vulnerable human being. It is the most extreme form of oppression in denial of human rights involving a totally powerless person: a child.

Research has indicated that there may be certain types of children who are more apt to be incest victims within a family. These children often tend to be the undesired child, a child born of an incestuous relationship, a child who is an offspring of rape, an illegitimate child, a child born during a time of great economic need, a child with a parent serving a prison sentence, a child born despite an abortion attempt, a child reminding a parent of a hated spouse, the child of a former marriage who resembles the other spouse, a deformed child who is considered a personal offense by the parent, and a child born to a mother who did not plan or wish other children.

ERICKSEN'S TYPOLOGY OF OFFENDERS

It appears that in many cases most fathers, stepfathers, or other relatives involved in incestuous relationships fit into one of three typological categories modelled after the theory of Dr. William Ericksen at the University of Minnesota:

TYPE 1. (PSYCHOTIC)

He marries a woman more dependent and inadequate than he. He marries and fails as a provider and sexual partner. His wife rejects him sexually, fears him. Neither seek extramarital affairs.

He seeks sexual contact with an available daughter . . . allows daughter "special" relationship with father. There is little threat of rejection for him. Allays wife's fear husband will leave her.

TYPE 2. (SOCIOPATH)

He marries a woman he sees as domineering and controlling. He fails as a provider and sexual partner. His wife rejects him sexually, finds another man *but no divorce*. He seeks sexual contact with teenage daughter seen as "seductive and promiscuous," who ultimately rejects him as mother has. The girl may enjoy special relationship without sex. The wife appears unaware and uncaring.

TYPE 3. (ENDOGAMOUS)

> He marries a woman he sees as domineering and controlling. He fails as a provider and sexual partner. Wife rejects him sexually and *divorces him*. He remarries, often to divorced woman with teenage daughter. He again fails as provider and sexual partner. He seeks sexual contact with available daughter, whom he sees as seductive and promiscuous, like her mother and his first wife. The girl may feel competitive with mother for him. Mother is usually unaware, or allows it to continue because she fears divorce.

Ericksen stated that most of the incest perpetrators fall into the endogamous category. These situations result from an interplay between the father's, mother's, and daughter's personalities and circumstances of time, place, and availability. The wide variety of personal dynamics and circumstances that results in sexual contact between father and child shows that biological fathers and stepfathers share a great many characteristics and can be considered to show common dynamics in sexual relationships; stepfathers should be considered to have been so involved for the same reasons and in much the same circumstances as biological fathers.

Frank X: A Case of Incest

Not all cases of incest involve overt sexual activity. A born-again Christian received a vision from God one afternoon in his garage when installing a new starter in his car. God told this man that the natural way to praise Him was to practice nudity in the home. Joyously, he related his vision to his wife, who was also a fundamentalist. Both convinced their two daughters, ages fourteen and two. Frank, his wife Betty, and Pam and Cherry, the daughters, practiced nudity in their home for the next two years. Frank took over 1500 pictures of his daughter of both the instamatic and 35mm color prints variety in various stages of nudity. He expanded his "call" to include Pam's best friend, also fourteen, a neighbor of the family. Both girls posed willingly. A social service agency was called into the case after a neighbor saw a nude picture of Pam atop the television in the recreation room. The social work agency, along with the police department, launched an investigation into this case, charged the father with sex abuse, and after a trial in which the father pleaded innocent because of the grounds that God had commanded him to take pictures of his daughter and also because his photography was "art," Frank X was given five years probation.

Pam, upon realizing that the arrangement with the father, even though no actual physical sexual activity had occurred, was a form of incest and not a commandment of God, became rapidly emotionally distressed and was committed to a local mental hospital. She became more and more disoriented and at the time of this writing is just starting to become more accepting of her own role in the pattern of incest and her feelings toward her father and mother. She has been released from the hospital and has returned to live with her parents. The father is receiving counselling, a condition of his probation. The mother was also encouraged to participate in the counselling situation.

SYMPTOMS OF SEX ABUSE

Symptoms of the sexually abused child may include physical and behavioral signs as well as indirect comments made by the child. Physical signs such as hematomas, lacerations, irritation, pain, or injury to the genital area, vaginal or penile discharge, difficulty with urination, pregnancy, venereal disease, and nightmares are many times present and should be a sign of possible sexual abuse. Behavioral signs such as one child being treated differently in a significant way than the other members of the family, running away, use of alcohol or drugs, sexual promiscuity, withdrawal from social relationships, and inability to make friends may alert a school counselor. Comments such as, "He fooled around with me," "I don't like to be alone with my father," and, "I'm afraid to go home tonight," may all be a child's way of alerting those who are sensitive to this particular social problem to notice a potential incest case.

Mindy: A Five-Year-Old Incest Victim

The case of a thirty-four-year-old white male who was convicted of Sodomy I and sentenced to twenty-five years in prison is an excellent example of a school counselor being aware of key words while listening to a five-year-old first-grader, Mindy. The offender was one of eight children born to a low income family. His background indicated that he has little formal education but a good work record as a blue collar worker. He had been married and divorced prior to the time of the offense and was residing with the

Figures 6a & 6b. Sexual child abuse: incest. The father of this child was sentenced to five years probation. The photos were released by the court to the author for educational purposes.

mother of the child in a common-law relationship.

The following is an official version of the crime for which he was convicted. The transcript was taken from police files as dictated by the child-victim to the social worker and police officer team.

A teacher from an elementary school notified the local police department that she had suspected that one of her students, a five-year-old female, was a victim of incest. The police came to the school and talked with the child in the company of the teacher, the school counselor, and the social worker from the social service agency. (All names have been changed.)

Ms. Miller (the teacher) stated that shortly after Christmas she became suspicious that something had been going on in regard to the victim. She told the detectives that the victim was in her kindergarten class and began drawing pictures; she would ask her to explain the pictures and she felt that something had been going on between the victim and the man who lives with her mother that she called dad.

Ms. Miller began telling the detectives what the girl had stated and that she had written them down from the victim's statements. She told the detective that when the victim drew a picture there was a man and a little girl in the picture and that the little girl's name was Charlotte and the man's name was Tom and she called him daddy. Generally, Ms. Miller stated, she would draw a picture of the mother, however, she was off to the side and when the victim would first draw the picture she would state the mommy was not at home.

The teacher went on to state that Charlotte would state, "this is the daddy, this is the little girl, they is in bathroom. The daddy is doing kiss. This is the toilet. Then he shakes it. The little girl isn't supposed to be in the bathroom with the daddy. The daddy keeps saying for her to come in, come in, the bathroom. The little girl gets a bad whipping. This is the bathtub, this is the towel. They been to spick and spanish. This is the daddy's bobo."

Ms. Miller went on to state that each time the victim would draw the daddy she would draw his penis and refer to this as daddy's bobo. "It has a hole in it, piss comes out of the hole and medicine comes out of the hole. Daddy likes the little girl to come in the bathroom. He says it's beautiful. It's O.K., cause the mama ain't home. The daddy says to touch the bobo. It's soft and nice, but then it's hard too and has like bones in it. It's good to touch the daddy's bobo. Sometimes the daddy gives the little girl a bath with him. He washes her good. He rubs and rubs and rubs. She gets nice and clean. He washes her hair too. She has to keep her eyes tight so soap doesn't get in. He gets her nice and clean. She looks pretty. This is daddy's bobo. It's nice, it's really nice. The little girl touches the daddy's bobo. She doesn't want to. If mama comes home and they is in the bathroom again, the little girl gets a bad whipping."

"But daddy says to touch the bobo. It's good to touch the bobo. The medicine is good. The daddy touches the little girl with the bobo. The bobo touches her all over. On her head, on her tummy, on her legs, and her toes." At this point, Ms. Miller stated that there was a lot of giggling and wiggling on the part of the victim. "Mama says it's bad, terrible, but daddy says it's good. There is the bobo. There is the hole, that's where the piss and medicines come out. The bobo goes in the girl's mouth. It's big, real big, it chokes, the medicines comes out, it tastes terrible. The little girl wants to spit it out, but she has to swallow it. It's good for her. It makes her well. The daddy says it's heavenly. Beautiful. If the mama comes home, the little girl gets another bad whipping, but the daddy keeps saying, 'come in, come in, come in.' "

"The daddy says it's good to touch the bobo. It's good to put them in the little girl's mouth. He puts it in all the time, all the time. Every day he puts it in her mouth or somewhere else. That's the daddy's bobo. It's little then gets big. It's soft and wonderful. It gets big. It's hard. It has bones in it. It's red. The daddy puts it in here. He puts it in here too. That's good too."

At this point, Ms. Miller stated that the child points to the area between her leg in the private area. "He puts it in the front of her butt. You know, down there. But when daddy puts it in the front of the butt they have to lay down. That's how you get the shot. It doesn't hurt too much now. She gets lots of shots. The more times she gets the bobo, the more it don't hurt."

"If you get enough bobo and don't tell, don't have to go to the hospital and get them shots in the finger. The little girl goes in the bathroom lots with daddy. Lots, lots, lots. He tells her to all the time. Every day, every day. When they is through, they gets dressed right way, right away. That's the mommy. If she catches them in the bathroom, the little girl gets a bad whipping. The daddy says he's going to take the little girl in the bathroom and the mama says she's going to beat her. The daddy says he's going to take her back in the bathroom. They fight about the little girl. The little girl runs away from home."

The victim also told the teacher that "other boys and girls don't know about all these bad words and that they shouldn't know," and stated that, "it's bad for them to know. It's O.K. for the teacher to know about all the bad words. The teacher shouldn't never tell mama that the little girl told about the bad words."

By the alertness of the teacher, her actions were able to hopefully circumvent a long history of child abuse by this man on Mindy. The police officers were able to ascertain some dates that Mindy had been forced to perform oral sodomy and have anal intercourse. With this information from the child and the teacher, the offender was arrested and later convicted.

SUMMARY

To be aware of the practice of incest, those in the criminal justice system should be cognizant of the signs to look for. The signs may be physical, behavioral, verbal, or a combination of all these. In addition, there are other possible contributing factors beyond the lack of impulse control and confusion of social roles. These factors may include prolonged or habitual absence of either the mother or the father, assignment of a "mother" role to a daughter (for example, caring for other children, looking after the father), loss of the wife by divorce, separation, or death, history of child abuse in the background of one or both parents, conditions of overcrowding, alcoholism, drug addiction, intellectual limitation of parents or child, and an inability to establish social and/or emotional contacts outside the family because of eccentric belief system, extreme poverty, or remoteness of the area in which the family lives.

The interviewing of a child who has been a victim of incest certainly entails a great deal of sensitivity and care. A guideline for interviewing child victims has been developed by Fred Drenkhan for this very purpose. The guidelines are attached.

The focus of the interview should center around the unique situation of the child victim, speaking with the child on the child's level and using the language of the child. The setting, establishment of the relationship, obtaining a history of the sexual assault, the child's statement of what, who, when, where, and the closing of the interview are all considered to be integral units of the interview.

The child is the important element in the total scheme of the involvement of the criminal justice system. The contact with the child must be approached from a different perspective and with special understanding.

The treatment approach for the adult involved in incest has with it an added dimension since the family is intimately involved. Any treatment plan should involve the entire family. The father who is sexually involved with the daughter should not be treated in a vacuum. The daughter needs special care and attention to ease her feelings of anomie, guilt, and shame. The wife needs someone to help her with her general feelings about the situation and to evaluate those feelings. It must moreover be realized that the father (or the mother if she is the incestuous parent) is the responsible agent for the incest behavior regardless of the contributions made by the child. This responsibility must be emphasized and be a focal point for therapy. In the past, it has been historically true that the incestuous parent has been separated from the family. Newer points of view and relevant research tend to point out that the better approach may be a total family therapeutic plan.

INTERVIEWING CHILD VICTIMS*

Guidelines for Criminal Justice System Personnel

Background Information

The following issues affect the child's ability to give a history of sexual assault and influence the cooperativeness of victim and family.

I. **Child's Developmental Level**

A child's cognitive, emotional and social growth occurs in sequential phases of increasingly complex levels of development. Progression occurs with mastery of one stage leading to concentration on the next.

Cognitive—Preconceptual, concrete, intuitive thinking in the young child gradually develops toward comprehension of abstract concepts. Time and space begin as personalized notions and gradually are identified as logical and ordered concepts.

Emotional—The young child perceives her/himself egocentrically with little ability to identify her/himself in a context. S/he is dependent on the family

*From materials prepared with Federal Grant No. 77-DF = 10-0016.

to meet all needs and invests adults with total authority. The child often reflects the emotional responses of the parents. S/he gradually shifts to greater reliance on peer relationships and emotional commitments to people outside the family.

Behavioral—The young child is spontaneous, outgoing and explosive with few internal controls and only a tentative awareness of external limits. S/he has a short attention span. A child most often expresses feelings through behavior rather than verbally. As the child grows, s/he develops internal controls and establishes a sense of identity and independence. Peers and other adults have increasing influence on behavior.

II. **Sexual Assault**

Characteristics of the assault affect the child's emotional perception of the event and to a great extent determine the response. The closeness of the child's relationship to the offender, the duration of the offense, the amount of secrecy surrounding the assault, and the degree of violence are the factors which have the greatest impact on the child's reaction. The child may very well have ambivalent feelings toward the offender or be dependent on him for other needs.

III. **Response to Child**

The child is fearful of the consequences of reporting a sexual assault. The response of the family support system and official agencies will directly affect the resolution of the psychological trauma and her/his cooperativeness as a witness. The child fears s/he will be disbelieved or blamed for the assault and almost always is hesitant about reporting.

Interviewing Child Victims

I. **Preparing for Interview**

Prior to interviewing the child, obtain relevant information from parents/guardian, and if applicable, Child Protective Services caseworker, physician, and/or Sexual Assault Center/Rape Relief counselor.

A. Explain your role and procedures to above personnel and enlist their cooperation.

B. Determine child's general developmental status: age, grade, siblings, family composition: capabilities, ability to write, read, count, ride a bike, tell time, remember events; any unusual problems: physical, intellectual, behavioral, knowledge of anatomy and sexual behavior: family terminology for genital areas.

C. Review circumstances of assault (as reported already by child to other person): what, where, when, by whom, and to whom reported; exact words of child; other persons told by child; how many have interviewed child: child's reaction to assault; how child feels about it and what, if any, behavioral signs of distress (nightmares, withdrawal, regression, acting out) have occurred.

D. Determine what reactions and changes child has been exposed to following revelation of the assault(s): believing; supportive; blaming; angry; ambivalent; parents getting a divorce; move to a new home.

II. Beginning the Interview

A. Setting—The more comfortable for the child, the more information s/he is likely to share.

1. Flexibility—A child likes to move around the room, explore and touch, sit on the floor or adult's lap.
2. Activity—Playing or coloring occupy child's physical needs and allows her/him to talk with less guardedness.
3. Privacy—Interruptions distract an already short attention span, divert focus of interview, and make self-conscious or apprehensive child withdraw.
4. Support—If the child wishes a parent or other person present, it should be allowed. A frightened or insecure child will not give a complete statement.

B. Establishing a relationship

1. Introduction—Name, brief and simple explanation of role and purpose: "I am the lawyer (or legal person) on your side: my job is to talk to children about these things because we want to them to stop happening."
2. General exchange—Ask about name (last name), age, grade, school and teacher's name, siblings, family composition, pets, friends, activities, favorite games/TV shows. (It often helps to share personal information when appropriate, e.g., children, pets.)
3. Assess level of sophistication and ability to understand concepts—Does child read, write, count, tell time; know colors or shapes; know the day or date; know birthdate; remember past events (breakfast, yesterday, last year); understand before and after; know about money; assume responsibilities (goes around neighborhood alone, stays at home alone, makes dinner, etc.)

III. Obtaining History of Sexual Assault

A. Preliminaries

1. Use language appropriate to child's level; be sure child understands words. (Watch for signs of confusion, blankness, or embarrassment: be careful with words like incident, occur, penetration, prior, ejaculation, etc.)
2. Do not ask WHY questions ("Why did you go to the house?" "Why didn't you tell?") They tend to sound accusatory.
3. Never threaten or try to force a reluctant child to talk. Pressure causes a child to clam up and may further traumatize her/him.
4. Be aware that the child who has been instructed or threatened not to tell by the offender (ESPECIALLY if a parent) will be very reluctant and full of anxiety (you will usually notice a change in the child's

affect while talking about the assault). The fears often need to be allayed.

—"It's not bad to tell what happened."
—"You won't get in trouble."
—"You can help your dad by telling what happened."
—"It wasn't your fault."
—"You're not to blame."

5. Interviewer's affective response should be consonant with child's perception of assault (e.g., don't emphasize jail for the offender if the child has expressed positive feelings toward him.)
6. Ask direct, simple questions as open-ended as allowed by child's level of comprehension and ability to talk about the assault.

B. Statement

1. WHAT

—"Can you tell me what happened?"
—"I need to know what the man did."
—"Did he ever touch you? Where?"
—"Where did he put his finger?"
—"Have you ever seen him with his clothes off?"
—"Did you ever see his penis (thing, pee pee, weiner) get big?"
—"Did anything ever come out of it?"

Once basic information is elicited, ask specifically about other types of sexual contact.

—"Did he ever put it into your mouth?"
—"Did he ever make you touch him on his penis?"

2. WHO

Child's response here will probably not be elaborate. Most children know the offender and can name him, although in some cases the child may not understand relationship to self or family. Ascertain from other sources what is the exact nature/extent of the relationship.

3. WHEN

The response to this question will depend on child's ability, how recently assault happened, lapse between last incident and report, number of assaults (children will tend to confuse or mix separate incidents). If the child is under six, information re: time is unlikely to be reliable. An older child can often narrow down dates and times using recognizable events or associating assault with other incidents.

—"Was it before your birthday, the weekend, Valentine's Day?"
—"Was it nighttime or daytime?"
—"Did it happen after dinner, 'Happy Days', your brother's bedtime?"

4. WHERE

The assault usually occurs in the child's and/or offender's home. Information about which room, where other family members were, where child was before assault may be learned.

5. COERCION

What kind of force, threat, enticement, pressure was used to insure cooperation and secrecy?

—"Did he tell you not to tell?" "What did he say?"

—"Did he say something bad would happen or you would get in trouble if you told?"

—"Did the man say it was a secret?"

C. Assessing credibility and competency

1. Does child describe acts or experience to which s/he would not have normally been exposed? (Average child is not familiar with erection or ejaculation until adolescence at the earliest.)
2. Does child describe circumstances and characteristics typical of sexual assault situation? ("He told me that it was our secret"; "He said I couldn't go out if I didn't do it"; "He told me it was sex education".)
3. How and under what circumstances did child tell? What were exact words?
4. How many times has child given the history and how consistent is it regarding the basic facts of the assault (*not* times, dates, circumstances, sequence of events, etc.)?
5. How much spontaneous information can child provide? How much prompting is required?
6. Can child define difference between truth and a lie? (This question is not actually very useful with young children because they learn this by rote but may not understand the concepts.)

IV. Closing the Interview

A. Praise/thank child for information/cooperation.

B. Provide information

1. Child—Do not extract promises from child regarding testifying. Most children cannot project themselves into an unknown situation and predict how they will behave. Questions about testifying in court or undue emphasis on trial will have little meaning and often frightens the child (causing nightmares and apprehension).
2. Parent—Provide simple, straightforward information about what will happen next in the criminal justice system and approximately when, the likelihood of trial, etc.

C. Enlist cooperation—Let them know who to contact for status reports or in an emergency; express appreciation and understanding for the effort they are making by reporting and following through on process.

D. Answer questions: solicit responses.

Chapter 7

CHILD PORNOGRAPHY

There is perhaps no social problem involving the use of children that causes as much emotional upheavel and a sense of moral disgust as child pornography. Many citizens have a feeling that if adults wish to involve themselves in adult pornography, either as models or as customers, it should be their business. However, this same thought is not present when children are involved. In the first instance, the customer of child pornography is viewed as someone perverted and "sick." There "must be something wrong with a person who wishes to see children in poses that are supposed to arouse erotic feelings." Children are supposed to be asexual and pure, and those who violate this premise are people who are degenerates and dangerous to the functioning of society. In the second dimension of this discussion, the children who are involved in child porn are certainly not modelling as a free choice. Many are forced into child porn because they are runaways and this is the only manner in which they can earn money for survival. Others are involved because a parent is receiving money for their performance. Still others have been abducted by a pornographer and threatened with great physical harm. There may be some truth to one or all three of these arguments. There are some children who are involved in kiddie porn because they are runaways, and this is the only fashion in which they can earn money for food and lodging. There are also some parents who sell the services of their child, and, of course, some children are kidnapped and used as performers in child pornography.

WHAT IS CHILD PORNOGRAPHY

Of course, to discuss the whole social problem of child pornography, it is necessary to discuss and come to some operational definition of pornography in general. This is not an easy task. When people view the statue of David, there are not too many who become sexually aroused. Certainly there is nudity and the male genitalia is exposed. Does this in and of itself mean that the statue is pornographic? One would have a difficult time in suggesting to most citizens that this is truly a type of adult pornography and should be banned from public view. The same argument might be tried concerning the statues of Venus DeMilo. Truly the bust of the model is shown and may be erotic for someone who is a partialist or one who has erotic feelings for women with no arms. But to the general population, again, this is a work of art and not a statue that was deliberately made by an artist to arouse sexual feelings. The truly pornographic picture, statue, or film is one with the manifest purpose of arousing erotic feelings in the viewer. This same feeling is true when one is speaking about reading material. The writings of Rimmer (*Proposition 31, The Harrard Experiment, Thursday, My Love*, and others) may be pornographic, or the writings may be an indication of the changing sexual mores of the society. In this case, maybe only the writer knows the true purpose. However, there are many other instances in which it is very evident that the purpose of the book, the film, the play, or the pictures are deliberately manufactured, filmed, or written for that express purpose. This is true, I believe, in the cases of *Playboy, Oui, Nudist Moppets, Nudist Angels,* and *Lollitots*. The Johnny Wadd movies, "Deep Throat," "Behind the Green Door," and many other films are "pure" examples of pornography.

The real problem results when one tries to define obscenity. The definition of obscenity is something disgusting to the senses. War, poverty, child abuse, and hunger are all realities that to the typical citizens are obscene. Not all cases of obscenity involve sex and sex behavior. One cannot say the same thing when it comes to pornography.

This dilemma was faced without resolve when the President's Commission on Obscenity and Pornography was formed by President Lyndon Johnson. The general findings of the Commission were that there was no scientific evidence to show that exposure to erotica caused any antisocial behavior. As a matter of fact, there may be some positive effects (Kant & Goldstein). There were two sets of questions asked of three groups of men. One group was composed of men who were termed as "normal;" that is, those men in the course of the last year who would see some form of pornography (see an X-rated movie, pick up a magazine containing nudity, etc.). A second group was composed of men who were termed as "users;" those men in the course of the last year who normally subscribed to or purchased some pornography material. The last group was the so-called "deviant group." This group was further divided into three subgroups. Each of the three subgroups had been in a mental hospital for the criminally insane for the last several months. The deviant group was composed of rapists, child molesters who molested female children, and child molesters who molested male children. The first questions posed to the three groups was, "As adolescents, how much pornography did you see?" The group that had seen the most was the "normal" group, and the group that had seen the least amount of porn was the sex criminal group. The second question concerned itself with how much pornography did the person see in the last year. The reason for asking "in the last year" was that all of the sex offenders had been free in the "last year." The group that had seen the most pornography was the "user" group, and the group that had seen the least amount of pornography was again the sex criminal group. So, in both instances, the sex criminal had seen less porn as an adolescent and as an adult.

As a reaction to this study, Wolfgang and Larsen offered a minority statement to the general statement of the President's Commission. Their recommendation was that pornographic information should be available to all those who are interested in purchasing or viewing it. There should be, in essence, no age restriction to the availability of the pornographic material. This particular recommendation does appear to have some validity to it if the findings of Kant and Goldstein are accurate.

The majority recommendation of the President's Commission was that since the only measurable consequence of the exposure to erotica was an increase in masturbation, the availability of pornography should be the age of eighteen. Regardless of the general findings and the recommendations of the committee, President Nixon dismissed the contents of the report with a very simple statement: "We know better, don't we?"

As stated earlier, there is little public furor raised regarding adult pornography other than a periodic parade against adult bookstores that crop up in some areas of a city. But when it is found that a bookstore is selling child pornography or a parent is involved in selling pictures of their child, the general apathy toward pornography is ignored and a feeling of social rage is directed toward the perpetrators.

Child pornography is the use of children in movies, pictures, books, etc. as sexual beings, in the same way that adults are depicted in adult publications. The debate over obscenity and child pornography is usually a heated one. The child, with no voice in the process, is viewed as a victim, not a person with a choice to become involved in such an activity. McCaghy offered an argument that in 1977 a moral crusade began in the United States. The crusade was short-lived and ended when President Carter signed Public Law 95-225, an amendment to the United States Code concerning the use of children in obscene material. Because of the general tone of the law, there were few people who were publicly opposed to the use of children in pornography, although there were few who opposed the legislation because of First Amendment rights.

The social impetus recognizing that children were indeed unwilling victims in the industry of child pornography was the publication of Robin Lloyd's *For Money or Love: Boy Prostitutes in America.* The *Washington Star*, the *Washington Post*, and other elements of the media responded to the crusade. Not at all times did they agree on the issue of child porn. The overriding concern centered around the First Amendment, censorship, and over the priorities of the crusade.

Regardless of the pressures on both sides of the issue, spokespersons for the crusade against kiddie porn have emerged. Lloyd Martin, Los Angeles Police Department, Dr. Judianne Densen-Gerber, Odyssey Center, New York City, and John Rabun, Exploited Child Unit, Louisville, are only a few of those who have become nationally known in the fight against child porn and exploited children. New buzz words have even been coined to acquaint the public with this social problem: sexploitation, chickenhawk, kiddie porn, etc. All of the above advocates in the march against the victimization of children have appeared before the nation's lawmakers in Washington to acquaint the powerful with the extent of the problem and the possible effects of the involvement of the child in kiddie porn. They, and others, have been effective in obtaining new laws.

THE LAW AND KIDDIE PORN

Before 1977, there were few laws either on the state or federal level that attempted to regulate the sexual exploitation of youth. Today, almost all states and the federal government have legislation that prescribes penalties against those who abuse the child. The Protection of Children Against Sexual Exploitation Act, Public Law 95-225, extended the federal government's role to include prosecution of both the producers and the distributors of child pornography. Also included in this law was some prohibition against the transportation of children across state lines for the purpose of sexual exploitation. This law provides punishment for anyone who uses, employs, or persuades a minor (anyone under the age of 16) to become involved in child pornography, either visual or printed material, that depicts sexually explicit material. Punishment is also provided for parents, guardians, or other person having control or custody of the minor who knowingly permits the child to be used in kiddie porn.

It should be remembered that most of the time child pornography is a state problem and not a federal one. Forty-eight of the fifty states have some legislation concerning child porn. Some states have merely amended their adult pornography laws to suit this particular social concern, but most have adopted new laws with stiff penalties. Moreover most of the offenses are considered to be felonies. In spite of, and even because of, such cases as *Miller v. California*, *Prince v. Massachusettes*, *Ginsberg v. New York*, and *The People v. Ferber*, it appears that child exploitation laws are having some effect. It would appear immature to say that the laws are "working." In San Francisco only two years ago, this author was able to purchase child pornography over the counter. Today, it is becoming very difficult to purchase this same material without gaining the trust of the bookstore manager or owner. The laws have at their base a vital concern for the welfare of the child by punishing the adult. Sadly though, the laws are not concerned with providing some type of treatment programs for the child-victim.

TYPES OF KIDDIE PORN

It should be obvious that there would be no social problem of child pornography without a demand for the product, a method of producing the product, and a distribution system for the product. Of course, whenever there is a need, in this case kiddie porn, the enterprise system will develop the methodology and distribution system.

Of one immediate concern is the extent or the prevalence of child pornography. There is no way to exactly measure the extent of this social problem. There are some guesses, some educated and some others quite uneducated. It is unfortunate that the uneducated guesses, the SWAG guesses, are the ones that capture the media and the ones the population grabs onto to measure the extent of the problem. Testimony presented at the House Hearing on the sexual exploitation of children estimated that about 75 percent of the United States pornographic market involves sexual activity of children with adults. How accurate this statement is, and there is some thought that it may not be too accurate, is beyond validation. In the collection of child pornography at the University of Louisville, for example, only a slight percentage of the kiddie porn shows both adults and juveniles in sexual scenes. This is not the case in paperback novels. The majority of the themes in these books concern themselves with sex between parents and their children, strangers and children, teachers and students, and other relationships that amaze the imagination.

In an immediate breakdown into types of kiddie porn, there is a commercial product that has been produced for sale from an adult bookstore to a customer. This type of child porn is done in a slick fashion, and the contents of the publication will run the gamut of children in various stages of dress to the point of complete nudity. There are stories that often accompany the pictures written to arouse erotic feelings. The other form of child pornography is done by amatuers: relatives, friends, or pedophiles who will entice the child into a relationship with pornography, either through promises, threats, or other likely props that may meet with success.

In the latter form of kiddie porn, this writer has been acquainted with several forms of child pornography made by parents. In one case, two parents were involved in filming their two-week-old son performing oral sex on adult males through a two-way mirror in their bedroom. The movie was sold, and the parents made several thousand dollars before they were apprehended by the police. There are many other cases where some parents are involved in either selling or trading pictures of their children with other parents of similar interests. It is interesting to note that even though most of the pictures are of the instamatic variety some are processed through normal channels at the local drug store or drive-in photo processing center. This author talked with professionals in the field of film processing about the practice of developing pictures where the nude subject is obviously a juvenile. One owner stated that much of the developing and processing is done by automation and very seldom is the finished product seen by the human eye. Therefore, unless there is some indication that a juvenile may be the subject of kiddie porn, the film itself would not be inspected.

Commercial child pornography is an industry with a clientele that is, for the most part, hidden. In examining evidence that has been placed at the disposal of this author by the courts in Kentucky, it is apparent that there is a wide variety of different types of commercial child porn. The preponderant form appears to be centered around small children, especially when females are concerned.

Young girls featured in child porn are often featured in a facade of nudism. Publications such as *Nudist Children, Nudist Moppets,*

Nudist Angels, and others feature editorials that attempt to legitimize nudity and children. *Nudist Moppets*, for example, ran the following editorial:

> Although basically we are all in our most natural state of being when we are nude, it is our children who are least concerned about the relative morality of degree of clothing. Left to their own devices, children would only dress for fun, style or comfort. Unless they have been indoctrinated into the regimentation of dress by their parents, young people frolic and uninhibitedly cavort with complete happiness . . . with or without clothing.
>
> Nudist children are the incontrovertable proof of the fact that our bodies exist in their entirety, with no reason to feel shame for any component or the exercitation in nudist freedoms.

There are editorials in other magazines that pontificate the same theme. The stories inside of the magazines that pertain to little girls tell the reader what the small child wants to be when she grows up. "Karri wants to be a policeman when she gets big. But that means she will have to keep clean and she likes to get dirty now." Or, "Carol is a pretty little girl with a love of all-day suckers and bedtime stories."

The by-lines and short stories surrounding the pictures of the small girls tell the reader of the simplicity of being a little girl and her virginity and purity. Most of the kiddie porn of females shows little actual sexual activity. The poses are asexual, and many show group scenes. Among the pseudonudism magazines, a young girl and an adult female, supposedly the mother, are often posed in an outdoor scene. There are, however, exceptions to this general rule. In some publications, such as *Child-Love*, a foreign publication, there are many pictures of overt sexual activity that depict young girls in acts of mutual masturbation, tribadism, and kissing. There are but a few kiddie porn publications that depict a boy and girl in sex scenes. In a *Moppets* magazine recently there was a centerfold picture with a short story of a brother and sister who were pictured nude, but there was no overt sex involved.

There also appears to be a mail order business that deals expressly with the distribution of child pornography. Confiscated evidence in a child molestation case showed an order for a packet of professionally-done glossy pictures of an eleven-year-old girl, Lynne. Gallery Portfolios advertised:

Figure 8. Example of child pornography available accross the counter. Photo by author.

> Perhaps the most beautiful child model ever photographed.
>
> Like a rosebud at first hint of bloom Lynne radiates delicate elegance . . . A classical grace and charm ordinarily found only in the rhythmic sophistication of the adult high fashion model.

For a grand total of 21.00 dollars, the customer could obtain two 8x10 bordered mounting prints, four 5x7 glossy framing prints, and eight 4x5 quad bookmount prints. All of the photos were contained in an "equisitely illustrated folio to preserve them for treasured viewing."

Figures 9a, 9b, 9c, & 9d. Examples of child pornography available accross the counter. Photos by the author.

Figure 10. These photographs were confiscated as evidence in a child molestation case and were released to the author for educational purposes.

In kiddie porn that depicts the young boy, the sex acts are usually well shown. Most of the pictures show at least two males involved in a variety of sexual acts from mutual masturbation and fellatio to anal sex. There is some hint in many photos of sadism and masochism with whips, chains, and other items for pain and torture. What is so interesting in both male and female juvenile pornography is the relative lack of adults in the scene with the exception of the "mother" in the "nudist" magazines. The young boys in the kiddie porn are viewed as active participants, engaging in a variety of different sex acts with other boys of relatively the same age. In paperback books, the theme often switches to older men engaging in sex with young boys, boys initiated into "sex rings," and sex occurring in public areas such as parks, bus stations, and public restrooms. What seems to be a common theme in many pulp publications is the young boy, a virgin, being forcibly initiated into sex with an older man, and after the act has been consummated, the younger male becomes so much enamored with the homosexual acts that he becomes the pursuer of further sex.

In the past, it was found that many publications featured models who were made to look younger; that is, a female obviously well past her eighteenth birthday but dressed in preteen clothing and wearing pig tails. But in today's society, with the market for kiddie porn being what it is, child models are available and the necessity for "faking it" is no longer necessary.

KIDDIE PORN'S EFFECTS ON CHILDREN

Intuitive knowledge would have us believe that those children who are involved in child porn would be eternally psychologically and emotionally damaged. This might truly be the case. However, it must be noted that there are no full-termed, scientific studies that could verify this point of view. For the most part, the children who are involved in the production of kiddie porn are invisible to the criminal justice system. The adults also are not well known, and the relationship between the adult, the child, and the system must be examined and the prognosis for adjustment as far as the child is concerned must hinge on the relationships developed in his/her social world.

There has been much literature that shows some relationship among the variables of childhood prostitution, runaways, and child pornography. In a study of over 235 youngsters involved in the criminal justice system in Kentucky for the above three offenses, the children were asked about their involvement with kiddie porn. Less than 11 percent admitted any involvement in child pornography, and most of this involvement was of the noncommercial variety. It may be that commercial pornography is more prevalent in larger cities around the coastal areas of the nation.

The effect on the child from his/her involvement in kiddie porn may lie in several different dimensions. First of all, there may be extreme social repercussions from peers if it is found out the child has been involved in pornography. An added dimension may be other problems presented by the adult who is responsible for introducing the youth to kiddie porn. The adult may introduce the youth to alcohol, drugs, etc. to entice the youth into the porno scene and, once into the situation, use the same to keep them. Some researchers tend to believe that child pornography is the first step in many children's runaway process. This particular author tends to believe that pornography more often occurs after the child has become a runaway. In the same way that juvenile prostitution often follows the juvenile's runaway, kiddie porn is yet another fashion, admittedly a limited one, to obtain money for survival.

Some view pornography as a victimless crime. There may be some validity to this point of view when the model is an adult and freely chooses for one reason or another to become so involved. When the model, however, is a juvenile and cannot freely choose his/her own course of action, the victim is clearly identified and perhaps marked for life. The final analysis of possible harm to the child must wait on the scientific inquiry process. It may be, as in the case of child molestation, that the judgment of the significant others be more important in the adjustment pattern of the youth than the actual kiddie porn experience.

Chapter 8

PORNOGRAPHY

One social concern that has emerged is the whole issue and debate over obscenity and pornography. Pornography is not necessarily obscene and not all obscene things are pornographic. The word obscenity comes from the French word meaning disgusting to the senses or abhorent to morality. Pornography, concerning its etymological definition, literally means the writings of harlots. The obvious purpose of pornography is to arouse the sexual appetite, while obscene things may have nothing to do with sex.

Anthropologists such as Margaret Mead believe that pornography is found in every culture and carries with it some form of value judgment. These value judgments are necessary, as are deviants, to define the limits of society. Every culture does not necessarily believe that there is something wrong with pornography. The attitudes toward pornography and obscenity in Sweden is obviously different from the attitudes concerning the same phenomenon occurring in rural southern United States and among the Trobriand Islanders.

It is also quite evident that the manifest purpose of pornography has to be considered in order to be defined. In this particular case, pornography has created a great problem for the legal system as well as public concern. If one would accept the basic operational definition of pornography as anything that has been made to deliberately arouse erotic feelings and obscenity as that which is disgusting to the senses, it can be easily seen that there is a basic difference in these two words. Pornography inately involves sex and obscenity may or may not involve sex. There are many things that are obscene that do not deal with sex or sexuality at all: child abuse, war, famine, plague, epidemics, etc. These occurrences are certainly disgusting to the people who are intimately involved as well as those who are only tangently involved. But as stated above, there are certain behavioral patterns, such as bare-breasted women, that some societies believe are not erotic-producing at all; yet if this same behavior was manifested in other cultures, it would cause public outrage and demonstrated furor. So the basic difference between pornography and obscenity should be clear.

Throughout history pornography has been a source of concern only because some believe that some detrimental effect may be experienced by those who view, read, or are otherwise exposed to such material. This obviously makes some sense when one uses intuitive knowledge. However, scientific facts and research do not necessarily substantiate these feelings. *Fanny Hill*, an English novel of the early 1820s, was the first piece of purely erotic literature that was found to be legally obscene. From that moment on, laws have been passed from one country to another that have dealt with obscene and pornographic materials. The battle continues.

In the play *Hair*, in the last scene, there is complete male and female nudity. Among many critics of the theater, there is some agreement that nudity in and of itself has nothing to do with pornography. Nudity may become totally asexual, and some consider it to be just another form of costume. So it is possible for art to be pornographic but not obscene. Other items may be objectively pornographic but not subjectively so. A film intended to be pornographic may be so tacky that it turns people off. These films', which depict complete male and female nudity, original mission may have been to arouse erotic feelings, but they may be so poorly done and in "such bad taste" that it turns out to be not pornographic at all but "only" obscene.

In this particular section of pornography as a sex crime, it must be stated that the victim of pornography may not share the same characteristics as the victim of child molestation, rape, or other types of sex crimes. The victim may be the viewer, and the particular effects of pornography, while not completely researched and validated, may lie only in being stimulated to become involved in antisocial and/or sexual activity. To be considered here is a general overall treatment of the legal aspects of pornography and obscenity, the types of pornography, and possible effects of these phenomenon.

LEGAL CONCERNS

It has been conservatively estimated that by the age of eighteen about 80 percent of the males and 70 percent of the females have seen some form of pornography. Others have estimated that at least one of two adult men and one of four adult women have been exposed to pornography within the last two years. These sets of data are probably outdated and newer research would possibly show a great increase in the numbers who have seen or at least been exposed to pornography. There may also be an increase in the numbers of people who regularly purchase this material.

Most of the patrons of adult bookstores, according to this writer's research, are white males, in the late thirties or early forties. Many are businessmen on their lunch hours, sporting a wedding ring. In addition, there appears to be a group of people who have been termed as being on the fringe of society, those who loiter around the adult bookstore area for a variety of reasons, and some of their reasons may center around prostitution and pandering.

The legal dilemma surrounding pornography centers around the famous Comstock Law of 1873. Chapter 4 of this law excluded the selling of contraceptives and contraceptive information through the mail by defining the material as obscene. A forty-year battle against pornography was launched by Anthony Comstock, a small man with a big crusade. His law banned, "... obscene, lewd, lascivious, indecent, filthy, or vile articles, matter, thing, device or substance." Comstock joined with the Young Men's Christian Association, and the legislation has remained basically the same since the turn of the century. This crusader became a special agent for the U.S. Post Office in charge of the enforcement. States that did not have particular statutes regarding obscenity passed such laws, and by the early 1900s, at least thirty states had prohibitions against pornography.

In recent times, the whole question concerning the issue of control of pornography has been connected with censorship. In *Roth v. U.S.* in 1957, obscenity to the Supreme Court is not protected by the First Amendment. The First Amendment says

> Congress shall make no law respecting an establishment of religion, or prohibiting the free exercise thereof; or abridging the freedom of speech, or of the press; or the right of the people peaceably to assemble, and to petition the government for redress of grievances.

In addition to this, the Supreme Court also stated that not all such sexual materials are obscene. Obscenity is, then, "... to the average person applying contemporary community standards the dominant theme of the material as a whole appeals to purient interest." Obscene material, then, is sexual matter that appeals to the purient (lustful) interests. The total criteria for determining whether the material is obscene offered by the Supreme Court in the *Roth v. U.S.* were

1. For the average person, the dominant theme of the material taken as a whole must appear to the "purient" interest in sex.
2. The material must be "patently" offensive because it affronts "contemporary community standards" regarding the depicting of sexual matters.
3. The material must be "utterly lacking in redeeming social value" (Lipton).

But what are community standards? This is a particular concern that has added fuel to the fire in trying to ascertain and evaluate "current community standards." In the mid-1960s, a citizens action group was initiated in Jefferson County, Kentucky. Similar groups were also started in other communities throughout the United States. This committee of citizens held town meetings throughout their community. At each of the meetings, heated and sometimes violent dialogue was the ordinary scenario, the dialogue of interested citizens and representatives of various social and religious groups. One of the speakers asserted that in no fashion did he want others to act as a censor for him. The next speaker, a housewife, born-again Christian, launched into a long discourse concerning her responsibility as a Christian and a mother and to act to the best of her ability to clear the pornographic books from the shelves of the schools and public libraries. The end product, after several thousand dollars and many hours devoted to the topic, was that this committee could not develop current community attitudes concerning pornography and obscenity.

While attitudes and public standards for obscenity and pornography vary from one area of the country to another, it also seems to vary within a community from one location to another. It would also appear to be almost an impossible task to develop a set of community standards that would include the moral values of all of the citizens within even a small town.

The famous Ginsberg case of 1966 was a further deviation from consideration of the material itself. In this case, the motive of

Figures 11a & 11b. Examples of pornography, both sadomasochistic (top) and kiddie porn (bottom). Photos by the author.

the purveyor was examined and less emphasis was placed on the material itself. As evidence of Ginsberg's true motive, it was brought up in this case that Ginsberg tried to get his mailing address changed to Blue Ball or Intercourse, Pennsylvania, and this was the "proof" of his motive. He was successful in obtaining a mailing address of Middlesex, New Jersey.

In *Miller v. California* a very important change was made from "utterly without redeeming social value" to "(lacking) serious literary, artistic, political or scientific value," and again emphasized the local community standards. This particular case allowed for prosecutions under state laws rather than federal laws. Within this opinion in this case, there appears to be a burden placed on the defendant to prove that the material does indeed have "serious literary, artistic, political or scientific value."

President Lyndon B. Johnson, in the latter stages of his presidency, enacted the President's Commission on Obscenity and Pornography. This Commission, composed of an interdisciplinary membership, attempted to analyse and evaluate obscenity and pornography on four levels. These levels were

1. To analyse the laws pertaining to the control of obscenity and pornography and to pass on the recommendations for defining obscenity and pornography.
2. To determine the means used in distributing of obscenity and pornography materials and to study the nature and volume of the traffic.
3. To study the effects of obscenity and pornography on adults and children and its relationship to crime and other antisocial behavior.
4. . . . to recommend such legislative, administrative, or other advisable and appropriate action that the Commission deems necessary.

The war never dies. Only has the emergence of the Moral Majority (and this may not be a majority at all) been felt in their fight on obscenity and pornography. The battle is being waged with new vigor and sometimes with almost fanatical dedication.

TYPES OF PORNOGRAPHY

There are several types of pornography that are very visible and thus apparent. When one visits an "adult bookstore," there is immediate visual confrontation and emotional shock by the sheer physical display of movies, magazines, books, "marital aids," live stage shows, and rubber goods including vibrators and inflatable dolls. This section will briefly identify the various kinds of pornography.

Movies

Porno movies, or stag films, have been on the American scene for many years. Until only recently the stag films have been shown to private groups at civic gatherings of the Veterans of Foreign Wars, the American Legion posts, or other such places. The audiences have traditionally been the college-age young people and the upper-lower and lower-middle class males (Gagnon & Simon)

The early stag films were as a general group poorly filmed and "acted." The actors themselves were often emaciated and visually unattractive. The lighting and photographic techniques were usually lacking in imagination and skill. Actual coitus was seldom completed since erection was usually not shown. In recent years, there has been a tremendous stride in both techniques and skills of the actors. Early films were often preceeded by a pseudoscientific statement declaring the film to be an educational endeavor for the viewer to gain knowledge and insight into human sexuality and sex techniques. The plot itself was usually quite simple and straightforward. What was, and still is, a theme is a fantasy that centers around a solitary female, often in flimsy attire, in a scene where she is erotically aroused, masturbates, is interrupted and seduced by a man, and becomes random in her rapture. Of course, there are variation to this theme, and one can cite numerous exceptions.

Another common scene is the one where two females are involved in kissing, tribadism, and oral-genital sex. The lesbian scene is not directed to other lesbians but rather caters to heterosexual males who are erotically aroused by viewing women having sex with other women. Only rarely are films produced that depict males involved in homosexual acts. *Vir Amat,* an exception to this rule, depicts homosexuality in a light that attempts to show love and caring between two male adults. The preface to the film advertises its merits to be its educational focus and "true message of homosexual love."

The performers in today's pornographic movies appear to be younger, more attractive, and less sexually inhibited than their predecessors of just a few years ago. Linda Lovelace, John W. Holmes, Marilyn Chambers, and others are examples of today's stars of porn. The classic films of today, "The Devil in Miss

Jones," "Behind the Green Door," "Deep Throat," plus some others depict a wide variety of sex acts. In "Deep Throat," Ms. Lovelace is convinced by her doctor, played by Harry Reems, that her clitoris is actually in her throat, thereby accounting for her inability to reach orgasm. Performing fellatio on her sex partners, coupled with her ability to repress her gag reflex, won her national acclaim. Ms. Lovelace has recently claimed that she was forced into acting in porn movies.

In some of the porn movies, there is a pretense of a moral. In "The Devil in Miss Jones," for example, the heroine is allowed to live again for a short time after she had committed suicide. In the former life, she was a recluse and a virgin. In her reprieve, she is involved in a wide range of sex activities, including group sex, sodomy, bestiality, etc., before she is "recalled" to serve her everlasting sentence in hell.

X-rated movies have emerged into the local theaters as well as the living rooms of private homes via cable television. These movies are usually rated X because of sexually related materials and not because of violence or brutality. "Caligula" created a stir in a midwestern town when the Moral Majority picketed and actually convinced the management to stop the showing until certain scenes were removed. By having the movie rated X, this almost guarantees a full house and a profit. The X-rated label serves the purpose in the same manner that the Scarlet Letter did in the early days of our country. By wearing the Scarlet Letter, the interested party did not have to shop around. He was certain of the situation. This is true of the modern movie-goer. By looking at the daily newspaper, the citizen can see which movies are showing and which ones are rated X. There is little left to chance.

Live Sex

Usually not included when one discusses pornography is the exposure of the human body. The many methods, as well as the wide variety of means of exposure, are certainly nothing new in our culture. The history of strippers (obviously usually females) is replete with a theory of exposure and an explanation of the structural opportunity.

There exists within this economic structural system a group of people who expose their body for money. The range of exposure situations will vary from one situation to another and probably from one time to another. In our early history, the exposure of the female breats was enough to warrant arrests by the police. In later times, the G-string became the artificial criteria for pornography. The G-string could be lowered thereby exposing the pubic area, but it could not be totally removed from the body. In other words, the G-string could be taken down to the ankles without the risk of arrest but no further. One must be careful here to differentiate between exposure of the body by a stripper or entertainer and the exposure of the body by the person who is a nudist. The motive behind the exposure must be taken into consideration. The latter case of exposure is for "psychological" reasons, not for reasons of erotic stimulation.

The stripper, for example, is a person involved in nude erotic stimulation, and she has a motive behind her activity, a motive probably coupled with the economy of the act and a measure of exhibitionism. In many large cities, there are ads in the newspaper constantly wanting young girls for erotic dancing opportunities.

The only prerequisite is that the girl have an erotically pleasing body. The females, especially in economic hard times, are placed into a social situation where they can earn relatively good money for a job that requires no special training or particular skill.

Women involved in the exposure of their body for pay can presently choose a variety of different work scenes. There are adult book stores with separate small rooms that feature strippers. The customer will enter a small cubicle, deposit a coin into a slot, and a female, usually already nude, will dance in front of his lighted window. The movement of the woman will vary from one dancer to the next, but the dance is designed to arouse erotic feelings. The girl may also ask for a "tip" to be inserted through a small hole in the wall. The more the tip, the more the erotic suggestive movements performed by the dancer.

Burlesque has an old history in American society. The dancers involved in burlesque may rebell at being called strippers and probably prefer the terms "exotic dancer" or entertainer. More and more females are moving away from the burlesque hall scene and into more contemporary arrangements such as described above.

There is yet another form of occupation that has recently emerged that features female nudity as a form of erotic stimulation. The massage parlor features a female therapist and operates often with the manifest purpose of impersonal and commercial sex. The operator will certainly give a "straight" massage if that is what the customer desires. However, through the system of nonverbal communication, and not in outright solicitation, the customer may receive a massage from the operator while the female is topless, and if more money is exchanged, more sex will be exchanged. Optional sexual activity is available, varying from masturbation to sexual intercourse.

Other forms of body exposure will vary from one section of the country to another. In California only recently this writer went into an adult book store that had a wall composed of telephone booths. On the wall inside the booth itself was a glass wall that permitted visual contact with a woman, nude, sitting by a telephone. The operator of the store informed this writer that there were some customers who would come into this store, use the phone to make obscene telephone calls, and many would masturbate while talking with the girl. The role of the female in this relationship was to answer the phone, act surprised, disgusted, but slowly become erotically stimulated and "masturbate." The manager of the store believed that this was a service to the community because the obscene telephone callers would come into this store and make calls and not be "forced" into making such calls on other women.

The manifest motive for the dancer, the female in the massage parlor, and the girl in the telephone room is erotic stimulation of the customer. There can be no doubt of this. Of course, coupled with erotic stimulation may be an economic motive. The "bump and grind" of the stripper simulates sexual intercourse, and these movements are not easily misunderstood.

Novels

Pornographic books take a variety of different forms. Usually the very hard-core porn books are short in terms of length, but there appears to be a price tag that is much higher than on non-porn books. The great majority of the books and novels are for male customers who are heterosexual, and the contents of the books deal with topics that run the entire range of sexual behaviors.

The plot of the novel is often slight or almost nonexistent. The general tone itself runs from one sexual encounter to another, and in some books there is a different sex act on every page. The theme of an inhibited young housewife who becomes gradually less inhibited as the novel progresses and as she is exposed to her first adulterous relationship, often as a rebellion to her learning of her husband's unfaithfullness, thereby becoming a "liberated woman," is often a reoccurring thread. Of course, there are many other stories that center around incest, rape, swinging, and sadism/masochism.

Within the novels there is little or no mention of any problems that result from the various sexual behaviors that are part of the novel itself. Venereal disease, divorce, and mental or emotional problems are all disregarded. The panacea to all of life's problems are solved by the various escapades and the relationships developed because of the sex happenings.

A very disturbing set of novels has been discovered by this writer during his investigation of pedophilia. There appears to be a set of novels directed toward the gay, sadistic pedophile.

These books are apparently intended for devotees of pain and describe in great detail manners of punishment and the pleasures derived from the infliction of such pain. The contents centers around the infliction of pain from a wide variety of methods and the pleasures of receiving terrible pain.

Figure 13. Paperback books depicting sadism and masochism with children and young adults. These books are part of a collection of child pornography, School of Justice Administration, University of Louisville.

> . . . the pain was pretty bad, but the pleasure of looking at a huge cock, so terible, strong and sexy, was even better as he started to fuck me. Even sexier than just watching him do it to some other kid. My asshole opened up wider than I had ever had it before in my life . . . burning my flesh. Then I could feel the muscles of my assring starting to rip and tear apart like dozens of little rubber bands breakin (sic)" (Love).

The presence of homosexuality in books is usually centered around two major reasons. The first reason is manifestly intended to arouse the homosexual erotic feelings of gays who might happen to read such materials. These homosexual novels concern themselves with materials of love and homosexual activity. Female homosexuality (lesbianism) is written for the purpose of arousing erotic feelings in males, not females. Female homosexuality is written therefore for the heterosexual male who receives some pleasure centering around women who are involved in sex with other women. However, from the content analysis of the pornographic library that is available it appears that among homosexual pornography there is more literature devoted to the

Figure 14. Gay-oriented paperbacks devoted to the practice of sadism. Photo by author.

treatment of sadism and masochism than in the heterosexual pornography. Further study of this assumption is certainly in order and needs to be examined. What can be said with some validity and verifiable research documentation is that most of the pornography is written for the heterosexual male, and there is only a very small market for the female interested in pornography. The presence of women in pornography appears to be a theme that is more erotic among the better educated male (Bell).

EFFECTS OF PORNOGRAPHY

It appears that one of the main objections to pornography is the possible harmful effects it has on people, especially children and the sex offender. The purpose of this section is to attempt to analyze the studies that have been done in this area.

Adult pornography has been criticized historically because of additional factors as well. The most critical statement is that it is demeaning to women, and porn treats them as sex objects. Susan Brownmiller's book, *Against Our Will,* acted as a catalyst in its rejection of pornography and was instrumental in the initiation of two groups: Woman Against Pornography and Women Against Violence Against Women. The beliefs of these two organizations, as well as some other groups, center around the way women are viewed by men. The demeaning status of women, mechanical sex, impersonal sex, and many other reasons are offered for the prohibition of pornography. But the central issue remains. The claim is "Pornography causes sex crimes!" Pornography becomes the critical factors in the rising rate of sex crimes against women and children (Brownmiller).

There can be no doubt that pornography exploits and demeans women. But does it cause sex crimes?

As was previously stated in the section on child porn, the President's Commission on Obscenity and Pornography was initiated under President Johnson with a charge of ascertaining the effects of pornography upon sex crimes. The general findings were offered to the American public. One of the general findings was that exposure to erotic materials does produce sexual arousal in a substantial proportion of males and females. The extent of the effects depend on various personal, psychological, and social characteristics of the viewer and the type of material present. Obviously, some patterns and content of the pornography itself may be conducive to arousal while other forms may be repulsive to the viewer.

The Commission stated that the younger viewer is more aroused than the older viewer, the college-educated more erotically influenced than lesser educated, the religiously inactive more "turned on" than those who are regular church-goers, and the sexually experienced more influenced than the sexually inexperienced. The sexual behavior found to be more erotically pleasing featured conventional sex behavior rather than homosexual sex and petting and coitus rather than oral sex.

The Commission offered a finding that there is no increase in sex behavior other than in onanism. The Report also offered some information in the area that some married couples find that pornography adds to their marital sex life. It must also be said that, according to their findings, exposure to pornography has little or no effects on extant values.

Concerning cross-cultural studies, many experts in the field of sex crimes argue on either side of the academic fence regarding the experience of Denmark and sex crimes. In 1967, Denmark legalized the sale of pornographic books and magazines to persons sixteen years of age and older. Pictures and movies were made legal in 1969. The rate of sex crimes dropped drastically as measured by available statistics. Rape decreased 16 percent, exhibitionism dropped 58 percent, voyuerism dropped 80 percent, and child molestation by 69 percent. The critics reacted to the available statistics by stating that the general attitudes toward sex crimes may have been ameliorated by the change in attitudes in law enforcement and the changed laws themselves. The other side of the argument offers the discussion that pornography serves as a safety valve, and other than the increase in the frequency of masturbatory activity, no antisocial sexual activity is evident.

Phyllis and Eberhard Kronhausen offered that, "... it is extremely doubtful whether even continued exposure to specific pornographic stimuli will result in behavior changes, unless they are accompanied by actual contacts with individuals who are so predisposed." The attitudes appear to be more shaped by contacts with those who are judged to be more significant than exposure to erotic materials. Kotzman reported that among a group of patients he studied, he found no detrimental effects because of their exposure to erotica. But does it affect children in the same fashion? The Commission asked, "Do you think that reading obscene books plays a significant role in causing juvenile delinquency?" Twelve percent of professionals responded in a positive fashion while 58 percent of police chiefs answered in a similar manner. The Commission's findings were,

> In sum, empirical research designed to clarify the question has found no evidence to date that exposure to explicit sexual materials plays a significant role in the causation of delinquent or criminal behavior among youths or adults. The Commission cannot conclude that exposure to erotic materi-

> als is a factor in the causation of sex crimes or sex delinquency (Report of the Commission on Obscenity).

Because of the lack of empirical data concerning the detrimental effect on either adults or juveniles, the Commission recommended a sex education program be initiated on a national scale:

> regarding materials which depict explicit sexual activity stems from the inability or reluctance of people in our society to be open and direct in dealing with sexual matters . . . Failure to talk openly and directly about sex has several consequences. It overemphasizes sex, gives it a magical, nonnatural quality, making it more attractive and fascinating (Report of the Commission on Obscenity).

Closing then, it appears that there are no empirical data that link pornography and sex crimes. The important linkage appears to lie more in the manner in which sex education is handled in personal, primary group relationships. One additional dimension to the problem may lie in the area of some to accept counterintuitive knowledge and their battle against porn. The proponents of porn may be just as interested in the politics of the battle than in the substance of the matter, and maybe, " . . . Our problem is not that pornography represents such a danger—it's far too minor a phenomenon for that—but that the kind of thinking prevalent in dealing with pornography will come to be prevalent in controlling the advocacy of other ideas as well" (Gagnon & Simon).

Chapter 9

DANGEROUS SEX CRIMES

Terror abounds in any city where there has occurred a particularly horrible and sadistic sex crime. The case histories of any large city police department is replete with cases where a victim has been horribly mutilated and killed after being savagely sexually assaulted. The cases of Ted Bundy, John Wayne Gacy, Dean Corll, and a multitude of others merely substantiate the case in point. There is a societal reaction to those who violate the rights and the person of another in such a despicable manner.

In the case of John Wayne Gacy, for example, there was evidence and testimony that showed that he sadistically debased many of his victims when he killed them. There was also additional testimony that lent credence to the allegation that after he had buried some of the bodies he later retreived the corpses and had sex with them (necrophilia).

Ted Bundy was especially cruel and unfeeling in his dealings with his victims. His teeth marks on some of his victims, especially the two coeds from Florida State University, provided the physical evidence that was instrumental in his conviction. Gerald Stano, a self-confessed murderer of thirty-two young women, stated that killing the females after demanding sex from them left him with no more of an emotional feeling than, "... stepping on a bunch of cockroaches."

What captures the imagination of the public is the utter appraisal of senselessness of the crimes, the inability to understand the mind of the perpetrator, and our vulnerability as potential victims. When one understands that he or she could be a victim, the message becomes clear. Something must be done. But what is it that "must be done?" Clearly, one approach is the understanding of the extent of the problem and the dynamics of the behavior. The humor of the exhibitionist is lost when the lust murderer is on the loose. It is no longer an issue of two adults involved in a consenting relationship. Now one of the members of the dyad is being placed in a potentially dangerous situation where bodily harm and even death may be the outcome. The values and the attitudes regarding the lower end of the sexual continuum now become fixed around the evaluation of danger. The danger now becomes personal. It may happen to a friend. It may happen to a relative. It may happen to oneself.

The attitudes thus held are significant in the formation of the sexual psychopath laws. In the development of such laws, the public's realization of a few serious crimes serves as a catalyst for public action. The knowledge of the acts on other citizens is essential as far as an initiation of a legal process. As the knowledge base is expanded and the seriousness and particulars become public, the interested and affected citizens become agitated and dedicated to do *something* about the sex crimes and the sex criminals. As in almost any human activity, a societal committee is formed to investigate the situation, develop a suitable plan of activity, and attempt relevant action to combat the problem.

The media constantly reminds the reader that a dangerous offender is on the loose and the citizens should prepare themselves against possible attack. But are the people in the towns and villages truly prepared for a Ted Bundy or a John Wayne Gacy?

Recognizing that rape is truly a crime of violence and not a sex crime, rape has been deliberately included in this chapter on dangerous sex crimes. Probably among all of the dangerous sex crimes, rape is one of which most are aware because of the space that the media devotes to it. Do we really know that rape is fifteen times more prevalent than cancer? Do we know that atrocious acts of sadism and necrophilia are more prevalent than we know or even care? It is simply not true that all of the acts of the sadists are with those who are masochists. The most blessed union may be between the true sadist and the pure masochist—that is, if the sadist doesn't kill the masochist. The dangerous sex crimes are those of rape (recognizing that it is not a sex crime), necrophilia, piquerism, erotic hanging, pyromania, vampirism, cannibalism, and sadism/masochism. Each of the topics will be covered in some detail similar to the chapter on nuisance sex crimes. What is an added dimension is that those who are involved in most of these forms of deviant sex acts also involve other people, and these partners in these acts are usually unwilling. The repercussions are often severe and detrimental to the emotional and physical well-being of the victim. Sexual hanging is an exception to this rule. Erotic ritualism is one dangerous sex crime that usually involves only the deviant himself.

SADISM/MASOCHISM

Sadism is a sexual perversion where the pleasure is received by inflicting pain on another. The particular type of sexual perversion is probably more in fantasy than in reality. Regardless, however, of the number of persons involved in this sexual perversion, the activity is dangerous to their victims. The polar type of perversion is that of masochism. The true masochist is one who receives pleasure from pain. Of course, the pleasure received can come from actual physical abuse or it can be verbal; for example, Ray, a homosexual, related that he can only receive sexual gratification when his "master" forces him to crawl, beg, and plead for him to sexually service his superior. Ray often is covered with welts from the whip of his master. He is manacled with chains and other special devices that he is forced to wear during his sexual scenes with his master.

The term sadism was devised from an eighteenth century French nobelman, Marquis de Sade. De Sade was noted for his cruel and savage sexual activity. He was imprisoned for his sexual escapades with ladies of the court, and after his release from prison, he wrote his memoires and novels depicting graphically his sexual activities. Masochism comes from a lesser known character, Leopold von Sacher-Masoch. He authored novels about his methods of achieving sexual gratification by having women inflict pain on him. The masochist is one who receives sexual pleasure by being tortured, physically abused, or verbally humiliated. It is true that the pain hurts. The masochist who has been whipped hurts in the same fashion that a nonmasochist hurts. But it is the anticipation of the pain and the feeling of humiliation that triggers the feeling of sexual excitement.

There are organizations that have been formed to promote the causes of sadism. The Eulenspiegel Society is a noncommercial association of individuals devoted to the bringing together of those people who are devotees of pain. This society also has a newsletter entitled *Prometheus*. For a small fee, the society offers a booklet, ". . . dedicated to foster public understanding and give a forum for both a philosophical and practical treatment of B & D as well as sadism and masochism."

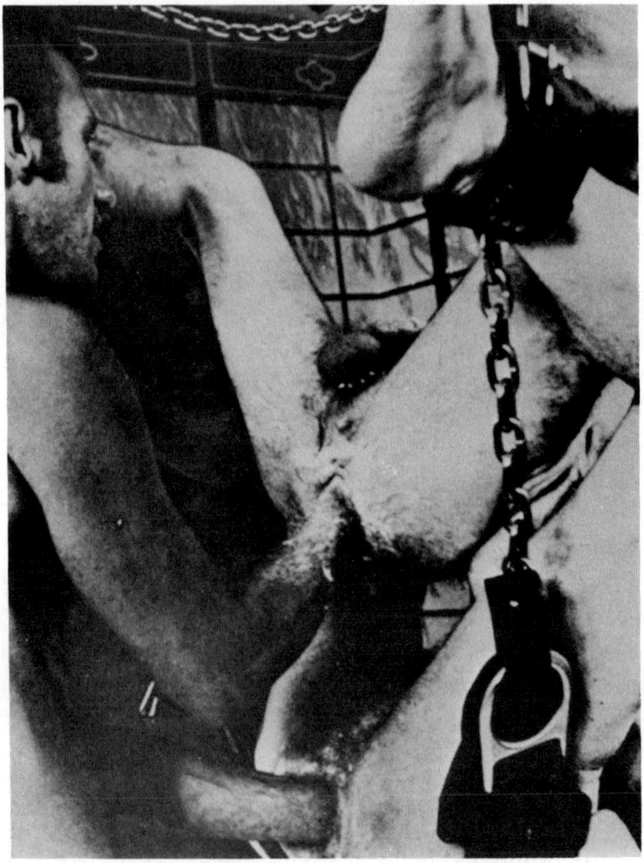

Figure 15. Sadomasochistic parlor activity featuring anal "stimulation."

There are also other organizations into which one can enroll that inform the interested party about sadism and masochism. In a recent advertisement in *Screw*, those people who are interested in being a "slave" and in being treated as a slave could call a number to be in touch with Dominatrix Velvet. Her place of business is called Dominatrix Velvet's Dungeon in New York City. The slave calls the listed number and arranges for an appointment with a dominatrix. In an article explaining the procedure, Ms. Velvet related that she will administer any form of punishment that the slave wishes; that is, any form of punishment that will not do any permanent physical damage. The charge is 100 dollars per hour (naturally, slaves do not haggle over any fee). Walls of the dungeon are covered with whips, chains, harnesses, dildos, hoods, and masks.

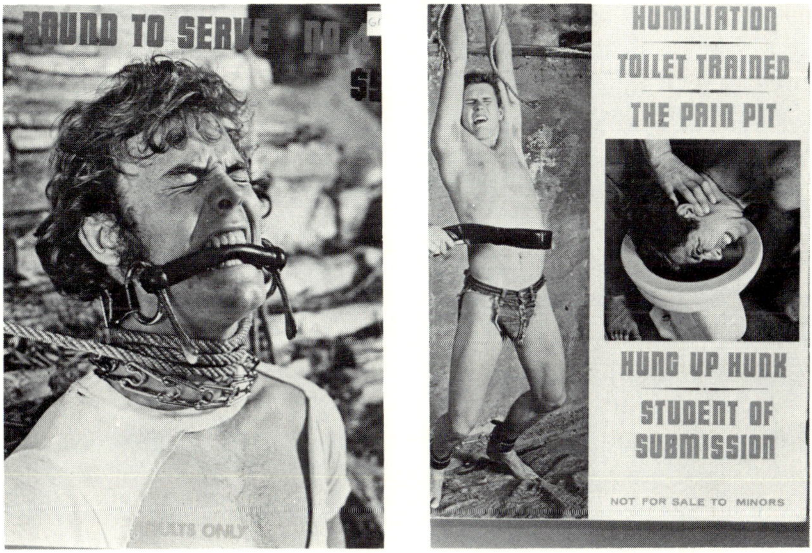

Figures 16a & 16b. Popular magazines for the devotee of pain. Photos by author.

There are also clamps designed to attach themselves to various parts of the body, and their main purpose is to inflict pain. Velvet stated that most of her clients come from the professional businessman ranks. It was her opinion that such men who are in the seats of power and authority have a need to let someone else dominate them occasionally and let someone else make decisions for them. It is not believed that this is the sole reason that one would want to be dominated in such a fashion. There must be some form of masochism involved. These slaves, sometimes called prisoners when they are the property of masters, are sometimes traded off and sold like used cars. There are ads that appear in many publications advertising for sale or trade a person who is a slave. Sometimes there is a sale price, and other times goods can be exchanged for the slave. In a recent issue of *Screw* magazine, the slaves advertised came from across the nation and included states such as California, Florida, New York, Washington, and Indiana.

The author is aware of a marriage where the husband is a sadist and the wife is a masochist. This is the usual case. They are also swingers. The word among the other swingers in this community was to stay away from Jerry and Rita (not their correct names). They like to tie people up and beat them. Before they became swingers, Jerry would get so excited that he would reach an orgasm when he and Rita would practice their own S & M behavior. On several occasions, Rita found herself in the local hospital with broken ribs, broken leg, a dislocated shoulder, and a variety of other ailments. Rita told this writer that she liked the pain because it made her feel good.

Infibulation is a form of sadism whereby the masochist pierces the flesh of his own genitals and in the process receives sexual satisfaction. There is no other person involved in this act of sexual perversion, but the dangers are real to the victim, the perpetrator himself.

There appears to be a great deal of ritualism involved in the sadism and masochism. The bracelets of leather studded with brass stars, cat-of-nine tails, leather stockings, and other apparel items signal to many others that they are involved in the sadism/masochism scene.

Of course, as with other forms of sexual behavior, sadism and masochism are on a continuum. A strong hug from a loved one feels good. Most of the forms of sadism, it is granted, is far from a strong hug. Most of the forms of sadism comes in the form of light spanking, scratching, or other forms of corporal discourse. It is only a perversion when the sadistic treatment or the masochistic demands interfere with the normal sexual functioning. When one inflicts pain in order to achieve sexual gratification and can only receive sexual gratification when pain is present, in one form or another, a perversion is present. What accounts for the dangerous sex crime is that the presence of maltreatment, pain (either physical or verbal), and humiliation become integral parts of the sexual activity. The hostility, aggression, and pain become associated with sex, and gratification can only be fully realized when these elements are present. In rape, lust murders, anthropophagy, and necrophilia, there is a thread of violence present. This is visible in all of the dangerous sex crimes. However, the level of hostility and aggression is only barely below the surface and only surfaces when the sex becomes an active agent. In necrophilia, for example, many have a history of killing their victim before having sex with them.

The etiology of the sadist is not clear. There are some who believe that the sadist is a person with a great deal of hostility or aggression that is directed to others because of their own history of personal rejection. In these cases, the sexual dimension seems to play a secondary role in the relationship between the sadist and his victim. Another possible explanation of the etiology of the sadist may lie in the person's feeling that sex itself is something dirty, sinful, and personally degrading. By punishing others for engaging in this particularly despicable type of behavior, he is fulfilling a mission to punish others for their actions. A learning theory might suggest that the etiology of this perversion may stem from the point of view that the person has early in his life situation learned a connection between sexual satisfaction and the administering of pain. The hostile and violent stories learned through various forms of communication may in fact offer some valuable learning situations to the young person in his ability to make this vital connection.

In the psychodynamic model, the sadistic impulse is first experienced in the oral and anal stages of psychosexual development. A person learns some pleasure through biting and the withholding of feces and if this behavior is fixated at these stages, then later in life because of the aggressive instinct in all humans he will turn to sadism as a manner of expressing himself sexually.

There is also some thought that the sadist is a person who is shy and timid, not at all gregarious in behavior. His sense of power may be limited, and indeed he may experience impotency in his sexual relationships with others unless there is some evidence of pain involved and his partner expresses some reaction to this sadistic treatment.

Of course, there are some people with asocial personality types who experience violence in their daily lives that many times are not at all involved in the sexual area. The violence exhibited in their interactions with others in personal relationships may also be carried through into their sex relationships. Their uninhibited behavior and amorality may account for their behavior, regardless of their sexual history as a youth.

The masochist's history tends to be an expression of a tendency to react to frustration, disappointment, and failure by feeling sorry for oneself. The suffering may be an acceptable way of a means of relieving a sense of guilt. Historically women traditionally have been taught that sex is dirty and bad. Women, then, if they truly like sex, must have some ability to legitimize their feelings. Some may require the application of pain prior to indulging in sex behavior. This is the price to pay for their participation in what they have learned to be dirty.

Some parents may try to prevent their children from experiencing sex too early by telling their daughters that sex is painful, first intercourse is unbearable, and masturbation causes blindness, senility, or mental illness. The child's experience with menarche, monthly periods, and other sexual things may confirm the parents' teachings. Therefore, all sex must have some pain associated with it. Social learning again may account for establishing a relationship between sexual gratification and masochism. Early experiences among some children have at least a tangent theme of pain, e.g. tickling, hair-pulling, and spanking. The masochist may not be sexually aroused unless there is some pain present in the relationship. As already stated, some masochists may go to adult parlors and houses of prostitution that are especially equipped with ingenious devices for torture. Others may go to extreme ends to satisfy their own masochistic tendencies. They have been known to mutilate and castrate themselves. Origin, an early Church bishop, castrated himself in front of his congregation one Sunday morning during his sermon. The castration was an "example" of the evils of the flesh. Hardly an example most of us would want to follow but an excellent example of the highest caliber of the true masochist.

In an interesting case in Kentucky, the nude body of a young housewife was found by her husband upon his return from work one evening. The police investigating the case arrested the husband on suspicion of murder. The wife had been severely beaten about her face and had shown signs of being sexually assaulted. The husband tearfully denied any knowledge of the murder and claimed their marriage of less than a year was very happy.

Upon further investigation into this case, a swinger's magazine was found in the bedroom of the woman.

The husband again denied any knowledge of swinging behavior

Figure 17. Various swinger's magazines available either in adult book stores or through the mail. Photo by author.

on his or his wife's part. An ad had been circled with her picture appearing. The ad related that she was a young housewife who was interested in light sadism and masochism. A reply was found among her personal belongings that showed a name and address of a man who was a self-described sadist. This man was later arrested by the police and admitted that he had met the female in her home after the husband had left for work. He stated that she asked him to spank her, which he did. They then had intercourse both vaginally and anally. After several sessions of this form of light sadism and masochism, she requested that he hit her in the face with an open hand and later with his fist. He gave testimony to the police that she had a strange look on her face after he struck her and kept demanding that he hit her harder and harder. Finally he hit her too hard, and she died.

Because of skillful and careful investigation by the police department, a dangerous sex criminal was discovered and convicted. The man was sent to prison and, hopefully, some form of rehabilitation is in the offering.

NECROPHILIA

Among all of the very dangerous sex crimes, none is perhaps more repulsive and so unknown than necrophilia. Necrophilia is the sexual desire to have sex with a corpse. The activity may only be fantasized, but in some cases the act itself is real; that is, sex does truly take place with a dead body. There is some confusion about necrophiliacs and their propensity to kill their victim in order to have sex with them after the victim is deceased. As far as this phenomenon is concerned, there is another added dimension, and this particular form of perversion, a propensity to kill and later have sex with the body, is called a necrosadistic sex offense. This latter form of sex offense is rarely noticed and little has been written about it in the professional literature. The necrophiliac occupies most of the sparse literature, and most of the knowledge is gleaned from very few studies.

Regarding the history of necrophilia, there is some anthropological evidence that ancient man practiced necrophilia. The writings of the ancient Egyptians, for example, indicated that special palace guards were placed around the grave sites of the dead to protect the precious goods as well as to protect the royal deceased from those who might be involved in necrophilia. From that time to the present, there appears to be no evidence that necrophilia occupies any approved sexual pattern. Kraft-Ebbing wrote,

> This horrible kind of sexual indulgence is so monstrous that the presumption of a psychopathic state is, under all circumstances, justified; and Maschka's recommendation, that the mental condition of the perpetrator should always be investigated, is well founded. In any case, an abnormal and decidedly perverse sensuality is required to overcome the natural repugnance which man has for a corpse, and permit the feeling of pleasure to be experienced in sexual congress with a cadaver.

The obvious pejorative point of view of this writer reflects the attitude of many when it comes to necrophilia.

Necrophilia tends to be a male perversion. The only verifiable cases have always been male and for obvious reason. The sexual activity to occur in coitus naturally entails erection if penetration is an object of the act. Female necrophiliacs only exist, it appears, in the minds of man. It may make for sensationalism and raise the reading number of some tabloid publications, but the fact remains that the cases known are male only. It is also true that the necrophiliac or the necrosadistic offender may be either heterosexual or homosexual. There are police cases that show that offenders had sex with a corpse of the same and the opposite sex.

It appears then that the true necrophiliac very seldom actually kills his victim. He commits sex with a corpse after the fact. For that reason, there are some occupations that may be more attractive to the necrophiliac than others because of the possibility of having access to dead bodies. Funeral home personnel, hospital employees, and other like occupations may serve as a facilitator for access. This is not to say that all morticians and hospital workers are necrophiliacs. This is only to say that there are certain occupational roles that permit more ease to the sex object than others. This same statement can be said for other roles that permit access to sex crime choice; for example, shool teaching for pedophilia, firefighter for pyromania.

There is another group of necrophiliacs who do not have sex with dead bodies. This group can actually be divided into two subgroups; those who have sex with a living person but the partner pretends, for whatever reason, to be deceased, and the other subgroup that only fantasizes about having sex with the dead. In the first instance, the offender may pay a prostitute to play the part of the deceased in their prostitute-john relationship. Jackie, a prostitute, related to this writer her experience with a necrophiliac:

> He asked me to take a cold shower, lie very still on the bed. The man then put baby powder all over me and told me not to move a muscle. I have been with him a couple of times, but the first time I moved, and he lost it (his erection). He got mad. He acted like he was going to kill me. The next time I made sure I stayed still. Man, he's weird.

In these cases, the offender may lose his ability to sexually perform if the partner moves the slightest bit. The appearance of the partner visually approximating a corpse is of paramount importance. The cold bath, even to the point of being placed in a tub of ice water, the application of talcum powder to produce the ashen appearance, and the absolute insistence of immobility are essential elements in the successful completion of the sex act for the necrophiliac.

It appears then that the most common behavioral activity as far as the necrophiliacs are those that center around their sexual fantasies regarding necrophilia. "Necrophiliacs frequently dream about dead bodies and show a morbid interest in funerals, cemeteries (taphophilia), morgues and autopsies" (Goldenson).

The necrosadistic offender is one who kills his victim, the ultimate in sadism. This offender will later have sex with his victim. The necrosadistic sex criminal appears to be very rare as far as necromania is concerned. There are, however, examples of the necrosadistic offender. John Wayne Gacy, the killer of more than thirty young men in Chicago, on several occasions retrieved the bodies of some of his victims from their graves on his property. The graves were located in his home, attic, under the driveway, under the patio, and otherwise scattered around his premises. The purpose of the retrieval was of course to engage in sex with them. Joseph Vache, a Frenchman of the latter 1800s, killed over twenty women and then performed sex with each of them. Bruno Luske, a German, confessed to the killing and then raping of eighty-five women.

The investigator in the criminal justice system must be alert to the possibility of a necrophiliac victim when a body is discovered and there is some evidence that a sex crime has been committed. The murder may have been a result of sexual excitation that accompanied the necrophiliac fantasies.

As with most sex offenders, the exact etiology of the necrophiliac or the necrosadistic offender is unclear. There appears to be a need on the part of the offender to express himself in terms of total domination over his intended victim. This domination plays an essential part in the total scenario of this sex criminal. If a movement is made, this in itself may signal that the victim is not in total submission and the offender is not in total control. The act by the offender is not within his total power. By having the victim in total subjection, the offender does not run a risk of rejection or humiliation. He is in total control. He has no fear of failure. But this fear of failure would not be sufficient in and of itself to sufficiently explain this sexual perversion. The disorder, with its obvious distorted object, may lie more in the direction of a form of psychosis. If this theory is correct, and there is so little professional literature to support this position, traditional therapy would seem to be of little benefit and long-term treatment would be the better alternative rather than incarceration. The protection of society, however, must be considered to be of the utmost importance.

RAPE

Forcible rape according to the Uniform Crime Report is, "the carnal knowledge of a female, forcibly and against her will." It includes rape by force, assault to rape, and attempted rape. This particular definition does not include statutory rape.

Statutory rape is operationally defined as, "intercourse with a person of the same or opposite sex under the age of consent with or without their consent." Forcible rape on the other hand is, "intercourse with a person of the same or opposite gender over the age of consent without their consent."

In the first instance, statutory rape, some studies have shed some information on the statutory rapists and their victims. Gebhart discovered that the median age of the men convicted of heterosexual offenses with females under the age of consent was twenty-five years of age. Eighty percent of these rapists were first offenders, and few of them had any signs of psychopathic conditions. In the majority of the cases, the victim herself did not discourage the rape nor report the rape (Gebhart). In statutory rape, the crucial factors to be considered are the age of the victim and whether or not there was consent. The age limitation is an artificial legal point and is considered to be an age when the person has the maturity to give consent and to understand the consequences of the behavior. These ages will vary from one state to another, but most of the states require either the age of sixteen or eighteen. Thus, if the courts finds that an adult male has been sexually involved with another person under the legal age of that state, this man can be charged with statutory rape.

Most of the information regarding rape in the last twenty years has not been focused on the perpetration of statutory rape. Rather the research has focused more on aggressive or forcible rape. Historically, women have been considered the property of a man, subjugated to the demands of the men in her tribe. The Old Testament as well as other early writings stated that a married woman who was raped was not only guilty of the act but was also guilty of bringing the act of defilement upon herself. The role of woman from property to private being has not been totally successful. Many men still view women as chattel. In the time of war, women in villages, towns, and cities are viewed as another form of spoils to be ravished, abused, and discarded. This point was well-illustrated in the atrocities in Viet Nam. As the military advanced from village to village, women were raped and in many instances died of the physical damage heaped upon them by the "enemy."

Rape Statistics

There are some interesting statistics when one considers the rapid increase in reported rape. The obvious concern here is whether there are in fact more rapes being committed or more rapes being reported. With the advent of various "hot lines" and rape relief centers, it would appear on first impression that more women are reporting rape than ever before. The true situation may never be known. Rape, regardless of either alternative, is considered to be the fastest growing violent crime in the United States today. The FBI believes that one woman in five will be sexually assaulted in their lifetime, and a further estimate calculates that only about one in ten rapes are reported. Nationally, only three in one hundred rapes result in some conviction.

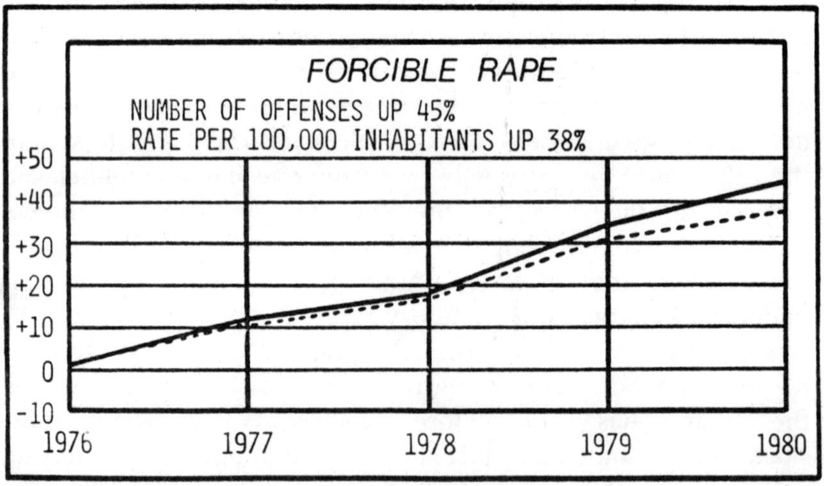

Figure 18. Source: Uniform Crime Report, 1981.

Grace Ericksen, Director of the Rape Relief Center, Louisville, Kentucky, estimates that fifteen times more people are being raped than are stricken by cancer. Less than twenty percent of the rapists are "punished," and one in sixty receive some form of prison sentence. For the rapist, sex is not the reason for the act. The motivation behind rape tends to be in the feeling of hostility and aggression directed toward women. There does seem to be, however, an increase also in the number of males being raped. Some states define rape as sexual penetration of a woman by a man, not her husband, without the woman's consent. This law appears to be behind the times because of recent developments in some other states that have lead to significant changes in the scope of their particular rape laws. In other words, a husband may be held legally liable for rape if he forces sexual intercourse on his wife (Barlow). The 1978 Rideout case was a much publicized case in which the husband was acquitted of the rape charges brought against him by his wife.

Profile of the Rapist

The profile of the rapist can in some part be gleaned from the information by Amir. In his study, twenty-five percent of the rapists were single offenders who did not plan their rape. The statistic in his study, which attacks the myth that rape is an impulsive act, is his finding that seventy-five percent of all of his cases of rape that he examined, either those which involved gang rapes or single rapes, were indeed planned. For many rapists, the sexual pleasure may be heightened through the planning and the perpetration of the rape. The majority of the rapists were young, the median age was twenty-three, black, and from the lower socioeconomic class (Amir). Brownmiller observed that almost three of four rapists had prior arrest records, and almost ninety percent repeat other crimes, including rape. Furthermore, Amir has reported that the majority of the rapists were married, had children, and outwardly at least lead normal sex lives. It is very difficult to obtain a true profile of the rapists, especially since ninety percent are never reported. In the same manner that one speaks of developing characteristics of the criminal by accumulating data of those who are incarcerated, to say that all rapists possess certain characteristics by studying only those who have been apprehended, what we actually have is a profile of only those rapists who have been caught.

There is another myth concerning the rapist: he is a stranger to his victim. Most rapists and their victim live in the same neighborhood or area. They often run into each other shopping and at social gatherings. Almost fifty percent of the rapists are known to the victim, and in some instances, they may be friends.

Typologies of Rapists

It would be erroneous to think that all rapists are similar. There may be an individual who because of his immaturity or lack of social skills and understanding of his social role may not be aware of the proper form of sexual behavior. He may involve himself sexually with a partner unaware of the "rules of the game" and force himself on her. This type of rapist may be quite different from the person who rapes because of his hostility to women. There is also a belief in our society that when women say "no" they actually mean "yes." To stretch the meaning of "no" to "yes" is no great distance to make when a person only hears what he wishes to hear. The three above types of rapists need to be examined in light of their behavioral patterns and their expectations of women. Moreover, the sadistic rapist is certainly different from the above types. His reason for rape, mutilation, and even murder is directed not through a misunderstanding of the social role, the inability or unwillingness to understand the spoken word, or even the general hostility of most rapists but rather to a general feeling of extreme aggression and sadism. All need to be carefully examined, and if treatment is a possibility, the direction and modality of treatment needs to be modified for the unique needs of the rapist.

Some rapes occur in a gang situation, when several males sexually assault a woman, taking turns with her in a savage sexual rape. This form of rape must also be viewed differently. The process of interactional amplification among the group members is intensified and may be viewed by the perpetrators as not rape at all. In many cases of gang rape, there may be erections as far as the rapists are concerned but in only few instances is semen present. In other words, there is penetration but not ejaculation.

Captain Jerry Beavers, Louisville Division of Police, has made a career dedicated to the study and apprehension of the sex offender. Beavers in his lectures to professionals involved in the criminal justice system in dealing with the sex offender throughout the United States likes to use a schematic representation of five different types of rapists. The first rapist is what he calls the Assaultist Rapist. This rapists uses force in his relationship with his victim, and in his initial contact he may tear her clothing, strike her with his hands and fists, and grab her private parts. The assault is actually on two levels: physical assault and psychological assault using violent and abusive language. This particular type of rapist strikes sporadically and infrequently, and many times the rapes occur after he has undergone a drinking spree. His frustration tolerance appears to be low, he appears to be a social isolate, and he lives in a world of sexual fantasy where he can control women and dominate them. His contact with women tends to be unfulfilling in the real world.

A second type of rapist is termed the Sexually Inadequate Rapist. This particular type of man through his rape seeks reassurance of his manhood and has some fear of homosexuality. By dominating women in rape, he is able to assure himself that he is truly not homosexual. This man is very much aware of the sex involved in rape, and he goes to great ends in an attempt to erotically arouse his victims, wanting them to enjoy the forced sex with him. During the course of the rape itself, he will conduct the victim's activities to create his own fantasies. He may be impotent and require considerable assistance from his victims to obtain an erection and ejaculation. For this reason, he may need verbal encouragement and oral sex. He engages in extensive conversations with his victims and may ask a variety of personal questions in order to maintain some form of psychological intimacy. He may also elicit a pathetic need for attention, and in many cases, the victim may respond in a sympathetic fashion to his "needs." Regarding his background, this rapist may be well-educated and come from a middle- to upper-class residential area. He may, however, be experiencing some domestic or personal problems at home. This rapist expresses great feelings of guilt and remorse and at times feels a compulsion to confess his sex offenses.

The third type of rapist is the Predator Rapist. This person has a life-style of exploited behavior, particularly against women. He has also a history of burglary and robbery as well as other types of criminal acts. He is quite skillful at exploiting women, and he does not see his attacks as being serious. He can, therefore, easily rationalize his behavior. This man holds great contempt for women, and in general, he exhibits a great deal of distrust for both sexes. His environment changes continually because he is involved in constant trouble with the authorities and may move from one area of the country to another. What is still further interesting about this rapist is that there may be some significant others who may know of his rapes but may in some fashion support his behavior. His psychological personality may be narcissistic and preoccupied with self-gratification.

A fourth type of rapist is the of the Sadistic Rapist. This man inflicts a great deal of mental and physical pain. He has a need for control and domination. He has a need to control the situation and his victim. He is known to torture, making his victim suffer through physical methods, verbal threats and insults, and by demanding degrading sexual acts. By involving himself with the victim who is truly intimidated and dominated, he is apparently acting out his hostilities. He may come from a background where he was considered to be bright and successful in his social and occupational life. Kidnapping is frequent with the sadistic rapist, and he poses a great problem for the members of the criminal justice system.

Beavers' next example is the Polymorphous Perverse Rapist. This man is unpredictable and has had various sexual experiences throughout his life. His background may show that he has been a victim of child molestation and sexual abuse. He may also molest children. His sexual orientation may show some vacillation between heterosexuality and homosexuality. Often his sexual behavior will show extreme sexual patterns. He may have a history of mental illness, and incarceration throughout the United States is often a predictable pattern. He is also considered to be somewhat of a social isolate, the "oddball" of the community. He experiences an inconsistent and irregular pattern of sexual behavior and may have a long and extensive arrest record for sex crimes.

Regardless of the point of view extended to the rapist, be it an evaluation that he is a sex criminal or that he is mentally ill, it must be kept in mind that the victims have been violated both physically and emotionally. The victim will never be the same again. Debbie, a rape victim, told this author that even after five years, she is still afraid to go into her home alone. If she comes home too early, she will wait in her car until her husband arrives. Sometimes she will wait for more than an hour. The trauma for this victim, as well as many other victims, causes problems that will take many years to resolve. The husbands, boyfriends, and others who share a primary group relationship with the victim also have to deal with the rape. A common theme among the friends and the relatives, although rarely verbalized, is that the victim somehow "asked for it." This feeling must be examined and resolved. There can be no instance where a human being asks to be raped. There can be no justification for being sexually assaulted.

Developmental Factors For the Rapist

There has been an increased interest in the interactional effects of early life between the sex offender and the significant others. The relationship between the mother and the future rapist has been the major focus. The relationship with the father appears to be less significant. The mother is usually described as rejecting, excessively overcontrolling, dominant, punitive, overprotective, and seductive. There are also combinations to these themes. By contrast, the father is usually described as uninvolved, aloof, distant, absent, or passive, but occasionally punitive and cruel. The mother is sometimes described as distant and emotionally isolated. Some researchers suggest that in the case of the sex offender, as opposed to the nonoffender, parental cruelty, inconsistency, envy, and sexual frustration as well as overstimulation or seduction were the main factors that influenced their sexual life-style and criminal behavior (Rada, 1978; Hartogs, 1951).

Parental seduction, usually involving the mother, occurs continuously from covert seduction to actual sexual involvement. There may be a history of early prolonged sharing of the bed with a sibling or a parent, which may sensitize the child's imagination unduly to sexual stimulation. In some cases, sharing of the bed with the mother is prolonged into puberty. Although actual incest is quite rare, other forms of incest within the family have been reported with some frequency. Early sexual seduction can lead to overstimulation of the immature person, which can lead later into antisocial sexual acts. This child may be amenable to the sexual advances of an adult, and his experiences with an adult later in his life may indicate some pathological learning situations stemming from this period in his life.

Many rapists also have a history of severe physical punishments by their dominating, sadistic, and castrating mothers. The father, because of his personality, may not lend the support to the child when really needed. If the mother is cruel, dominating, and all of the other characteristics mentioned, the future hostility may be more directed toward women in general because of the pain suffered from women in particular.

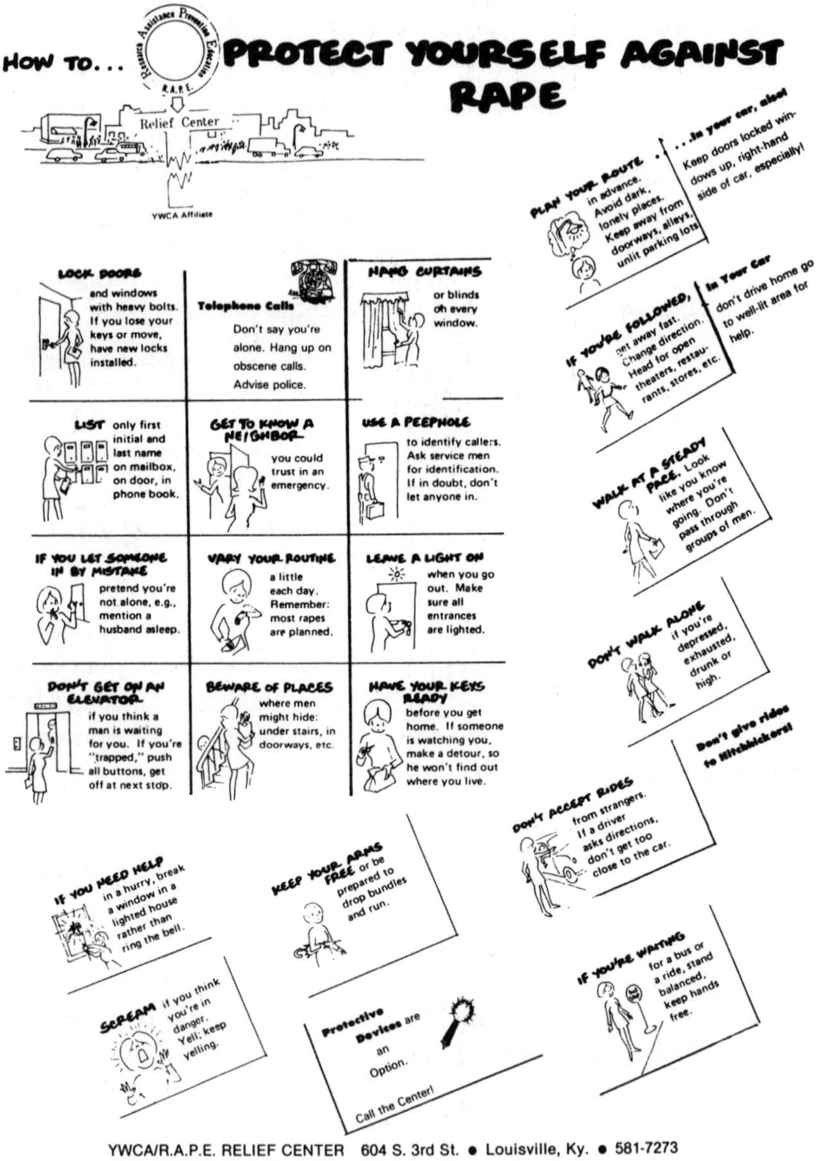

Figure 19. Courtesy of R.A.P.E. Relief Center, Louisville, Kentucky.

"WAS HE ASKING FOR IT?"

Recently, *Harper's Weekly* carried an item from the American Bar Association *Journal* declaring that few rapists are punished for their crime: only one in five rapes is reported and only one out of eight reported rapes ends in conviction. In a dialogue to demonstrate why most rape victims prefer not to press charges, the article asks us to imagine a robbery victim undergoing the same sort of cross-examination that a rape victim does:

"Mr. Smith, you were held up at gunpoint on the corner of First and Main?"

"*Yes.*"

"Did you struggle with the robber?"

"*No.*"

"Why not?"

"*He was armed.*"

"Then you made a conscious decision to comply with his demands rather than resist?"

"*Yes.*"

"Did you scream? Cry out?"

"*No. I was afraid.*"

"I see. Have you ever been held up before?"

"*No.*"

"Have you ever *given* money away?"

"*Yes, of course.*"

"And you did so willingly?"

"*What are you getting at?*"

"Well, let's put it like this, Mr. Smith. You've given money away in the past. In fact you have quite a reputation for philanthropy. How can we be sure you weren't *contriving* to have your money taken by force?"

"*Listen, if I wanted—*"

"Never mind. What time did this holdup take place?"

"*About 11 P.M.*"

"You were out on the street at 11 P.M.? Doing what?"

"*Just walking.*"

"Just walking? You know that it's dangerous being out on the street that late at night. Weren't you aware that you could have been held up?"

"*I hadn't thought about it.*"

"What were you wearing?"

"*Let's see—a suit. Yes, a suit.*"

"An *expensive* suit?"

"*Well—yes. I'm a successful lawyer, you know.*"

"In other words, Mr. Smith, you were walking around the streets late at night in a suit that practically advertised the fact that you might be a good target for some easy money, isn't that so? I mean, if we didn't know better, Mr. Smith, we might even think that you were *asking* for this to happen, mightn't we?"

Figure 20. Courtesy of R.A.P.E. Relief Center, Louisville, Kentucky.

It is also interesting to note that many rapists accept parental cruelty as being deserved. He may have seen his siblings receiving similar punishments, but he sees himself more deserving of the pain from the beatings.

In some rapists, the cruelty experienced from the parents becomes eroticized. This seems to be particularly true if the mother insists on administering beatings to the bare buttocks. Some rapists recall developing an erection during the beatings and experienced their first pleasurable sexual experience.

The relationship with the father appears to be one of absence or deprivation. In one study, fifty percent of the fathers were absent from the home at some point in early childhood. If he was not physically absent, he was at least psychologically absent (Rada).

In summary, the professional literature suggests that parental rejection, domination, cruelty, and sexual seduction are important factors in the early life experience of the rapists. During the "latency" period, mild to moderate social maladjustments are evident by fighting, temper tantrums, truancy, and stealing.

EROTIC ASPHYXIATION

Erotic asphyxiation, or ritual hanging, is yet another form of dangerous sex crime. The general student of criminal behavior and sexual behavior is unfamiliar with this form of sex crime. In this sex practice, the offender is himself the perpetrator as well as the victim. The danger to himself is relatively great, while the danger to society is minimal.

This offender is either a male or a female. The emphasis is equally devoted to ritualism of the practice as well as the hanging itself. What often occurs in erotic asphyxiation is a situation where the person may tie a rope around his neck and slowly bend his knees until the pressure from the rope creates a feeling of physical lightheadness. This feeling, plus the sexual fantasy, enables him to become erect and ejaculate. The simple scenario is usually not the case, as in the picture of the young Air Force lieutenant who was found in his room. He had some erotic materials in his possession that featured sexual hanging.

What often happens is very complex indeed. Since the ritualism is very involved in complex situations where everything must be in its place, the asphyxiate will often manipulate complex sexual scenes whereby he is able to successfully fantasize. The local police files relates the following case of a young man who was found hanging from a rafter in his bedroom. The scenerio was appropriate for the complex asphyxiate. He had been very careful.

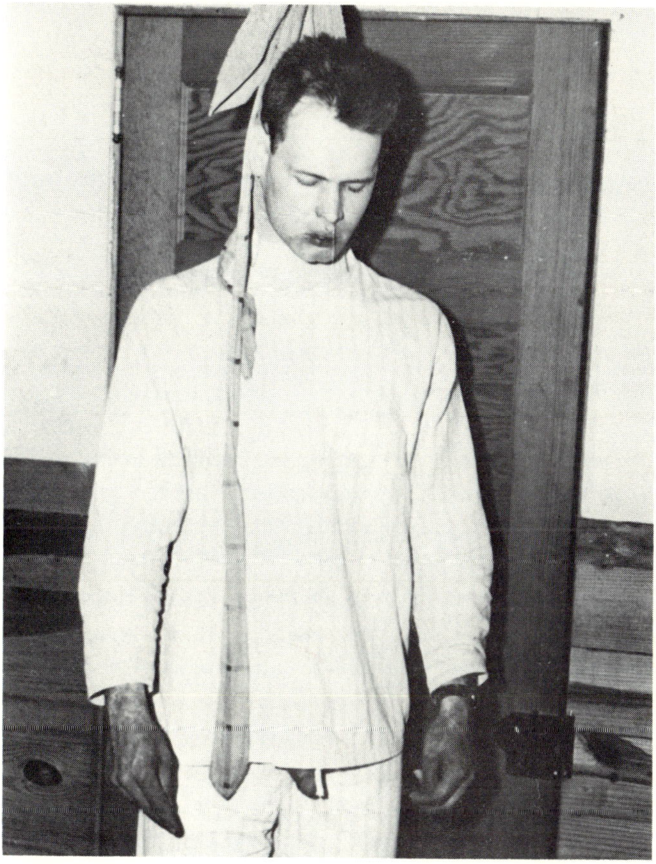

Figure 21. Accidental death due to erotic asphyxiation. Usually there is more sophistication in dress.

He had very neatly tied leather straps to both legs and had bound his chest in a similar manner. The symmetry was both impressive and important. The slip knot had failed to slip, and he accidentally hung himself. The concept and the practice of symmetry appears to be important to most of this form of sex practitioners. They will often adorn themselves in straps, parts of garments, and other paraphernalia that shows perfect symmetry. If one ties a shoe on the right foot in a certain way, the left shoe must be tied in the same identical manner.

Voyeurism, then, also appears to play an important role, and fantasy is only one part of voyeurism. Often on the scene of the hanging, a mirror may be found close to the body where he could see himself from his hanging position. He could view his rising state of sexual excitement. He would finally reach an sexual orgasm.

To illustrate the popularity of this form of sexual perversion and dangerous sex practice, a convention was held this past summer by a sadism and masochism society. The manifest purpose of the convention was to acquaint those interested in erotic asphyxiation with the joys and dangers of the practice. Over five hundred people attended the conference, and many purchased a special rope with an apparatus that automatically disengaged when over fifty pounds of pressure was exerted. The latest invention greatly reduces the possibility of accidental strangulation.

The police should pay particular attention to this form of sexual activity in the investigation of "suicide by hanging" cases; for example, the police were called into a case to investigate an apparent suicide. A factory worker was found in a storage room hanging from pipes in the ceiling. The hands were loosely tied behind his back, and he was wearing his undershorts and an undershirt. He had also placed plastic sheets around his head, face, and genital area. The rope had been tied with one end attached to the pipes and the other around his neck. The noose itself appeared to be sturdy but with a particular knot. One detective stated that it looked like a slip knot. What was also unusual and deserved special attention was that the body was not suspended in the air, but rather the man's knees were only sightly buckled.

Upon further investigation it was determined that, looking through his personal belongings, the victim had pornographic materials, ropes, belts, and other materials, including bondage and erotic asphyxiation magazines. In the home, there were many rope burns on the rafters in the ceiling where he had practiced his ritualistic hangings. It has been estimated that some erotic asphyxiates practice their perversion up to four times a day.

Alert investigators, through their investigations and their knowledge of this form of sexual perversion, were able to solve a case that had been originally suspected of being a suicide. A man's insurance company had originally refused to pay the settlement on his insurance claim because it was thought that the victim had committed suicide. Because of the thorough and professional job done by the police in this case, the insurance company was forced to pay double because it was accidental death.

Those within the criminal justice system may be well-advised to pay particular attention in a suspected case of erotic asphyxiation. The presence of an elaborate system of escape from possible strangulation, including complex slip knots, pictures and magazine in the home of the victim concerning erotic hangings, semen guards, or other such material, may serve as indicators of a possible accidental death due to erotic asphyxiation. The offender may also be interested in transvestism and possess women's nightgowns and underwear as well as pornography that depicts this form of sexual deviation. There is also some indication that some people who are involved in erotic asphyxiation are also involved in pygmalionism and anal stimulation.

Causes of Erotic Asphyxiation

There is no direct explanation of the etiology of the person who is involved in erotic asphyxiation. There appears to be some indication that this form of perversion is learned at an early age. One possible explanation can be that the person as a youth experienced some form of sexual excitation and at the same time was almost to the point of passing out or fainting. It must be pointed out, however, that there is no supportive evidence to this point of view, and this is theory only. Of course, there is also the feeling that humans are always experimenting with different ways of reaching sexual gratification, and pornography devoted to this topic may be picked up, read, and acted upon. As it has been stated, experimentation along with fantasy occupies a special place in many people's sex lives. It may also occupy a special place in many people's sex lives who are sexual deviants.

Regardless of the etiology of the person who is involved in ritualistic hanging, it is important for the people in criminal justice to be concerned with the special problems presented along with the discovery and the practice of the erotic asphyxiate.

PYROMANIA

Pyromania is an irresistible urge to set fires. In the process of setting the fires, the pyromaniac receives some sexual satisfaction from watching the fire, flames, and smoke.

Historically, it has been thought that the pyromaniac is one who suffers from severe emotional problems. He is at least considered to be neurotic and at the other extreme psychopathic. This behavioral obsession of "impulsive firesetting" only has been recognized as a sexual perversion and a sex crime within the last century.

Causes of Pyromania

With the advent of psychiatry and the examination of the unconscious, there has been directed attention to possible causes for behavior that are not readily visible to the casual observer. The etiology of the pyromaniac is unclear. There are some who believe, for example, that the offender is an obsessive-compulsive personality type. He seems to be compelled to set fires and, at the extreme end of pyromania, is preoccupied by the thoughts of setting fires. He becomes almost totally involved in the fantasy centered around setting fires, watching fires, and all of the other things centering around the total situation. A probation officer recently told this author a story about one of her clients. The man had been stopped on many occasions from setting fires using toilet paper, which he threw fully lit into a garbage can. The can was in his living room of his multiunit apartment complex. Despite his refusal to admit any compulsion to setting fires or having a problem with pyromania, he had to be rescued by the local fire department because he had set the apartment ablaze and suffered smoke inhalation on at least five separate occasions.

Psychiatry and Pyromania

The psychiatric model concerning pyromania appears to center around three dimensions:

1. Defiance of authority;
2. Expression of hostility and aggression; and
3. Attempting to resolve deep-rooted sexual conflicts.

In this psychodynamic model, the target chosen for the fire may be an example of an attack against authority; for example, if the parents' home has been set on fire, it would not be difficult to ascertain the unconscious motive(s).

In the second dimension, expression of hostility and aggression, the base for this hostility and aggression would be the early childhood expression of parental rejection and emotional deprivation. The reason for the fire-setting may be a substitute for an expression of hostility.

There is another school of thought with an explanation of the pyromania phenomenon. In an attempt to resolve the deep-rooted sexual conflict, the "impulsive fire setting" personality symbolically attempts to resolve this conflict through urethral eroticism. The components of sexual thrilling and pleasurable urination may be an additive factor in the etiology of the pyromaniac. The person in some fashion learned to express his erotic feelings through the medium of fire.

Fire, Power, Passion, and Sex

Fire is a common cultural symbol of passion and sex. Many times it has been heard that one lover tells another that "my heart is on fire for you," and many popular songs mention fire as a synonym for erotic feelings. The tendency to set fires may in itself be a learned response, subtly reinforced by cultural cues. The symbol of fire becomes an integral part in erotic expression.

In addition, there are other elements present in the personality that may account for the tendencies toward pyromania. From various contacts with pyromaniacs, it is evident that many are socially, sexually, and vocationally inadequate. They appear to have a self-concept of powerlessness. The setting of a fire enhances their self-image on two levels: the elevation of their own status and a direct erotic arousal.

In the first instance, the setting of the fire serves as an index of his power. By commanding a multitude of public servants, e.g. firemen, police officers, etc., he then may have the occasion to reevaluate his own subjective status in a more favorable position. He often appears to have some difficulty in social intercourse, and by being such a powerful creature he will, in his own mind, become a person with awesome authority.

The pyromaniac uses the "impulsive fire-setting" as a substitute for normal sexual functioning. The offender may be "the fire truck chaser" and go from fire to fire, becoming sexually excited and having an orgasm simply by viewing the flame and smoke. This is an important point to make as far as those in the criminal justice system is concerned. Whenever there are a series of puzzling fires, the origin unknown or at least suspicious, the wise arson squad investigator might be well-advised to pay particular and special attention to the crowd. Is there a familiar face in the crowd? It is apparent that many fire-setters go from one fire to another, fires that they themselves do not set, and experience sexual arousal and gratification. Some others may leave the fire scene and masturbate because of the arousal stemming from the fire. Of course, there are some who choose not to chase fires but simply set their own.

The pyromaniac also appears to be somewhat vocationally inadequate. The reason for this generalization (and it is a generalization) does not lie in his native ability to satisfactorily perform his job but rather from his obsession for his sexual perversion. By his preoccupation with pyromania, his skills in the areas of social and vocational development are neglected and subsequently retarded.

Pyromania and Public Safety

The reason for including pyromania into the dangerous sex crime category is really quite simple. It has been suggested, and this author believes with creditable research, that there is a sexual component with pyromania. The added dimension of defiance of authority coupled with the components of hostility and aggression only add additional reasons for the behavior. It is with the possession of the latter two dimensions that danger presents itself and poses a great problem to society. By involving himself in pyromania, there is a great chance that others may be in the burning building he has just set ablaze. There are many people killed annually in public and private buildings set afire by the compulsive fire setter. Therefore, regardless of the feeling of society about the etiology of the offender or the personal mental health of the offender, the danger to others in the community looms as a paramount concern that overrides individual concerns. Many more persons will be victims of the fire setter, and these victims are usually killed or at least horribly burned.

LUST MURDERS (PIQUERISM)

Usually in the investigation of murders, the motive for the homicide rests in the area of love, revenge, or sex. Nationally, statistics show that as many as three cases of four involve those where the victim knows the offender. This is certainly the case where a jealous husband shoots his errant wife. Such was the case of a young husband, age twenty, who came home early one afternoon from work. The couple argued over her flirting with other men at a local tavern. The argument erupted into a violent dispute over her alleged infidelities. In the heat of the argument, he ran into their bedroom for his shotgun, ran back into the kitchen, and shot her. She bled to death and was pronounced DOA at the local emergency room.

Such murders appear too often in the files of the police department. However, there are fewer cases where murders are committed not during the course of a domestic argument or in a commission of a robbery. These are murders committed by a person who receives a sexual thrill by the killing of another human being. These murders are sexually motivated and become investigated all too often as "simple murder cases."

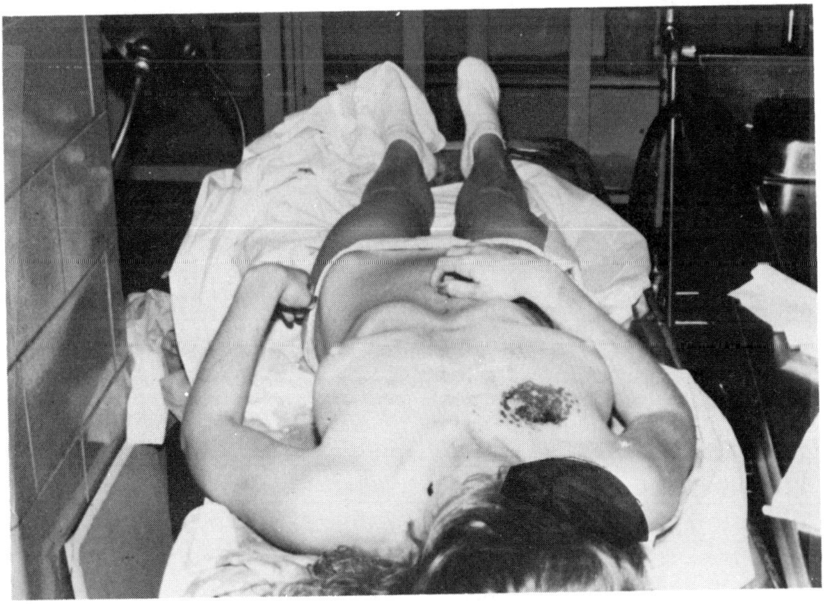

Figure 22. A young housewife murdered by her jealous husband.

The lust murderer is one who can only be sexually excited when violence of a sexual/physical nature precedes or accompanies the sexual act. The violent, savage mutilation often serves as a psychological aphrodisiac to the murderer. The lust murderer does not kill out of a fear of being apprehended. He kills because the violence is an added dimension to the sex act and sex scene. It serves as a heightened experience, one that enhances his sexual energy and feelings of power and virility.

Piquerism, then, is usually perpetrated on others within some close physical proximity. Some theorists believe that there exists some piquerers who use a projectile from a gun to tear the flesh of another. After the victim is wounded or killed, he may then move on to another victim at another locale and commit the same offense without discovery.

Those within the criminal justice system should be alert when there is a homicide where the number of bullet holes, knife wounds, etc. are more numerous than needed for killing. A woman was recently found in her home, an apartment located in a housing project. The body had fourteen knife wounds in it. Upon closer examination, semen was found on the crime scene. This case has not been solved at the time of this writing, so further details cannot be given. It is suspected, however, that the murder was possibly connected with piquerism.

Kraft-Ebing was one of the first researchers to offer insights into lust murderers. He reported a case of an offender who related that,

> I opened her breast and with a knife cut through the fleshy parts of the body. Then I arranged the body as a butcher does beef, and hacked it up with an axe into pieces of a size to fit the hole which I had dug up in the mountain for burying it. I may say that while opening the body I was so greedy that I trembled, and could have cut out a piece and eaten it.

Jack The Ripper, although never found, was possibly a piquerist. From 1877 to 1879, bodies of women were found in the streets of London. He cut the throats of his victims first and later opened their stomachs to examine the intestines. In some cases, the intestines were removed from the crime scenes and never found.

Recently a body was found on a military reservation. The nude body of a thirty-year-old housewife was found tied by her arms and legs to a football goalpost, where she was properly centered. She had multiple cigarette burns over parts of her body and more than twenty knife wounds. Inserted into her vagina was a pipe that had been rammed up into her stomach cavity. This case had all of the characteristics of a lust murder. The federal investigators, after careful and expert work, determined that this was the case of an ordinary homicide. The woman had a long history of affairs with other soldiers on the base. Her husband, jealous and in a fit of rage, took his wife to the abandoned football field and killed her. The alertness of the investigators solved the case. If the detectives only had been looking at one thing, looking at the murder as a sex crime, then the case could not possibly had been solved.

Early in this writer's criminal justice practitioner career as a probation/parole officer, a case was assigned to him by his supervisor. The body of a seven-year-old girl was found in a vacant house. The young girl had been killed by a thirteen-year-old boy. He had admitted to stabbing this female repeatedly with a kitchen butcher knife, and she had more than thirty-seven stab wounds on her body. The boy was diagnosed by the court psychiatrist as schizophrenic, undifferentiated type. The juvenile was committed to the state department for juvenile services and released after serving six months in a juvenile institution. The psychiatric evaluation admitted that the prognosis for success was dim, but because of limited resources he was released for supervision. Only six years later, he was arrested for a brutal sex crime-burglary-homicide, which resulted in his conviction and a sentence of death.

Not all cases of piquerism involve the death of the victim. There have been some cases reported where a woman has been slashed with a razor in her buttock area. Only after the offender has left the scene does the victim realize she has been cut. Sometimes the cutting bares muscles in the legs or parts of the body. The piquer also will use hat pins, ice picks, and various other sharp instruments. There have been other reported cases where acid and chemicals have been used in place of knives and razors.

Lunde (1976) carefully catergorizes two types of murderers, the single murderer and the mass murderer. The second type is of concern to the present discussion. The mass murderer is further divided into two subgroups, one being the sexual sadist. Sexual sadism, "... in its extreme form is a deviation characterized by torture and/or killing and mutilation of other persons in order to achieve sexual gratification" (Lunde).

The sexual sadist appears to be quite skillful in his ability to elude the police and others in the criminal justice system. He is, however, thought to be a repeater, and he will kill again and again. Ted Bundy, an attractive, well-educated former law student, admitted privately to killing more than the three young girls in Florida. His sexual assaults were vicious and deadly, the bodies of his victims were brutally bitten, beaten, and killed. His psychological evaluation of women appears to place them in an extremely low status and as only sexual objects.

Brittain suggested that the sadistic murderer is an introverted sort who may go off on a campaign of sexual murderers when he experiences personal rejections. Bundy's case is an excellent example of this characteristic. He apparently launched into a series of sex murderers when he was rejected by his fiance (Brittain).

Other characteristics listed by this author include a carefully planned operation and fascination with the occult, vampires, and horror-items themselves. The offender receives sexual satisfaction in seeing his victims suffer, and usually he will kill his victims by strangulation. Bundy is an exception to this last characteristic; he usually bludgeoned his victims to death. In many cases, the lust murderer will slowly kill his victim to show his power and mastery over her. As he slowly kills, he experiences an erotic sensation. The sadistic offender will often mutilate his victim. After the killing episode, he will experience no sense of guilt or tension.

It appears then that the lust murderers may be characterized by the following:

1. a period of personal rejection by significant others;
2. a history of commonality by cutting, stabbing, and/or biting of a victim, which is sometimes combined with vampirism or cannibalism;
3. an absence of semen on the scene (often there is no ejaculation since the offender may later masturbate, but there are many exceptions to this rule); and
4. a feeling of normalcy surrounding the psychology of the perpetrator and his environment.

The lust murderer is very dangerous not only because of the acts he commits but also because of his elusiveness. He may be considered to be a model citizen (Bundy was a volunteer at a crisis center in Seattle and an advisor to the governor of Washington), and the epiodes are not predictable. He may move from one area of the country to another and apprehension is thereby drastically reduced. But the danger cannot be stressed too highly.

> The piquer is a very dangerous person. Police must be alert at all times to his activity. He frequently gets his complete satisfaction from the nature of his attack. Erection and ejaculation are many times not present. Some of

> the worst mutilation cases law enforcement investigators (investigate) are the work of the picqueruer. The body is horribly disfigured, frequently the head and the breasts amputated.
>
> Usually there is some effort to cut part of the genitals out or at least to remove some parts of the skin which support public hair. In other cases, the lower stomach is opened and the intestines are pulled out. The picqueruer may disrobe and wrap parts of his body in the still-warm entrails (Morneau & Rockwell).

One form of picquerism is anthropophagy. This consists of eating human flesh (cannibalism) or drinking human blood (vampirism). By eating flesh and drinking blood, sexual satisfaction is reached. There are obvious religious overtones to this practice. The Roman Catholic Church, for example, dogmatically believes that bread and wine are miraculously changed through the process of transubstantiation into the body and the blood of Jesus Christ. The faithful, eating the host and drinking the wine, will ingest the qualities of Christ and become closer to Him. When the cannibal eats the heart of his victim, he eats not necessarily of necessity, but by eating where the courage lies (the heart in many cases) he will inculcate the best of the valued enemy and become stronger in the process.

The sex offender who is involved in cannibalism has a different motive in the eating of human flesh. The "moon maniac," Albert Fish, killed apparently scores of young men and cannibalized them. Probably psychotic, Fish embarked upon a career of killing over four hundred children, and upon a psychiatric examination at Bellevue Hospital he detailed his bizarre activities. Following the general pattern of the psychopathic offender, he looked forward to his own execution as, "the most supreme thrill of my life."

The "Orge of Hanover," Fritz Haarman, after World War I, kidnapped, murdered, butchered, and ate the bodily remains of many young boys. A blatant homosexual, Haarman was finally convicted and sentenced to die. Just a few years ago, a case was discovered in Wisconsin where a man had murdered several people, butchered their bodies, and stored their remains in his refrigerator and freezer. The police acting on a tip discovered the grim remains. Carl Denker, a Polish landlord, brutally murdered an estimated thirty people, butchered their bodies, and pickled their remains.

Throughout history, vampirism has been a continuing theme.

Figure 23. Albert Fish, cannibal, 1870–1936.

The myth of Dracula at the time of the full moon has little bearing on the behavior of the true anthropophagist, including the vampire. Peter Kurten, a German citizen and a moulder by trade, often stalked the streets at night searching for his victims.

His life story was told in a Hollywood production of "M." An obsessive-compulsive personality type, he was totally concerned about being clean and washed his hands scores of times a day. Although he confessed to killing nine children, he probably killed more than a dozen and drank their blood. Kurten was also a pyromaniac and reached orgasms by watching fires. He also walked the local cemetaries at night, visiting the sites of his victims and carrying on animated conversations with them. He died in 1930.

The exact etiology of sexual sadism is unknown. In a study of ten sadistic murderers, features of psychopathy, unethical and unreticent behavior, explosiveness of aggression in behavior, and signs of infantilism and developing chemical dependency were also discovered (Student & Drvota). It does appear that somewhere along the line of development, the sadistic murderer has made a connection between sadism and sexual gratification. It is not

Figure 24. Carl Denker, cannibal. He was executed for killing and eating thirty people.

simply a case of the connection between a religious symbolic ceremony and gratification. The connectors of violence, aggression, and sex somehow are all tied together, and erotic satisfaction can only be achieved by violence and the suffering of his victim. Truly, the acts are not to be tolerated because of the dangers they present to society. The atrocities demand unrelentless attention and dedication for the practioner in the field of criminal justice.

Figure 25. A Hollywood version of a vampire.

Figure 26. Peter Kurten, the terror of Dusseldorf, a vampire.

Chapter 10

THE VICTIM OF SEXUAL ASSAULT

There is a feeling among many people that the victim of a sex crime has somehow "asked for it." By her dress, demeanor, or body language, she is seeking to be a victim. Of course, in victimology there are some people who by their actions are "advertising" their availability. If one drives a car to a high theft area and leaves the keys in the ignition and the door unlocked, there does develop between the victim and the doer a sense of relationship. If the victim had not taken his car to the area, if the victim had not left his keys in the car's ignition, and if the victim had not left the car unlocked, there might be a good chance that his car would not be stolen. He certainly has the right to park his car wherever he wants as long as it is legal to do so. He may do what he wants, but it may not be prudent.

A solitary female certainly has the right to walk down a dark and lonely street late in the evening. It is probably not wise for her to do this, but it is her right. By her behavior, in this case walking down a dark street, she may be giving to a potential doer a signal that she is an available victim. However, it is stressed that this discourse does not in any way or fashion excuse what the perpetrator does to the victim. But by their own actions, some victims show more availability to become victims than other persons do.

It can be said with some certainty that some persons who are victims of sexual assault, for example, do by their own actions precipitate their own assaults. In addition, there are some other victims who are multiple victims simply because of their own actions. Either the behavior that resulted in their victimization was intentional or unintentional, or maybe they are people with bad luck. But there still exists in many people's minds a feeling that the woman "asked for it." To further illustrate this point, a judge recently set aside a conviction of a rapist because it was brought out in court that the woman was dressed in a most provocative fashion. The judge responded that the man would not have raped the woman if she had been dressed properly and modestly.

The professionals in the field of criminal justice, because of their role, come into almost daily contact with the sex crime victim. It must be kept in mind that there are victims who are victims in the "purest" sense of the word. Their own actions did not in any way precipitate their assault. It must be kept in mind that these victims have been violated, their privacy and personal being has been invaded, and they have been unable to act of their own volition.

CONCERNS OF VICTIMS

Victims have a wide range of personal, familial, medical, and social concerns. First of all, there appears to be an immediate medical concern. Did the victim contract a form of venereal disease? With VD being at pandemic proportions, this does have to be a valid and legitimate concern. The whole dehumanizing medical examination, for example, in some rape cases, does lead some victims to become anxious and upset because of the experience of being not treated as a person but rather as an object, a victim, and a nonperson. The question of where to go for medical help is yet another concern. Some victims refuse to go for such help because they are unaware of medical resources or afraid that word of their ordeal will become public knowledge.

Another concern of the victim may be a fear of the environment. The offender may know where the victim lives, her telephone number, her employer, and other social items. This does result sometimes in a certain amount of healthy paranoia. The victim may find that she is reluctant to pursue her otherwise daily activities such as a daily walk or going to the grocery. She may feel she is being watched and consequently becomes almost a recluse. A young mother, after being raped in her home, refused any social activities unless she was in the company of her husband. Until she received professional help and guidance, she was a prisoner in her own home.

The fear that others will think of her in a lesser light because of her victimization may result in problems in interpersonal relationships. The relations between herself and significant others may be damaged not only because of some real changes in perceptions by her spouse, relatives, close friends, and others but also may be changed by her evaluations of imagined perceptions of those people. The sudden, stressful act carries with it crisis impact, and this will have an effect on the victim's behavior. The victim needs social acceptance at this time. The violent attack may also have a detrimental effect on the victim's sex life with her loved one. This sex life between the victim and her lover may have to go through some stressful times. Careful personal counselling with both members of the sexual dyad is often the only thing that may keep them together.

Despite the violence of the crime and the circumstances of the violation, some victims still believe they have a personal concern about the offender himself. A real fear for many victims is the role they play in the possible incarceration of the perpetrator. The victim experiences almost a fanatical need to know the laws regarding the offense itself as well as community sentencing structure and the probable sentence itself. The victim may not be willing to be the one "responsible" for sending another human being to prison.

In addition to asking "why me?" the victim may express some concern for being at least partially responsible for the sexual violation itself. It should be encouraged to believe that he/she is not at all responsible for what happened. They do not share any culpability of the actions, and they have a personal right not to be sexually assaulted.

Many victims have yet another concern and that is a need to know how "the system" operates. What does the prosecution involve? How long will it take, and is it really worth it? As a victim, will she be forced to testify in court? If this is true, what does she really have to say? If the case goes to trial, will she have to quit her job and will it take her away from her family and support network for an extended period of time? Will the victim's name or picture appear on the TV news or in the newspaper? Is there someone the victim can call anytime of the day or night if she needs to? Is there a crisis center? These are all valid concerns for the sex victim. The competent investigator must be aware of the personal concerns of the victim and be able to secure the needed information for the victim to successfully proceed in the investigation of the case itself.

THE INTERVIEW OF THE VICTIM

In the investigation of the sex crime, the experienced sex crime professional, and in this case it is usually a police officer or a social worker who comes into the initial contact with the sex crime victim, a first concern should be the capacity to understand "who" the victim really is. The reality of the situation is that this is a person of integrity and worth. The victim may have, and probably has, suffered extreme physical and emotional trauma. The direction of the interview should, therefore, be guided by whether or not the victim is male or female or adult or child. If the victim is a female, the male investigator may also be treated with some distrust and suspicion. This should be expected and not taken personally. The criminal justice system's personnel must take extra steps to gain the victim's trust and confidence. The investigator must not be overly aggressive and push too hard, too quickly.

In the initial interview with the victim, the fact should be stressed that the focus of this interview is that of trying to establish some form of trust. The establishment of rapport with the victim should be given the highest priority, and the manner in which this is done will of course vary from one victim to the next. The key to the manner and contact should be the result of an instant evaluation of the entire situation and circumstance (understandably not an easy task), and the direction of the interview should depend on that evaluation. The investigator should be in a position to say that he is aware of some of the feelings of the victim. To say to a person who has just undergone a traumatic episode such as rape or a sadistic assault, "I know how you feel," is bad and it will fall on deaf ears. Of course the investigator does not know how she feels unless the investigator has also undergone an identical experience. But the investigator can say that he is aware of some of her feelings and fears and can help her deal with these by making her aware of the resources available to her and also helping her come to grips with her anxiety. Of course, this may be beyond the expertise of many investigators; that is, to provide counselling or psychological help; but at least the person during the initial interview should be able to provide the victim with a knowledge of community resources and self-help agencies. In the movie, *The Reality of Rape*, a police officer tries to calm a rape victim, telling her that he knows that she has been through a lot and that if she feels up to it he would like to ask her a few questions in order to help catch the person who did this to her. His demeanor was calm, nonaccusing, and nonjudgmental. Competent and compassionate investigators should also be nonjudgmental and patient.

By attempting to put the victim at ease, this will facilitate the victim's recall of the situation and perhaps this may enable the quick capture of the offender.

The victim personally should be encouraged to talk and ventilate feelings. She should be asked to tell the story in her own words. After that has been done, going back over the story may help in truly reconstructing the story, clarifying details that might not have been clear. The original story as told by the victim might not have been deliberately distorted, but because of the personal trauma, some details may have been forgotten or imagined.

The investigator should be well-aware of his own sexuality and feelings toward sexual assaults as well as the victims of these sexual assaults. He should not be easily embarrassed. If the victim sees that the investigator is embarrassed, the information received may be limited by the emotional display. When the story has been told to the best of the ability of the victim or when it is related under the best of present circumstances, the story should be reiterated to try to clear up any fuzzy points. The victim should be made aware of the necessity to continually check the story. The purpose is not to catch the victim in a lie but to make certain that all of the details are constant and verifiable. The success of the investigation and arrest will depend on the reliability of the story.

It should not have to be said, but the victim should ordinarily be interviewed in private, away from family members. The family should, however, also be interviewed, and the investigator could take this opportunity to stress to the family that the victim is simply that, a victim. In no manner whatsoever should the victim be considered responsible for the crime of sexual assault. At this time, the family members can be solicited for potential valuable information. After a period of time, and this time will vary from one family to the next, it might be possible to interview the victim and the family together to see if anyone can add valuable testimony. The reason for this joint session is to join the stories to see if there is additional information that might be significant. Also by asking the victim to recount the experience, the victim may ventilate her feelings and inform the other family members about her experience. Additionally, the family members will be helped to alleviate their feelings of helplessness in the investigation of this case. By helping with the case itself, the family member may finally feel like a person who is a contributing member of the total team.

PSYCHOLOGICAL REACTIONS OF THE VICTIMIZED

The victim should be helped once again by the investigator not to fall into a situation where she feels somewhat guilty over what has happened to her. The feelings of guilt when she states that, "I should not . . . ," must be dismissed because she is not culpable in the attack. Misdirected anger, questioning "why me," must also be a focal point of discussion. There are other victims who totally repress their attack, and they often never recall the incident itself. These victims obviously need psychological help. Often, they are beyond the normal range of services of the ordinary person in the criminal justice profession. And yet, other victims may feel somewhat "dirty" or "tarnished" because they have been "violated." What has happened to them is not their fault, and this point has been stated several times before. It must be stressed strenuously to the victim because of the feelings many of the victims have over their attack.

Other victims become hysterical, and this response is typified by exaggerated emotional responses. Crying, screaming, and other extreme forms of reactions must be allowed to occur, because with these responses the victim can ventilate her responses. Of course, when these spells of crying or screaming appear to be beyond the normal range of reactions, other professional help should be secured.

There are some who believe that those people who are severely depressed, those who do not cry or otherwise show some form of emotion, were truly not sexually victimized. There are some victims who appear to be quite detached from the scene and circumstance of their sexual assault; they become observers. They carry on normal conversations with relatives and friends, and they appear to be able to clinically relate the occurrence. The investigator should be made aware of these people who have the ability to relate their experience in this manner. It does not mean that they have not been victimized nor does it mean that the experience itself was not painful, traumatic, and an invasion of their privacy and being. It only means that they are dealing with the invasion in a different fashion, and it is a manner of dealing with the problem in the same way another victim would become hysterical, suffer amnesia, or experience some other form of defense mechanism.

THE VICTIM AS KEY TO SUCCESS

The victim is the key to the investigation. To judge the attack by the reactions of the victim to determine if there was truly a crime committed or not is foolhardy. All victims do not react in the same manner. The success of the investigation will depend on the skill of the personnel of the system. The knowledge of victimology and the psychology of the human personality is imperative for success. It must be kept in mind that the victim is a real person, a complex person. It has been said that sex is only one part of a person. The sex offender, as well as the sex victim, is a complex person, and deviance is usually only one part of his being. The pedophile may be a prosocial, professional, and contributing person in society. His pedophilia is only one part of his personality. In some other pedophiles, for example, the love of children becomes a totally encompassing obsession, and all daily activities center around the quest for children. But from the professional research, the latter case tends to be the exception rather than the rule.

The victim, because of the sexual assault, is eternally changed. The person will never be the same either emotionally, physically, or psychologically. What happens to many victims is that while sex previously occupied only a part of their life the sexual attack now becomes a focal point. The attack serves as an unfortunate stimuli that centers their daily activities. Their routine of shopping, recreation, and being home alone has undergone a change, and the activities can never be the same. The self-evaluation has been altered, and special care and attention must be given to the victim because of this situation.

CONCLUSION

Too often, books have been devoted to the offender with little attention and mention of the victim. To some extent, this book has been equally guilty. While great care has been extended and devoted to the description of the offenders themselves, little has been devoted to the victim and the victim's concerns and problems. This must change.

Chapter 11

TREATMENT OF THE SEXUAL CRIMINAL

It is the final goal of the criminal justice system to change the sex offender into a contributing citizen. Regardless of the seriousness of the offense, unless it is a capital offense, there are the purposes of sentencing, punishment, and rehabilitation (habilitation). The punishment response stems from a society's feeling of its right to extricate a measure from the offender. To use punishment as a form of rehabilitation is nonsensical. If the philosophy of punishment rests on revenge, retribution, deterrence, or protection of society, rehabilitation is ignored. Rehabilitation and reintegration, because of humane considerations and practicalities, must be truly reckoned with as far as philosophical goals of corrections are concerned.

Rehabilitation is probably not the correct term to be used. Habilitation is a better one. To rehabilitate one means to restore one to a prior condition. A person who suffers a heart attack undergoes therapy and a program of rehabilitation to restore him to a physical condition that existed prior to the heart attack. Habilitation means to change someone to a state of a desired attitudinal position.

Aversion therapy was especially prevalent in the 1960s and early 1970s. Barker, for example, acknowledged that sexual perversions are resistent to change and treatment. In some few cases, psychotherapy or drug therapy is helpful. However, this author believes that aversion therapy shows promise as a viable treatment modality and may represent a major treatment form for all abnormal sexual compulsions.

It appears that the predominant theme in the treatment world is that the offender is having some problems in the area of his total social world. Since this is the case, this person should be viewed as a total person, not in a tunnel-vision approach; that is, not only in the light of his sexual crime. The rapist, for example, may need professional and peer group help in controlling his frustrations and anxieties, and he may get from therapy an ability to control this detrimental impulse. The child molester, as another example, may need some help to change his sex object choice. Supportive therapy needs to be initiated to help the offender deal in a positive way with anger, anxieties, frustrations, and other feelings that are detrimental to functioning.

What is stressed here is an approach to a more humane and understanding climate of the sex offender. Realizing that his offense is only one part of his personality, and realizing that his personality needs to be in some fashion amended to suit a proper social adjustment, a conducive conduit for change must be made.

There are several traditional therapies available to convicted sex offenders. The utilization of the medical treatment team of psychiatrist, psychologist, psychiatric social worker, and some few others occupies a special status in traditional therapy. This approach supposes that the sex offender is "sick" and the ideal therapist is the medical professional. However, there is a movement away from the one-on-one therapeutic relationship and the medical approach because of a variety of different reasons. The high cost of traditional psychiatric therapy coupled with the ever-increasing numbers of offenders to deal with has necessitated a change to newer treatment modalities. Guided group interaction, developed by Harry Vorath, has been used with some success, especially with youthful offenders. The probation-parole officer and the client relationship is not conducive to therapeutic change. The presence of authority coupled with the size of the caseloads precludes any great significant strides in developing new attitudinal and behavioral changes.

In one prison, there has been introduced a new treatment approach under the direction of Claud Turpin, a clinical social worker. LaGrange Reformatory, LaGrange, Kentucky, has instituted a sex offenders group therapy session. The group, which is composed of rapists, child molesters, pornographers, and other adjudicated sex offenders, meets once a week in peer group counseling. To become a group member, the sex offender must admit his guilt to the group. Turpin believes that this is the first step toward rehabilitation (recognizing the deficiency of the word), and he will not accept anyone into the group unless he does so. This admission in group is called a part of the Therapeutic Agreement.

The group member must be willing to verbalize his own

feelings regarding a wide range of attitudes and behaviors, but naturally centered around sex. He is also obligated to confront group members if he observes behavior detrimental to the man's rehabilitation. If the adverse behavior does not stop, he then has an obligation to relate this behavior to the total group.

The group session itself is very intense. The composition of the group will change as old members leave the group and new members join. On one day, the group was composed of the following six offenders:

John, serving two consecutive life sentences for rape against adult females;

Jeff, serving five years for having sex with his twenty-three-month-old stepdaughter;

Silas, serving ten years for rape of a twenty-four-year-old female;

David, serving twenty-one years for rape and attempted rape of two adult women;

Hubert, serving twenty years for sodomy of his nine-year-old stepdaughter;

Irv, serving twenty years for sodomy of his nine-year-old stepdaughter;

Robert, serving ten years for 2nd-degree rape of a ten-year-old girl;

Earl, serving fifteen years for two counts of rape of two adult women.

On this particular day, the group session was concerned with examining the statements of several group members. John, a man in his late fifties, related that his motive for rape was not of the type that usually fits the average model of rape. An intelligent man, owner and president of an architectural engineering firm on the outside, stated that he raped not because of any great hostility to women but because he needed love and acceptance. He could not receive any affection from his wife because she was an invalid and terminally ill. He had three affairs, but his wife found out about them. He would not go to a prostitute because they were "too dirty."

His method of operation was to go into the home of women while they were asleep, carefully slit their nightgowns so that the breasts were exposed, and then masturbate. He was careful not to awaken them and, if they did stir, he would leave immediately. He did this to several women, and also raped two other women.

John articulates that all he wants is comfort from his victims. When he was young, John related that he was held by his mother to her breast. When he and his wife were sexually active, he would get quite erotically aroused by "her mammary glands," and all he wants now is to be held close to a "set of mammary glands."

The other men in the group basically do not accept John's explanation of his motive for rape. Jeff, for example, stated that he feels that rape is a vicious attack, but he did not use force on his twenty-three-month-old stepdaughter. Jeff said that he was high on drugs and alcohol when he sexually molested his stepdaughter and probably would not have done it if he and his wife "were sleeping together." Silas said that he did not use any force on his victim, he merely "conned" her into having sex with him. They were out in the country, and he had her pinned against a car door that would not open. He grudgingly admitted that because he was a man and because of his size she yielded to his demands.

There is nothing sacred in these group meetings. The participants are encouraged to verbally attack another member if the person believes that the member is not being honest in his responses to the problem. The model accepted by most of the group members was that they did not rape because of any great hostility to women and any particular feelings of aggression to women themselves. Rather they raped and committed sodomy because they felt at that particular time peculiar frustrations and a sexual assault served as a tranquilizing behavior. One rapist in another group admitted that he had raped over thirty women, although convicted of only three, and felt very relaxed after each rape. On several occasions, for example, he pulled off the side of the highway and took a nap after raping a young girl. The men said that they raped because sex was the manner in which they could deal with frustrations and their fears. This feeling is certainly opposed to the traditional theoretical theory, which holds that rape is a crime of violence directed at women, and sex is only the object used. This new information, while gathered from only a handful of rapists, may deserve further study and evaluation.

This sex offender group may serve as a prototype for new groups. The offenders have developed within the group itself a subculture with a prosocial climate. Of course, there is always a chance that there are some games being played by some of the group members; for example, one rapist stated to me that he would not have committed his rapes if his super ego had been able to contain the savage impulses of his id. But the social workers in the group have taken great care to try to strip the group of this form of game playing. What is also interesting with this group is that there is a female social worker in each group along with Turpin. Ms. Mary Ann Eaglin and Ms. Trudy North are the therapists in the groups at this time. The reason for including a female in each group is to introduce to the male group members that there are women who are not passive, are intelligent, and have qualities that demand human respect and caring. The female social workers confront the sex offenders in the group, and there is sometimes violent verbal confrontations among the group members or between a group member and a social worker. The supreme confidentiality of the group permits discussions not ordinarily heard among convicts and their workers. What impressed this author was the ease of disagreement expressed by the group members without any apparent negative repercussions from the therapists or the prison administration.

The members of this group have been "in group" for a period of time ranging from three weeks to almost four years. There are no accurate data that may support any great claim for success using this form of sexual counseling. It is an attempt, however, to use an innovative form of humane treatment, and that in itself should be praised. The group is based on an assumption that change is a possibility, and any possible change results not from punishment but from a humane consideration of the worth of all of us, not only the sex offender but also a major consideration of the victims. A great deal of discussion is centered around the concern and rights of the victims of the rapes and sexual assaults. This program deserves special attention in terms of research and evaluation.

It must be kept in mind that the majority of sex offenders are released back into the community. Some are returned sooner than others, and some receive more treatment than others. What is certain, then, is that unless something is positively offered to change the sex deviant, little can be expected other than the same behavior.

Each member of the society shares in the cost of the habilitation of sex offenders. But as each social member shares in the cost of habilitation, each member also shares in the benefit of habilitation. By the education and enlightenment of society and the sex deviants, society can feel some semblance of personal safety and responsibility.

The time has truly passed when the sex deviant should be seen as an animal. The sex criminal, especially the dangerous sex offender, is one who is a member of society and shares many common activities. But because of his propensity toward deviant sex, he will interact with the overall society. Something must be done to help the situation on both ends of the behavioral continuum. To this end, this book has been offered for the purposes of education, understanding, and a general offering of only slight pontification. Only when there is a movement from narrow-mindedness toward understanding, sympathy, and hope can there be a chance for habilitation and civilized living. This should be the goal—not only the goal of the "normals" but of the sex offenders as well.

Chapter 12

SEX OFFENDERS AND CHANGE PERSPECTIVES

Just what is "abnormal sex?" It must be more than simply unacceptable sex. Fellatio and cunnilingus are sex behaviors that are increasing in popularity and acceptability. It is thought that there will be an increase in the acceptability of other forms of sex, including homosexuality, adultery, and premarital sex.

Abnormal sex will vary, then, from one person to another. Social patterns will change from one period to another, and since things do change, people today are not shocked in the same way their parents would have been if the same things occurred a generation ago. So what is acceptable sexual behavior? Some forms of sex behavior are legally acceptable, and this reflect normally the attitudes and values of the model citizens of the society. Abnormal sex then appears to center around three main elements:

1. Satisfies neurotic needs for sex satisfaction;
2. Needed to achieve penile erection; and
3. Needed to maintain penile erection.

Certainly there must be some distinction between what is normal sex and what is abnormal or neurotic sex. There appears to be certain elements involved in all forms of sexual behavior; but these elements become more evident when one speaks of deviant sexuality.

The first element concerns that of fantasy. Fantasy is a phenomenon often connected with deviant sex. Of course, a certain amount of fantasy is normal, and most of us fantasize in order to eroticize the particular situation of the moment. Some fantasies may not be related to sex at all: for example, fantasies of power, authority, wealth, and a variety of other nonsexual situations. Fantasies serve several functions. For the normal individual, fantasies may serve as a drive reducer. In the sex deviant, however, the fantasy itself may serve as a producer for their deviant sexual behavior.

Another element of deviant sex concerns that of symbolism. It appears that a great majority of people have sex symbols. It may be legs, breasts, noses, ankles, or whatever. Of course, by the very operational definition of symbol, that being something that stands for something other than what it really is, some concern the body and some concern dress. There are people who are turned on by large bosoms, beautiful legs, a uniform, a split skirt, or a visible panty line. The problem results when items that are not normally associated with sex become a symbol in and of themselves. The symbols may be fireplugs, open windows, exhaust pipes, or anything else the mind can imagine. The psychopathic person who may be a sex offender may not be able to control this symbolism, as well as his fantasy, and may, when exposed to this symbol, lose control of himself and become involved immediately in deviant sexual activity. This particular point of view is well illustrated by the apprehension of a young man who, whenever he saw a girl with a short skirt, would become sexually excited and masturbate quite publicly. Considering the fetish of shoes, leather, and fur and the partialism of legs, breasts, and ankles, the consideration of the source must be examined. The sex criminal may attach a certain measure of sex energy to these symbols and never get back on "the right track."

Another element of deviant sex is that of ritualism. If one thinks of one's own sex history, thinking about when one first discovered the self as a sexual being and finding others as part of fantasies, one also discovered that some things were liked and some others were disliked. When the boy first kissed the girl down the street on the back of the neck, the girl may have found it pleasant and transmitted this feeling to the boy. Moving onward through the continuum of sexual behavior, within the range of "normal" sex, those behavioral patterns that one found normal and pleasant were probably rewarded by positive strokes. Those things found unpleasant, disgusting, or otherwise unrewarding were dropped from the repertoire of sex behaviors. In the course of experimentation, we find out what turns some people on and what turns other people off. This ritual becomes very set, not only for the sex deviant but also for the normal human being, the normal sexual human being. How often does the sex relationship between the husband and the wife become so ritualistic and so predictable that one could go through the sex act counting the stages, knowing what follows each step. With the sex criminal, this ritual becomes almost a method of operation and can be quite helpful to those in the criminal justice system in apprehension.

There appears to be other generalizations for the deviant sex offender. The senses, for example, seems to play a great part in the area of sex crimes. The sense of sight, for example, serves the voyeur very well, and he becomes very hypersensitive to this particular sense. The senses of touch, smell, and taste also play a great part. And for most of us, all of the senses play a part. This appears to be quite normal. However, with the deviant sex offender, the reliability on sense presence and sense fantasy plays a greater role and must be present for deviant sex to be performed.

There are other obvious generalizations for deviant sex. The lack of necessity for a love partner is common. This is particularly evident in the erotic asphyxiate and in the cases of deviant sex where the partner is not a willing participant. This can be seen in the nuisance sex crimes as well as the dangerous sex crimes.

There is some evidence, in addition, that there may be a progressive degeneracy among those involved in deviant sex. It was commonly thought that if a person were a voyeur, he would also be an exhibitionist. This may not be true, and it is believed among the researchers in the field of sex crimes that people do change from one stage of deviancy to another. Beavers, in his seminars, states that in his many years of law enforcement dealing with sex offenders he has detected a pattern of progression in sex degeneracy. Those people who start off by stealing underwear off the clothesline after some time find this is not enough to gain sexual gratification. They may then move on to obscene telephone calls, voyeurism, exhibitionism, and finally into some of the more dangerous sex crimes, including rape. Beavers further believes that most dangerous offenders stop at about the age of thirty-five, when he believes that the sex drive greatly diminishes. However, this is not always the case, and there are a great many exceptions to this general rule.

So, sexuality appears to be what feels good for a person at a particular time. We tend to view other sexual beings in the eyes of sexual normalcy. With certain forms of behavior that can be categorized as "pain" sex—bondage, flagellation, and erotic asphyxiation—there are certain needs for pain to be an integral part of the sexual functioning. However, as was stated earlier, the giving or receiving of pain is on a continuum. Certainly most of the normal sexual beings enjoy a strong hug during lovemaking. There may be some people who like a stronger hug than others, and there may be other people who enjoy being tied up and even whipped. However, the definition of deviancy depends not only on what is normal sex, as far as the present discussion is concerned, but also on the rights of the partner. Too often the partner in deviant sex is the victim, an unwilling victim.

Abnormal sex, then, is very difficult to define since often we don't know what normal sex is. Only just a very few years ago, coitus in the missionary position was considered to be the only acceptable form of marital behavior. Today our society is accepting a wide variety of alternatives and the movement is away from looking at sexuality in a narrow focus. It is the personal belief of this author that abnormal sex is a symptom of a variety of neurotic problems. In some cases, the deviant act must accompany the sex. The man who eats human feces is certainly enjoying sex. The infibulator who castrates himself excites himself.

It has been the general tone of this text to this point that sexual behavior is learned, normal as well as deviant sexual behavior. Most sex criminals express the desire to be understood, and even while the act is going on, the sex criminal may not know that what he is doing is wrong.

In dealing with the sex offender, it has become more and more of a societal, cultural, and criminal justice problem. There must be something done in the interest of society as well as in the humane concern for the sex offender to deal with this particular problem. There does exist in many people's mind a callous and uncaring attitude toward this unique offender. Those persons who have been adjudicated as criminals because of bank robberies, drug dealings, and a multitude of other types of offenses are not seen in the same vision as the sex offender. He is somehow viewed as a criminal of a different sort and one who needs to be locked up and the key thrown away. What could be done? Which would serve the interest of society as well as the offender?

Initially, there must be a different focus on the type of person the sex offender is. It must be seen that by and large the sex offender is not too different from other people. His attitudes toward a variety of social concerns and religious beliefs are usually not any different than any other people. His feelings toward God, country, and apple pie tend to be of a modal point-of-view and one shared, obviously, by many others. There must be, then, a general educational effort on many levels. On the first level it is believed there must be a general educational movement toward teaching young people about themselves, their bodies, and their sexual responsibilities. While sex education in the school has been encouraged over the years, there is no doubt that it has done some good. However, sex education by parents, if properly done in a caring and uninhibited background, would certainly be the preferred situation. However, recognizing the situation for what it is, a continued effort in the area of teaching children about themselves and their sexual responsibilities is a must. There must be another concentrated effort in educating the general population regarding the range of sexual expressions. It must be seen that all people do not behave sexually in the same fashion. This is not to say, by any means, that the normal citizens of our society should tolerate deviant sex to the point that it endangers or infringes upon the rights, the privacy, and the person of another member.

There also must be changes within the area of investigation of sex crimes. An interdisciplinary approach to this particular social problem would appear to be of utmost importance and should be given highest priority. A formulation of an interdisciplinary sex crime unit would be one that could serve as a model for other departments to follow; by utilizing the experts within a variety of fields, the police with their investigative skills, the social scientist, the behavioral scientist, and the legal experts, the apprehension of the offender, the service to the victim, and the possible rehabilitation of the sex deviant are possible.

THEORETICAL MODEL

The basic model for the theoretical construction of the sex crime unit and function is based on the nine basic characteristics of the open systems as defined by Katz and Kahn in their book, *The Social Psychology of Organizations*.

These characteristics of the open system are briefly encapsulated by this author as follows:

1. *Importation of energy*—there is some form of energy imported into any open system, and a social system must draw energy from other institutions, the people, or the environment.

2. *The through-put*—the social system provides a service, makes a product, processes materials. Work gets accomplished in a system.
3. *The output*—some export is made into the environment, the case is assigned into some department.
4. *Systems as cycles of events*—the system has a cyclic movement. In this instance, the police departments have a never-ending supply of inputs.
5. *Negative entropy*—a movement toward disorganization. This movement can grow with the importation of energy.
6. *Information input, negative feedback, and coding process*—the negative feedback arrests deviation from the stated course of the organization, and while the coding process is important in an organization, not all of the information into the system is capable of being absorbed into the system.
7. *Steady state and dynamic homeostatis*—there is a continuous inflow and export of energy into the system. With this inflow there is a move toward incorporating the external resources essential to survival.
8. *Differentiation*—there is a movement to the mean and elaboration of roles with the specialization of function(s).
9. *Equifinality*—a system can reach the final goal from differing initial conditions and by a variety of paths. The authors stated that as more regulation in the larger system occurs equifinality may be reduced.

CHARACTERISTICS OF THE CRIMINAL JUSTICE SYSTEM AS AN OPEN SYSTEM

1. *Importation of energy*—All reported crimes, including sex crimes, are reported to the police as one agent of the criminal justice departmental system. The corrections units are also involved in the input of energy as far as the adjudicated criminal is concerned. The police receives its input from the community; the corrections units receive their input of energy not only from the police but also from the courts and other agents of the system.
2. *Through-put*—After the receiving of the criminal report, the police departments will assign to the responsible units within the system, e.g. homicide, vice, etc. The entire criminal justice system will respond to the reported and adjudicated offenders according to the statutory dictates and philosophy of the organization.
3. *Output*—The police department officials and the other members of the criminal justice system will respond to the reported offenses as well as the persons who are already into the system, e.g. the parolee or the inmate of an institution.
4. *System as a Cycle of Events*—There appears to be a never-ending source of referrals from the community that deal with the criminal element in our society. The reported crime rate is increasing and this has exerted pressure upon the individuals in the system to provide services to a seemingly endless line of persons, a frustrating situation, to be sure.

5. *Negative entropy*—By the very nature of the criminal justice system, the system itself is self-perpetuating. This statement is predicated upon the fact that crime is normal in a class society or where the structure of a society blocks legitimate means to societal approved goals.
6. *Information input, negative feedback, and coding process*—The criminal justice system has an elaborate coding system that identifies the type of offense that has been reported not only on the very formal level, but it is also evident on the informal level, where the offenders within the system have a coding feedback system. The negative feedback into the system consists of the reported rates of recidivism. This rate will, of course, vary since the norm was utilized from one component of the complex to the next; for example, some in the system might use a year for a norm measuring recidivism, while another component within the system might use six months as a norm.
7. *Steady State and homeostatic*—The role of each member of the criminal justice system is so stated. Within the system as the roles intertwine one with the other, there is a steady flow of information in the form of referrals into the system. The system itself will be adjudication, parole, probation, plea bargaining, and other forms of discretion used to adjust the system to homeostasis. The system, in other words, will not explode by the sheer numbers. The system itself adjusts to new demands by utilizing methods, both formal and informal, legal and illegal.
8. *Differentiation*—The roles of the members in the criminal justice system will vary, but they have all been legally, both formally and informally, arranged. It may be that it is the policy of a police department that the head of a unit be a sergeant. The various large components in the sysem have functions that are supposedly differentiated by purpose and mandate. The police officer is not a parole officer.
9. *Equifinality*—To protect the community by neutralizing the offender; that is, the Social Defense School of Criminology.

COMPOSITION OF THE MODEL SEX UNIT

The organization of the Sex Crime Unit dealing with the sex offender must include both specialists and generalists within the criminal justice system. It should be composed of members from the following fields and/or academic disciplines:

Law Enforcement
Probation and Parole
Corrections
Psychology
Sociology
Social Work
Psychiatry
Medicine, and
Law.

The function of each area is envisioned to operate for the protection of the community and to the service of the offender.

Law Enforcement—the criminal investigation of the facts: interviewing the victim, talking with the witnesses, arrest of the offender, and generally the total police function of case preparedness.

Probation and Parole—the careful evaluation of the potential success probability of this manner of legal disposition utilizing the expertise of other unit members as well as being familiar with the resources available within its own organization outside the unit but within the criminal justice system.

Corrections—the purposive and professional evaluation of treatment modalities that the corrections discipline can extend to the offender should some form of incarceration be needed, e.g. farms, reformatories, halfway houses, etc.

Psychology—psychological evaluation of the offender using standardized tests, which would give the unit a basis for recommendation for justice. The WAIS and other tests would yield supposedly verifiable data attesting to the intellectual and social abilities of the offender in order to understand his situation and possible consequences of his behavior.

Sociology—the discipline would inject input concerning the subcultural influences of this behavior, the relationships extant in sex offenses, and the possible avenues for exploration for justice in the case at hand.

Social Work—the examination of the offender's social life is the laboratory for the social worker. This role would include the evaluation of the home situation, job, and strengths and weaknesses of a social nature, which have been learned through social case work investigation.

Psychiatry—in-depth analysis and psychiatric evaluation by this discipline should allow for a proper treatment plan predicated upon the understanding of possible pathological etiological processes. Projective testing and in-depth interviews with the offenders would certainly yield vital results that would serve as a trait in the total complex of the justice plan.

Medicine—a medical examination should be a priority to not only determine health status but to also asertain any possible causes for this violent attack due to organicity. A medical report will be an important element in the final report, which is viewed as the total document for appraisal by the court.

Law—the role of the prosecutor is vital to the success of the unit not only as a standard to insure the careful preparation of the case against the subject but also, and this is of at least equal importance, to insure everything is legally done so that the offender's, if truly guilty, legal jurisdiction can be established so that treatment can be established not only for the purpose of neutralizing the offender but also treating the offender.

PHILOSOPHY, GOALS, AND OBJECTIVES OF THE SEX CRIME UNIT

The philosophy of the Sex Crime Unit would be to provide a comprehensive service effort to the community at large. The philosophy should be that it would be a functioning unit within the criminal justice system.

The component function of the unit would not only make legal arrests for the sex crimes but also serve as a change agent for the criminal justice system in dealing with the sex offender. It would also serve as one type of treatment modality and protective component for the community. The introduction of the problem to the criminal justice system is to introduce to the system again the philosophy of the Social Defense School of Criminology and the particular area of etiology and treatment modalities with an additional resources referral function. In this perspective, the sex offender is viewed as a legal offender, but the impact of the perspective is of primary importance and is placed upon the understanding of the personality of the offender. The law is not a forgotten item in this instance. The return to the Positive School point of view is not indicated here; that is, there is no free will and the law is ignored since the criminal is a product of "... the savage genes from his savage ancestors." It is important, however, to neutralize the offender by removing him from the community, and some type of treatment indicated. In other words, this unit would be interested in more than simply the arrest as a function of the component but rather as another added dimension in the criminal justice system.

The overall goals of the Sex Crime Unit follow:

Goal—Comprehensive protection of the citizens of the community.

Objectives

A. Twenty-four hour unit functioning to insure prompt reactions from the reported offense.

B. Educational efforts at alerting the public to become aware of the danger of sex offenses.

C. Utilizing the various expertise of the members of the unit to devise plans for a comprehensive protection plan.

D. Speedy apprehension of the nuisance and dangerous sex offenders, utilizing the methods and equipment of the entire criminal justice system.

Goal—Extend to the sex offender the services of the Sex Crime Unit.

Objectives

A. Careful evaluation of the capabilities of the offender.

B. Blending the services represented by the Sex Crime Unit, evaluations made and recommendations offered to the courts.

C. Based upon careful evaluation by the members of the Unit, a careful treatment program is outlined as far as a follow-up program is concerned. This program will especially utilize the services of the probation, parole and social work.

Goal—Legitimizing the existence of the Sex Crime Unit concerning the viability, integrity, and worth as a valid tool of the criminal justice system.

Objectives

A. Develop and maintain a comprehensive public relations program to develop a general awareness of the purpose of the unit and its contributions both real and potential to the social problem.

B. Extensive research, both local and nationwide in scope, to verify the knowledge of the unit's experiences and to establish trends and possible preventative measures to be established based on the empirical evidence utilizing basic and advanced statistical computer operations.

C. Maintain a close relationship with other agencies of the criminal justice system to maintain credibility and open lines of communication.

Goal—Maintain an avenue for feedback as an evaluative method of the unit and as a measure for change within the unit.

Objectives

A. Establish measures for channels of communications through the various components of the criminal justice system.

B. Establish an instrument utilizing the expertise of the social and behavioral scientists concerning the structure of the instrument and also the pertinent input by other members of the unit.

PROBLEM EXPANSION

To briefly restate the problem, it is the manifest purpose of this model to demonstrate the imperative nature of using a treatment, nonpunitive approach in a nontraditional manner in neutralizing the sex offender. The police department is usually the first element of the entire criminal justice system to come into contact with the offender if the latter is apprehended.

There are at least two problem expansion possibilities with the interaction of the new philosophy and goals of a separate sex crime unit dealing with a radical treatment modality with the deviant. The rapist, for example, is committing a crime of violence against a person, which is not a sex act alone. The act of rape to the perpetrator is based on power and the humiliation of the victim. This is the traditional belief, and research may be needed to really substantiate this point of view. Sex is secondary. The victim is not selected as a sex object for sexual release because of the absence of other sex outlets. Indeed the vast majority of convicted rapists are married (Clinard).

The act of rape in American society carries with it a great deal of negative feeling. The agents of the criminal justice system are also members of the community and share many of the same attitudes and values of the other members who have been inculcated with these prosocial ideals. The basic resistance to change is based on ethnocentrism, religious or subcultural loyalties, and is certainly enhanced by these negative values and attitudes toward this act of aggression. The members of the criminal justice system are not immune to these thoughts.

It is theorized, however, that the members of the Sex Crime Unit, a newly created unit especially formed for a purpose unique in the system, would be carefully selected and differentiated to the point where only certain agents, who possess a more tolerant and educated viewpoint, are assigned certain offenses. The viewpoints will be enhanced by a philosophical position of rehabilitation and human concerns. If an agent is present with an attitude not conducive toward the philosophy of the treatment process approach, the area of the problem expansion will certainly grow because of the potential disruptive force this would have on the internal operation of the component.

The second major area of problem expansion potential lies in the new philosophy toward the deviant sex offender being introduced into the criminal justice system. The other members of the system may not be conducive to change. They may see this new attitudinal change agent as one that creates a new set of problems with a possible effect resulting in an increase in the rate of the sex offenses.

Members of the criminal justice system, e.g. police, probation officers, etc., are the ones who often reflect the moral viewpoints of society. The potential for conflict will not be as great as one would move along a continuum of treatment versus the simple arrest function. This is not to imply that the two must be diametrically opposed. Too often, however, they are.

With an approach toward the modification of the attitudes of the sex offense unit toward not only the apprehension of the offender but also of referrals and a better understanding of the sex offender, not ignoring the rights of the offender and the experiences of his background and the experiences of the victim, the area of problem expansion to the system becomes more evident. The apprehension and the arrest rate would certainly be one affected by a changing attitude by the investigating officers. The potential conflict situation of their social defense philosophy would have its repercussions upon the legalistic viewpoints of the court system.

To reverse the problem area, with the attitudes of the criminal justice system as an element, the problem restrictive aspect of this focus would be to the point that the structure would reflect a point of view in sympathy with the social defense school of criminology, a viewpoint that is not necessarily in congruence with the modal feelings of the community-at-large.

In analyzing the potential effect the philosophy of a multidisciplinary approach to the sex offender, let it be kept in mind and recall the nine basic characteristics of the open system while also realizing a perspective on the component of the model sex crime unit.

1. *Importation of energy*—As in the first section of this discourse, the model unit is the component of the criminal justice system that would receive all reported sex crime offenses. The further impact of changing attitudes with the model would be to further delineate the sex offenses, and these offenses would be assigned to those agents who have expressed a desire for working with this type of offender.
2. *The through-put*—The basic sex offenses are still processed in a similar fashion, but the processed materials, the sex offenses, are not directly processed to the interdisciplinary model.
3. *The output*—After receiving the reported offenses, the task force that has been designed for the purpose of dealing with the deviant would be activated.
4. *Systems and a cycle of events*—The model is in a constant state of receiving new referrals both from within and outside the system. The tremendous growth in only reported figures testifies to the need and justifies the existence of the unit.
5. *Negative entropy*—By the nature of the referrals, the violations of society's norms as formally and legally defined, the input of energy is guaranteed

not only by past experiences in the study of human behavior but also by theoretical knowledge regarding the inevitability of crime as a social phenomenon (Coser & Rosenberg).

6. *Information input, negative feedback, and coding process*—By the coding process and proper referral, the model is receiving those appropriate cases for attention and handling.
7. *Steady state and dynamic homeostatis*—As with past studies (e.g. author's unpublished study, "Synodic Lunar Patterns and Sex Offenses"), it is seen that there is a steady influx of cases that are referred daily for sex crime unit handling. One study shows high referrals as far as days of the weeks and changing patterns of a cyclical nature.
8. *Differentiation*—The roles of the members of the sex crime model will vary due to the discipline that each represents and the area of their expertise. However, they also will be concerned with the treatment, apprehension, and other handling of the offender.
9. *Equifinality*—To protect the community by neutralizing the offender is the goal, the fulfillment of the philosophy of an interdisciplinary unit.

CONCLUSION

In terminating this discourse using a systems approach to attempt to deal with a major social problem of our day, it has been the purpose of this section to utilize the systems model as a possible solution in the very difficult job of dealing with the sex offender, covering the full range of services. It is not enough for the police to arrest, the courts to try, and the corrections profession to warehouse and treat. Each component working in a vacuum is detrimental to society and the offender. It is not enough that a police department, as one component, house the sex crime unit in with another unit, such as homicide, and treat it as a stepchild. Only when police, the courts, corrections, the medical professionals, social work practitioners, and academicians all work together can they hope to make meaningful contributions to mankind's problem.

GLOSSARY

abnormal sex: generic term encompassing all criminalized or disvalued sexual behaviors, with the exceptions of adultery and fornication

abortifacient: oral medication taken with the intention of aborting the fetus; some abortifacients are chemical compounds, even proprietary products; others are derived from folk medicine or the inventiveness of desperation; few actually work and many are dangerous or lethal

abortion: terminating pregnancy without giving birth; spontaneous abortion is without deliberate inducement, and is generally known as miscarriage; therapeutic abortion, to save the life or health of the mother, was once distinguished from illegal abortion, but most jurisdictions are now much more permissive with restrictions limited largely by the state of fetal development

accost: term used by police and prosecutors to describe approaches in public, by males or females, for sexual solicitation

adultery: sexual intercourse between a man and woman at least one of whom is married but not to the other; compound or double adultery if both participants are married but not to each other

age of consent: statutory age, differing from jurisdiction to jurisdiction, which defines the legal capacity of a minor to give informed consent to sexual relations; to have sexual relations, even with consent, with a minor below the age of consent constitutes a crime (see statutory rape)

aggravated prostitution: operating a brothel or call girl business

algolagnia: sexual satisfaction derived from the anticipation of inflicting or suffering pain; a manifestation of sadomasochism

alienation of affections: the basis in some jurisdictions for civil action for monetary damages brought by a husband or wife whose spouse has been wooed away by another; less frequently applied in the case of engaged couples

ambisexual: bisexual; engaging in both heterosexual and homosexual activities

anal eroticism: sexual behavior focusing on the anus; oral-anal contacts (rimming); insertion of the penis into the anus (sodomy); digital insertion into the anus; one of the paraphilias involves sexual stimulation by anal odors

anal-genital: anal erotic behavior involving the penetration of the anus (male or female) by the penis

analism: preoccupation with the anus as a focus of sexual satisfaction

anaphrodisiac: a chemical preparation supposed to reduce or eliminate sexual erection in the male; saltpeter

androgen: male sex hormone

androgynous: possessing both male and female primary and/or secondary sex characteristics

androgyny: inversion of the sexual identity; masculinization of the female

androsterone: male sex hormone

anomaly, sexual: an aberration or deviation either in the sex organs or in the sexual focus

antuitrin: secretion of the anterior lobe of the pituitary gland important in the development of secondary sex characteristics in the male; injection or ingestion of antuitrin(s) is sometimes indicated in therapy for deficient sex drive and at one time was thought to be helpful in treatment of homosexuality

aphrodisiac: a chemical substance supposed to stimulate sex interest and capability; cantharides; Spanish fly; any sex stimulant

artificial insemination: technique of fertilizing the ovum with semen from the husband or a donor, inserted into the vagina by other than normal intercourse; sometimes used in cases of male impotence, sterility, impaired fertility, or injury to the genitalia

asexual: uninterested in sex

asexualization: castration

auntie: older effeminate homosexual

autoeroticism (also autoerotism): masturbation and other forms of self-gratification

auto-monosexual perversion: sexual actions performed on or with one's own body (e.g. self-fellation, self-abuse, self-mutilation)

auto-sexuality: perversions performed on oneself, including self-fellation and sadomasochistic practices; also includes masturbation

badger game: an act in which a prostitute solicits a client, takes him to her room, and while they are copulating her male partner enters, identifies himself as her husband or as a police officer, and shakes down the customer

basket: term commonly used by homosexuals to describe the visible bulge at the crotch made by the penis and testicles (see size queen)

bathroom (toilet) phobia: fear of falling into the toilet or fear of monster coming from toilet to attack one's genitals; said to be present in male anal erotics

beat the dummy (meat): masturbate

bestialism, bestiality: sexual contacts between human beings and infra-human animals; zoophilia

B-girl, B-boy: employee of establishment serving alcoholic beverages, often attractive and scantily dressed, whose duty it is to hustle drinks; frequently available for prostitution

bisexual: one who engages in or is interested in both heterosexual and homosexual behaviors

blow job: fellatio

body language, sexual: body gestures and/or postures that indicate to the knowledgeable observer a desire or readiness for sexual relations

bondage or discipline: sadomasochism; generic term used to describe both actual relationships and pornographic materials (plays, pictures, stories) emphasizing dominance by Amazonic females, scantily clad in leather, inflicting whippings and punishment on submissive males; less frequently sex-role reversal with dominant males using harnessed females to pull dog sleds, for example; also found in homosexual sadomasochism

bowdlerize: to excise (censor) unacceptable words from a manuscript, book, or other written material; usually but not always directed at words or phrases with sexual connotations

breach of promise: a basis at one time in many jurisdictions for a civil action for monetary damages based on an alleged promise to marry, later reneged on (see also seduction)

bubo: visible symptom of serious venereal disease

buggery: anal sodomy

bull dyke: masculine lesbian

buns: homosexual term for buttocks of other males

butch: masculine lesbian

call boy: male prostitute available for home or hotel visits through a central telephone answering service or registry

call girl: female prostitute available for hotel or home visits through a telephone answering service or registry; usually higher priced and more attractive than street walkers or brothel prostitutes

cantharides: an alleged aphrodisiac

carnal knowledge of a minor: charge brought against an adult who has had copulative or sodomistic relations, no matter how slight the penetration, with a child under the age specified in a given jurisdiction

castrati: male eunuchs castrated either for service in harems, to preserve the prepubertal voice range, for use as male prostitutes, or for religious reasons

castrating female: aggressive, dominating female who deprives or attempts to deprive males of their masculine identity

castration: asexualization; surgical excision of the male testes

castration, fear of: phobia experienced by some males that sexual intercourse with a woman will result in injury to their testes and hence their potency

cat house: house of prostitution

catamite: homosexual prostitute or kept boy

celibacy: state of sustained virginity; refraining from sexual relations and/or marriage, often for religious reasons (e.g. Catholic clergy)

chancroid: visible symptom of venereal infection

chastity belt: a device designed to prevent intercourse, at one time locked around a woman's genitals while her husband (father) was away

cherry: the hymen; a virgin

chicken: young male, usually in early adolescence, who makes himself available for sexual acts with older male partners, generally for money

chicken hawk: older male who pursues chicken

child abuse: usually physical abuse of young children, often by their parents, interpreted in some jurisdictions to include sexual assaults on child, carnal knowledge of child, etc.

child molester: person, usually male, who seeks sexual satisfaction from very young children

circle jerk: group masturbation; common in boys' boarding schools and in training schools of male delinquents; often a prize is given to first boy to ejaculate

circumcision: surgical removal of foreskin of penis for hygienic or religious reasons

clap: gonorrhea

clitoridectomy: surgical removal of all or part of clitoris

cock: penis

cocksucking: fellatio

cockteaser: female who stimulates the male to a state of sexual excitation and then evades or refuses copulation

codpiece: protective covering for the male genitals, worn by some externally; worn sometimes to exaggerate or advertise size of penis

cohabit: formerly used as euphemism for regular or at least repeated copulation between a male and female not married to each other; later tended to be restricted to such couples when domiciling together

cohabitation, lewd and lascivious: charge brought in some jurisdictions against those living together openly without marriage to each other

cohabitation, nonmarital: unmarried heterosexual couple domiciling together, usually without affront to community standards

coitus interruptus: withdrawal of the penis from the vagina before emission to prevent unwanted pregnancy

common-law marriage: relationship legally recognized in some jurisdictions in which certain legal rights inhere to the spouses and, in some cases, children after a statutorily defined period of living together openly, as if a marriage had taken place

community standards: phrase used by the U.S. Supreme Court in Miller decision (1973) which would define material as pornographic and subject to criminal sanction if patently offensive in a given area

companionate marriage: trial marriage; premarital cohabitation as man and wife to determine compatibility and suitability for a more permanent union

condom: contraceptive device placed over penis to prevent entry of semen into woman's body; also used for prevention of venereal disease (hence known as prophylactic); rubber

conjugal visit: sexual activity between a prison inmate and visiting spouse

consensual acts: generic term covering acts between two or more persons that take place by mutual consent, with no threat or use of force; usually restricted to acts between adults consolateur: a dildo; penis-shaped object utilized by females in autoerotic practices or lesbian activities

consummate: the process of completing the marital union by having sexual intercourse

continence: refraining from sexual relations by act of will

contraceptive: a device, medication, or method of preventing pregnancy

contributing to the delinquency of a minor: charge brought against an adult who exposes a child to situations that might result in delinquent acts (e.g. introducing a child to narcotics, suggesting that a child should commit a crime, encouraging homosexual activity or act with prostitute)

coprolagnia: sexual pleasure derived from handling feces

coprolalia, coprophasia, coprophilia: sexual stimulation and/or satisfaction from use of or listening to obscene language or stories, particularly those focusing on excrement

coprophagia: sexual deviation focusing on excrement and/or urine; watching others evacuate the bowels or urinate; being urinated on; could include stimulation from writing graffiti on toilet walls

coprophobia: fear of excreting or excreta

copulatio analis: pederasty, anal sodomy

Cornelia complex: incestuous desire of mother for her son

cornhole: anal sodomy

crabs: pubic lice

cross-dressing: transvestism

cruising: seeking stranger for sexual encounter, usually restricted to homosexuality

cuckold: husband whose wife has committed adultery

cunnilinctus, cunnilingus: oral contact with the female labia

daisy chain: three or more males engaging in simultaneous anal-genital or oral-genital relations

defloration: intercourse with a virgin

degenerate: police-prosecutorial term for a person engaging in almost any form of disvalued or criminalized sexual activity

demi-verge: literally a "half-virgin," used to denote a female who engages in many types of sexual activity except copulation; technical virgin

detumescence: the process of going from the erect to the flaccid of the penis, normally occurring following ejaculation

deviate, sexual: one whose sexual drive or focus is directed toward socially unaccepted channels; most often used for child molester

diaphragm: a contraceptive device inserted into body of woman to prevent fertilization

dicky waver: exhibitionist

dildo: artificial penis

dimorphism: having both male and female anatomical parts, sexual characteristics, or responses dirt: homosexual term for males who assault and/or rob homosexuals after having sexual relations with them

double standard: value system that is more tolerant of male sexuality or promiscuity than female

drag queen: effeminate homosexual who wears female clothing, jewelry, and may impersonate female

drag show: entertainment featuring transvestite performers, principally males in female costume

droit du seigneur: literally the right of the landholder; referring to the right to deflower female children of his serfs on their wedding night (see also jus primae noctic)

dyke: lesbian

eating pussy: cunnilingus

effeminate: being male and having pronounced feminine appearance and/or traits

ejaculation, premature: emission of seminal fluid either prior to penetration or prior to readiness of female partner; ejaculatio praecox

Electra complex: excessive, perhaps incestuous, interest of daughter in her father, including unconscious interest

emasculate: asexualize, castrate; used literally and figuratively

endowment: largely homosexual term for penis size, as heavily endowed, small endowment (see also size queen)

entrapment: vice squad technique in which either a plainclothesman or a decoy working with him inveigles homosexuals or prostitutes into soliciting, for the purpose of making arrest; widely used in criminal jurisprudence for nonsexual matters

eonism: transvestism; cross-dressing; drag

erection: the state of the sexually stimulated, tumescent penis; term is sometimes used when there is stimulation and hardening of clitoris or nipples

erogenous zones: areas of body particularly sensitive to sexual stimulation

erotographomania: conduct in which major sexual satisfaction is derived from viewing sexually explicit painting, sculpture, or other objects

erotolalia: deriving major sexual satisfaction from talking about or listening to talk about sex

erotomania: compulsive interest in sexual matters

erotophilic: strong interest in and concentration on erotic matters

erotophobic: afraid of sex; hostile to evidences of sexuality

estrogen: female sex hormone

estrus: in heat; ready for sex

eunuch: an emasculated male, asexualized, castrated

eunuchoid: like a eunuch (usually not castrated)

exhibitionist: one deriving sexual satisfaction from the showing of one's genitals to unwilling viewers; dicky waver, flasher extracoital: sexual connection between male and female not involving penetration of the vagina; may be oral, anal, intermammary, interfemoral, or other

extramarital: sex outside of marriage by a married person; adultery

extravaginal: extracoital

fag, faggot: pejorative term used either for an effeminate homosexual or for a homosexual regardless of outward manifestations of effeminacy

fag-bar, fag-joint: gathering place for homosexuals; gay bar

fairy: pejorative term similar in use to fag, faggot

feel: fondling of another, particularly of buttocks of a female by a male

fellatio, fellation: taking the penis into the mouth, the recipient can be male or female; cocksucking

fellator: male insertee in fellatio

fellatrix: female insertee in fellatio

fetishism: the focus of the sex drive on a part of the body rather than on the person (usually not on the genitals), or on some bodily function, or on some inanimate object, often clothing, odorous object, etc.

fetishist: one who has strong fetishistic compulsions

finger-fucking: digital stimulation of one's own or another's genitalia or anus

fish queen: male cunnilinguist

flagellation: a form of sadomasochism in which sexual satisfaction is obtained from whipping or being whipped

flasher: an exhibitionist

foreplay: stimulation by touching, licking, tickling, pinching, kissing, or in some other form, prior to copulation, and not as end in itself

fornication: copulation between a male and a female neither of whom is married

free love: term used to denote high tolerance for sexual promiscuity; sexuality and cohabitation without marriage

French envelope: contraceptive, particularly a condom

French kiss: entwining of tongues in kissing, also known as swapping spits; sometimes used as synonym for cunnilingus

French love: fellatio and/or cunnilingus

French tickler: a device attached to the tumescent penis to heighten sexual stimulation when inserted into vagina, often dangerous to female

frigidity: inability to respond to sexual stimulation

frottage: derivation of sexual satisfaction by rubbing one's genitals, even when fully clothed, against body of another; also known as dry fucking; in female homosexuality, rubbing of genital areas of two females against each other

frotteur: a person who frequents crowded places for the purpose of rubbing against the bodies of others

fruit: male homosexual; often restricted to effeminate male

fuck: to have sex, usually restricted to copulation and anal sex

full house: having gonorrhea and syphilis concurrently, and perhaps pubic lice and other venereal manifestations

gang bang: multiple copulation with one subject, male or female, who may be willing participant or coerced

gay: homosexual

gay bar: bar that is reputed to be a gathering place for homosexuals

gay liberation: movement to secure rights for homosexuals, destigmatize behavior, decriminalize homosexuality, and end discrimination

gerontosexuality: abnormal desire of a younger person for sexual relations with a much older male or female

gigolo: a male kept or paid by a woman for sexual favors

glory hole: homosexual term for an opening cut into the dividing wall between two public toilet cubicles, the male in one room inserting the tumescent penis into the hole so that it is fellated by the male in the adjoining cubicle

godemiche: dildo, artificial penis

go down on: to commit fellatio or cunnilingus

go-go girl (boy): attractive, scantily dressed or nude entertainer who performs sexually stimulating dances and gyrations

golden shower: paraphilia in which the subject permits himself (on rare occasions herself) to be urinated on by one or more males and/or females for sexual stimulation

gonorrhea: veneral disease characterized by an emission from the penis; clap

goose: pinching of the anal region of another person, or putting finger along anal region, usually of clothed person

granuloma inquinale: serious venereal disease

granuloma venereum: serious venereal disease

Greek love: anal sodomy usually with a young male as receptor

gymnopaedia: Greek athletic festival featuring nude boy atheletes; homosexual orgy with nude boys

gynandromorphy: having both male and female anatomical parts

gynandry: inversion of the female sexual identity; masculinization

gynecomastia: development of female-type breasts on a male; condition fostered in transvestites and transsexuals by hormonal treatment

hand job: masturbation, by oneself or on a person by another

hebephilia: focusing of the sex drive on very youthful boys or girls; Lolita syndrome

hebephrenia: mental disease at onset of menarche characterized by uncontrolled sexual promiscuity

hermaphroditism: possession of some male and some female sex organs by one person; ambiguity as to whether the individual is male or female

heterosexual: pertaining to individual or sex drive oriented toward gratification with other sex homoerotophobia: fear of being or being considered homosexual, also fear of homosexuality

homophile: homosexual, particularly associated with gay liberation movements; literally, love of same

homosexuality: pertaining to individual or sex drive oriented toward gratification with same sex

homosexual marriage: long-term monogamous homosexual relationship not recognized as legal marriages, but consecrated as marital union by a few homosexually oriented churches

homosexual panic: emotional crisis occasioned in some persons, particularly males, by fear of interest in homosexual gratification, by sight of male body that is stimulating, by solicitation for homosexual encounter, or by actual encounter, perhaps during state of intoxication

homosociality: intimate but not necessarily sexual social relationship between persons of same gender

hooker: a prostitute

horns, wearing: descriptive term applied to a cuckold

horny: sexual stimulated; if male, perhaps tumescent

hump: to copulate with a female

hustler: a male or female prostitute; also used for nonsexual connotations, as drug hustler

hymen: the membrane which closes the opening to the vagina in virgins; cherry

hypersexuality: oversexed; nymphomanic (female), satyriasis (male)

hypoplasis genitalia: very small genitalia; micro-penis

impairing the morals of a minor: charge brought against adults, lesser than carnal abuse, often but not always for sex-related offense, as fondling child's genitals, showing child pornographic material, or photographing a child engaging in sex play with other children

impersonator, female: a male transvestite; drag queen; one who cross-dresses, often an entertainer who cross-dresses

impotence: a condition in which the male is physiologically or psychologically unable to get or maintain an erection at the time of intercourse; occasionally used to describe the female

incest: sexual relations between persons of close blood kinship relationship; legally usually extended to relationships by adoption or through marriage, other than between spouses

indecent exposure: exhibitionism; exposure of the genitals in public even if no sexual motivation is present, as in public urination, nude swimming, or sunbathing

infantosexuality: focus of sexual desire on very young (prepubertal) children

insertor: in fellatio and anal relations, the participant whose penis is inserted into the orifice of partner instrumental masturbation: use of a mechanical or electrical device, as a cow milking machine, for example, to effect ejaculation

intercourse: term usually restricted to penile-vaginal copulation

interfemoral coitus: placing the tumescent penis between the tightly closed thighs of partner and reaching emission through friction; thighing

interfered with: police euphemism, particularly in England and Ireland, for rape

intermammary coitus: placing the tumescent penis between the breasts of partner and effecting emission by friction

intermarriage: marriage between persons of different races, religions, even nationalities; more restrictive term than miscegenation, which refers to sexual relations, with or without marriage, of such persons

intersexuality: hermaphroditism; possessing some of the physical and/or psychological characteristics of both genders

intrauterine device: contraceptive which prevents sperm from entering the womb; IUD

intromission: the act of introducing semen into the vagina; often used as synonymous with heterosexual copulation

inversion: term formerly used for homosexuality; later for having traits, characteristics, and manifestations of someone of the other sex (called sex-role inversion)

inversion, amphigenous: bisexual psychosexually

invert: term formerly used for a homosexual

irrumation: fellatio

jerk off: masturbate

jocker: an aggressive male who plays insertor role in anal sodomy

john: customer of a prostitute, usually used for heterosexual prostitution; trick is synonym used for homosexual and heterosexual customer

jus primae noctis: literally "law of the first night"; feudal right of the landholder to deflower the virgin females of his serfs or tenants on their wedding night (see also droit du seigneur)

Kama Kalpa: Indian sex manual

Kama Sutra: Indian sex manual

kept boy (girl): male (or female) supported, usually by older man, in return for sex favors

kept man: gigolo; sweet man; male supported and/or paid in return for favors, usually to older woman

ki-ki: sexual relations between two effeminate homosexuals

latent homosexuality: capacity for homosexual satisfaction without overt experience; unconscious homosexual desires

lay: to copulate; as noun, a female with whom one has (or wishes to have) intercourse; also get laid

leather bar: gathering place, particularly bar, for homosexual sadomasochists, rough trade, motorcycle crowd, and apparently virile type of homosexuals

lecher: one who is sensuous, lewd, grossly unchaste

lesbianism: female homosexuality, sapphis, tribadism

lewd or lascivious: police-prosecutorial term to describe criminalized, depraved, disvalued, and perverse sexual behaviors

libido: sexual drive

libido deficiens: lacking in sexual drive

line up: multiple copulation with one female, whether coerced or consensual; gang bang

living off the proceeds of prostitution: charge brought against pimps, procurers, brothel keepers, and others who receive funds from prostitutes or their customers

locomotor ataxia: tabes dorsalis, a venereal disease

loitering: charge brought against male and female prostitutes who solicit in public places; also used against males who seek sex partners in public restrooms

love child: child born out of wedlock; illegitimate child; bastard

lust murder: homicide for sexual satisfaction; differs from homicide in course of attempted rape or sodomy, or to eliminate victim as witness-complainant, in that the violence and killing is basic to satisfaction of perpetrator's lust

lymphogranuloma inguinale: venereal disease

lymphogranuloma venereum: venereal disease

madam: proprietor or manager of a house of prostitution; usually and traditionally woman heading female house; also used as male madam, for male heading homosexual house

masochism: deriving sexual satisfaction from having pain inflicted on oneself

masturbation: manual or instrumental stimulation of the genitalia, by oneself or another, to produce sexual satisfaction

Mattachine Society: organization devoted to gay liberation

meat rack: homosexual term for a place or area where homosexuals seeking partners display themselves, often in tight clothing emphasizing size of genitalia

menage a trois: two males and one female, or two females and one male, living in a sexual union; troilism

microphallus: extremely small penis

miscegenation: marriage or sexual relations between persons of different races, sometimes also applied to persons of different ethnic, religious, and national groups

misogynist: male who hates and/or fears women

mistress: paid or supported female companion; concubine

mixoscopia: deriving sexual satisfaction from watching other persons engage in sexual activity; some brothels have either viewing windows or two-way mirrors and charge fees to persons desiring this activity

mooning: displaying the bare buttocks as gesture of contempt

moral leper: degenerate, depraved, immoral, perverse (used for sexual and nonsexual descriptions) morals squad: vice squad

morphodite: hermaphrodite

muff diving: cunnilingus

multilateral sexuality: play-dominated sexual interaction; together sex, party sex; swinging; orgy; multi-sex, group sex

mutual masturbation: mutual stimulation of the genitals by two or more persons of same or different genders

narcissism: exaggerated self-love

narratophilia: deriving principal sex satisfaction or stimulation from listening to sex stories

necrophagia: see necrophilia

necrophilia: sexual fantasies about or overt sexual contact with dead bodies

necrosadism: deriving sexual satisfaction from defiling or mutilating dead bodies

nocturnal dreams (fantasies, ecstasies): sexually stimulating dreams, in male usually resulting in ejaculation

nocturnal emission (pollution): ejaculation during sleep as the result of dreams or fantasies, sometimes accompanied by friction of night clothing or bedding, or manual masturbation during sleep

noncoital: extracoital

nuts: testicles

nymphomania: compulsive, excessive desire for sexual intercourse in female

obscene telephone calls: use of forbidden sexual language over telephone by male to a female, usually stranger to caller, sometimes accompanied by verbal sexual advances; callers may be coprolaliacs or misogynistic sadists

obscenity: material dealing with the genitalia, excremental functions, or with the sex process, dominated by prurient interests, and not acceptable by large numbers of people in society

Oedipus complex: compulsive, excessive though usually unconscious sexual interest in mother by son

onanism: masturbation; term has also been used for coitus interruptus

one-night stand: term for one-time, nonaffectional, almost mechanical impersonal sex relationship, usually restricted to homosexual encounters

open cohabitation: unmarried couples living together without secrecy or circumspection

oral eroticism: fellatio, cunnilingus, rimming, or any libidinal drive in which gratification is centered around mouth, tongue, oral cavity

oralism: oral eroticism

orgasm: physiological reaction that takes place in male or female upon achievement of maximum sexual satisfaction; climax; in male, usually accompanied by ejaculation

orgy: group sex, swinging

out of wedlock: illegitimate, bastard

PG: parental guidance; rating given a film with explicit sexual language or matter, but short of hard-core pornography

pandering: pimping, procuring

paraphilia: classification of sexual aberrations including fetishism, coprophilia, sadomasochism, scatology, and others

parathesia: perversion of the sexual instinct permitting sexual excitement from nonsexual and generally inadequate stimuli

parerosia, homosexual: sexual inversion

partialism: paraphilia in which sexual satisfaction is derived by rubbing one's genitals against a part of another's body other than the genitals

passing: term derived from race relations, when light-colored black pretended to be white; used for homosexual pretending to be heterosexual and for impersonator pretending to be member of the other sex

passive homosexual: receptor in fellatio or anal sodomy

pasties: sequined patches pasted over the areola of the breasts of go-go girls, stripteasers, and others, to avoid arrest for indecent exposure

pederasty, pedication: love of boys (pedophilia), more commonlly anal intercourse between males of any ages; sodomy

pederosis, pedophilia: love of very young (prepubertal or early pubertal) boys or girls

pedomania: compulsive sexual drive toward boys

pedophiliac: person addicted to pedophilia, almost invariably male

penilingus: fellatio

penis envy: Freudian concept in which young girls were said to have strong emotional problems because of their alleged feeling of deprivation at not having a penis

perversion, sexual: generic term for criminal, disvalued, socially unacceptable sex behaviors; sex aberrations, sex deviations; generally used pejoratively, but sometimes in a more neutral manner to describe any deflection of the sex drive from heterosexual intercourse

pervert: a person who attempts, practices, or harbors interest in the practice of sex perversions

petting: sex foreplay or substitute, as fondling, touching, kissing, licking, and other stimulating noncoital behavior

phallicism: phallic worship; excessive interest in the phallus of oneself or another; priapism

phallic symbol: a substitute that brings to mind the phallus, because of form, shape, or meaning imputed thereto

phallic worship: use of phallic symbols in religious rites, particularly fertility rites; worship of reproductive process

philanderer: promiscuous male, restricted to heterosexual usage, and usually to describe married or betrothed man

picacism, sexual: heterosexual aberrations, anomalies, deviances pictophilia: deriving principal sexual satisfaction from erotic pictures of nude paintings, drawings, etc.

piece, piece of ass: a pejorative term about a woman, described solely as sex object

pimp: one who offers prostitutes to others; one who recruits, manages, and shares the earnings of prostitutes

pimpmobile: large, luxury-type automobile used by pimp to deliver prostitutes to assigned locations, supervise them, and collect their earnings

plainclothesman: vice squad cop or other policeman not wearning uniform and not readily identifiable as officer

platonic relationship: an affectional relationship without sexual involvement

play with oneself: masturbate

plural marriage: polygamy, polygyny, polyandry

pocket pool: manipulation of the genitals of a male by himself through side pants pockets; can also be conducted by anóther person

pollution: deriving sexual satisfaction by ejaculation of seminal fluid on a sex partner (rather than into an orifice), or by having fluid ejaculated on oneself by another

polyandry: one female with two or more husbands

polyerotism: deriving sexual satisfaction from a wide variety of sex objects and types of activity

polygamy: multiple marriage, most commonly used as synonym for polygyny

polymorphous perverse: wide range of sexual interests in a variety of objects and activities; believed by Freudians to be normal developmental stage of persons, particularly males, previous to narrowing of interest in heterosexuality

ponce: pimp, procurer

pornography: written or pictorial material with overt sexual portrayal in a manner generally unacceptable in a society

potency, sexual: virility; ability to have sexual (particularly heterosexual) intercourse

pouf: derogatory term, widely used in England, for homosexual

premarital sex: sex before marriage often used as synonymous with nonmarital sex

priapism: condition in which there is an almost continuous and sometimes painful tumescence

profanation: deflining and hence profaning inanimate objects for sexual stimulation or satisfaction; defiling a statute, particularly if it has religious meaning; defecating or urinating on the bedding of a sex partner; also called nihilisme de la chair

promiscuity: indiscriminate or near indiscriminate sex behavior with wide variety of partners, usually but not necessarily all of one sex

prostitution: sale of the body for sexual purposes to others for a fee, usually indiscriminately or nearly so prudery: extreme or exaggerated modesty; inhibition against being seen undressed, or against hearing discussion of sexuality

prurience: lasciviousness, lewdness

pseudohermaphroditism: condition in which there is partial anatomic development of both sexes

pseudohomosexuality: sometimes used as synonymous with bisexuality; also having some interests associated with homosexuality and hence confusing oneself with homosexual

psychic masturbation: ejaculation accomplished by deliberate fantasizing or daydreaming about sexually stimulating persons or situations

pubic hair: hair growth on the lower abdomen around the penis base and the vulva

public indecency: indecent exposure or lewd and lascivious conduct in public; may consist of public urination, fellatio, copulation, or other act

public morals, crimes against: generic classification for most sex crimes, as prostitution, sodomy, but usually not including forcible rape, which is classified as crime against the person

pull off: masturbate

punk: male passive receptor (insertee) in homosexual sodomy

puritanical: exaggerated and rigid code of sex behavior

pussy: female genitalia

put out: to make oneself available for sexual intercourse, usually to describe female, but may be used homosexually as well

pyromania: pathological fire setting, said to be frequently sexually motivated

queen: effeminate male homosexual

queer: homosexual (adj. or noun)

queer baiting: badgering and assaulting homosexuals by males, usually adolescents or young adults; dirt

R: restricted; rating for moving picture containing sexually oriented dialogue or situations, but not hard-core pornographic; children under 16 not admitted

rape, forcible: sexual intercourse with an unwilling female by force or threat of force; also used in unusual case of impersonation of husband

rape, sodomistic: anal intercourse accomplished on man or woman by force or threat of serious injury

rape, statutory: consensual sexual intercourse between a male and a female, when the former is over and the latter under the age of consent; in some jurisdictions, term applies when there is a custodial-patient or custodial-inmate relationship

ravish: rape

receptors: insertees in fellatio or anal intercourse

redeeming social value: standard set up by Supreme Court for judgment of pornography and obscenity cases; phrase used is "utterly without redeeming social value" red light area (district): section of a city or town in which prostitution is permitted either by law or by police policy

rimming: oral-anal contact, also called reaming; a major cause of hepatitis

rough trade: virile, masculine-appearing, often delinquent adolescents and young male adults who prostitute themselves for homosexual clients, often beating and robbing the customer; also used for rough-looking males who seek females for one-night stands

rubber: contraceptive, condom; also a frotteur

S & M: (sadomasochism): behavior in which sexual satisfaction is obtained from inflicting pain or having pain inflicted; algolagnia, metatropism, submissionism, flagellation, bondage and discipline

sadism: sexual satisfaction derived from inflicting pain on others

salacious: lecherous, lustful, obscene

saliromania: defilement or destruction of women's underclothing, or of nude statues or paintings of females

saltpeter: an alleged anaphrodisiac, said to eliminate or reduce sexual appetite

sapphism: lesbianism, tribadism

satyr: an extremely highly sexed male

satyriasis: compulsive male sexuality, almost always used for heterosexual; male counterpart of nymphomania; sometimes confused with priapism

scatological: dirty, filthy, preoccupied with excrement or with excremental functions

scoptophilia: deriving sexual pleasure and satisfaction from looking at the sexual organs of others; homosexual scoptophiliacs often loiter in public toilets, lockers and shower rooms; heterosexuals often become voyeurs; also scopophilia

score: term used by male and female prostitutes (and occasionally by males, homosexual and heterosexual, in nonprostitutive pursuits) to indicate success in getting a sex partner

screw: copulate, lay

scum: male ejaculate; also come

scumbag: condom; sometimes used as contemptuous term for prostitute or other promiscuous female

seafood: homosexual term for a sailor

seduction: act by which female permits intercourse only after a promise of male to marry her; her previous chastity was often considered sine qua non for act of seduction

self-abuse: masturbation

sex aberration: any of the sexual deviations or perversions; sexual anomaly, paraphilia

sex athlete: one who is reputed to be extremely virile; male having a reputation for ability to have repeated ejaculations

sex change: a reassignment of gender, by surgical operation, hormonal treatment, and other measures; transsexualism sex deviance: any criminalized, disvalued, or socially unacceptable sexual behaviors

sex education: program designed for use in elementary and junior high schools to acquaint children with human physiology and anatomy, reproductive process, birth control, and similar information

sexhibitionism: neologism indicating sexual satisfaction obtained from performing sex acts in front of audience

sex-induced guilt: feelings of remorse and often depression among some persons after indulging in or even fantasizing about sexual relations

sex murder: lust murder

sexo-esthetic inversion: sex role inversion; transvestism

sexology: science of sex, including reproduction, drives, relationships

sexopathy: sexual anomaly, aberration, abnormality

sex psychopath: legal term used in sex psychopath laws to classify those charged with certain sex-related offenses

sexual anomaly: a physical anomaly involving the genitalia, or an aberration of the sexual drive (paraphilia)

sexual assault: uninvited touching of the genitals, buttocks, or breasts of another; indecent assault

sexual equality: movement to end the double standard, giving equal freedom to women and men in sexual matters; also used by some to describe gay liberation

sexual freedom: movement to eliminate social prohibitions and inhibitions against previously disvalued sexual behaviors

sexualitis senilis: geriatric sexuality

short arm: penis

short arm inspection: examination of the penis in the military and merchant marine for evidence of unreported venereal disease

short eyes: prison jargon for someone incarcerated for carnal abuse of minor or child molestation; from shorties

situational homosexuality: engaging in homosexual relations in monosexual environment, although previously exclusively or principally heterosexual

sixty-nine, soixante-neuf: simultaneous oral-genital contact between two persons of the same or different genders

size queen: homosexual term for male with compulsive interest in partner with large penis, usually applied to effeminate homosexual; also basket queen

skinny dipping: nude swimming in public

sleep with: have sexual relations with

slut: prostitute or other promiscuous woman

snatch: female genital area, particularly pubic hair; muff, pussy

sodomy: anal intercourse, but often used to include all oral-genital relations, bestiality, and other acts

solicitation (for immoral purposes): police-prosecutorial term for making an approach to potential sex customers by male or female prostitutes; also applied to approaches by males to other males for nonprostitutive sex

sotadic zone: purported geographic area circling the globe in the warmer climates, in which homosexuality and other sexual aberrations were said to have thrived

Spanish fly: an alleged aphrodisiac; cantharides

sponge, collagen: contraceptive device which prevents fertilization; said to be more comfortable and effective than IUD

statuophilia: love of statues and other inanimate replicas of human form; attempt to effect sexual relations with inanimate replica of human body

sterilization: surgical procedure which prevents passage of the reproductive cells into male seminal fluid without interfering with copulation and ejaculation

stigma: negative labeling; descriptive classification that causes persons to be disvalued or discriminated against

streaking: running nude in public places

streetwalking: solicitation for prostitution on a public street or thoroughfare

striptease: entertainment in which dancer removes her clothing in a highly suggestive manner

stud: virile male, sex athlete

submission: masochism

superfixation: inability to gain sex satisfaction except with an extremely specific sex object (as a slender blue-eyed blonde) or in a highly specific manner (as in the canine position)

superstud: extremely virile male, with large and thick penis and ability to ejaculate repeatedly

swapping spits: French kissing; insertion of tongue into mouth of sex partner

swing, swinging, swinger: lack of sex inhibition, and specifically participation in mate swapping, group sex, and/or orgies

syphilis: venereal disease

syphilomania: insanity resulting from exaggerated fear of contracting syphilis

syphilophobia: exaggerated fear of contracting venereal disease, particularly syphilis, sometimes leading to continence or satisfaction via masturbation

syphilopsychosis: tabes dorsalis, venereal disease

tabes dorsalis (also known as tabes): syphilitic disease attacking central nervous system, called locomotor ataxia and syphilopsychosis

taboo (tabu): strongly held social mores, violation of which results in death, ostracism, or severe criminal punishment; originally referred to prohibition against incestuous relations

tearoom: euphemism for public toilet, first used in England, later among homosexuals in America

tenesmus penile: priapism, chronic erection of penis

testosterone: male sex hormone

third sex: term formerly applied to homosexuals

top man: insertor in anal sodomy

toucher: frotteur

trade: male with exaggerated masculine demeanor, who makes himself available to passive homosexuals for fellatio, particularly for money; also used for heterosexual male of similar demeanor

tramp: sometimes used as pejorative synonym for prostitute

transsexual: person who has undergone a sex reassignment operation and who now adopts the opposite gender; also used for a person having desire and drive for such an operation

transvestism: cross-dressing, eonism

transvestite: one who cross-dresses; drag queen, female impersonator (when male)

tribadism: lesbianism, sapphism

trick, turn a trick: the customer of the prostitute; the john; to perform the sex act with the trick

troilism: sexual involvement among three persons, simultaneously or seriatim; similar to menage a trois, but in troilism the sexuality is simultaneous or nearly so

undinism: urophilia; sexually responsive to the sight, smell, or taste of urine, or the sound of someone urinating

unisex: effacement of visible distinctions between the sexes other than anatomical

unnatural: sexual aberrations and/or deviations; has particularly been applied to describe homosexuality and bestialism

uranism: word formerly used for homosexuality

urethral masturbation: digital or instrumental stimulation of the urethra in the female

urninde: female homosexual, lesbian, tribade

urning: male homosexual (obsolete)

urophilia: deriving sexual satisfaction from urine, smell or urine, or being urinated on

VD: venereal disease

vampirism, pseudovampirism: sexual satisfaction from sight, smell or taste of partner's blood; act of biting until blood flows during sexual stimulation

vasectomy: sterilization of male by surgery which prevents the passage of sperm into seminal fluid

venereal disease: any of the diseases that are most commonly transmitted during sexual contact

vibrator: artificial penis, often electrically or mechanically operated; dildo

vice squad: police unit in charge of violations of laws relating to prostitution, homosexuality, pornography, and other sex matters

victimless crimes: consensual acts, sexual and other, in which there is no complainant, no victim except a willing adult participant, and on which there is no agreement in society that they are harmful modes of behavior

virgo intacta: virgin

virility: masculinity, potency, ability to copulate with females; also used to describe ability to impregnate females

voyeur: one deriving sexual satisfaction from viewing others in the nude, undressing, or in act of copulation, or by attending live sex shows or pornographic films; peeping Tom

watch queen: one who stands on the lookout in public restroom while two males are having sex contact, and who gives signal when someone is approaching

wet dream: nocturnal emission in response to sexually stimulating dream

white slavery: compulsory prostitution, usually involving transportation of the victims to foreign countries or at least to other than their home areas

whore: prostitute

whorehouse: house of prostitution, bordello, cathouse

wife-lending: custom in some societies to show hospitality to a guest by permitting him to enjoy sexual favors of wife; also of daughter

wife-swapping: early term for swinging, later changed to mate-swapping

wolf: male on the prowl for sexual satisfaction; used heterosexually for man seeking variety of partners and making frequent overtures; homosexually for one who seeks to subdue other, usually younger, male for sodomy

X rated, XX rated: rating applied to hard-core pornographic films depicting sexuality, and expecially sex aberrations

XYY: chromosome: biological anomaly in some males in which there is an extra Y chromosome, as distinct from normal chromosomal pattern in males of XY

zooerasty: zooeroticism

zooeroticism: deriving or seeking sexual satisfaction from relationships with animals

zoophilia: zooeroticism, bestiality

zoosadism: deriving sexual satisfaction from killing or inflicting pain on animals or birds

BIBLIOGRAPHY

Amir, Menachem. *Patterns in Forcible Rape*. Chicago: University of Chicago Press, 1969.

Barlow, Hugh D. *Introduction to Criminology* (2nd ed.). Boston: Little Brown & Co., 1981.

Bartell, G. D. *Group Sex: A Scientist's Eyewitness Account of the American Way of Swinging*. New York: Wyden, 1971

Bauer, G., R. Friedel, and K. Hagenbuchner. *Psychopathology of Sexual Contacts with Animals: Two Singular Cases of Sodomy*. Schweitzer Archives for Neurologie, 107 (1):109–121, 1970.

Beach, Frank A. (ed.). *Sex and Behavior*. New York: Wiley, 1965.

Beigel, Hugo G. (ed.). *Advances in Sex Research*. New York: Harper & Row, 1963.

Bell, Alan P. and Calvin S. Hall. *The Personality of a Child Molester: An Analysis of Dreams*. Chicago: Aldine-Atherton, 1971.

Bell, A. P. and M. S. Weinberg. *Homosexualities: A Study of Diversity Among Men and Women*. New York: Simon and Schuster, 1978.

Bell, R. R. *Social deviance: A substantive analysis*. Homewood, Ill.: Dorsey Press, 1976

Berg, Charles and Clifford Allen. *The Problem of Homosexuality*. New York: Citadel, 1958.

Blackburn, R. "Personality types among abnormal homicides." *British Journal of Criminology*, 1971, pp. 11, 14–31.

Block, N. L. and A. N. Tessler. "Transsexualism and Surgical Procedures." *Medical Aspects of Human Sexuality*, 7:158–161.

Block, R. *Violent Crime*. Lexington, Mass.: Lexington Books, 1977.

Blumer, H. *Symbolic Interactionism: Perspective and Method.*/Englewood Cliffs, N.J.: Prentice Hall, 1969.

Bodenheimer, A. R. "The Symbol as Eye-Catcher: An Interpretation of the Symbol and a Suggestion Regarding Therapy in Exhibitionism," *Psychotheropic Und Medzinische Psychologie*, 1977, July, XXVII (4), 125–155.

Brecher, E. M. *The Sex Researchers*. London: Andre Deutsch, Ltd., 1970.

Brecher, E. M. *Treatment Programs for Sex Offenders*. National Institute of Law Enforcement and Criminal Justice and Law Enforcement Assistance Administration, 1978.

Brittain, R. P. "The sadistic murderer." *Medicine, Science and the Law*, 1970.

Brodsky, C. M. "Rape at work." In M. J. Walker and S. L. Brodsky (eds.) *Sexual Assault: The victims and the rapist*. Lexington, Mass.: Lexington Books, 1976.

Brownmiller, Susan. *Against Our Will*. New York: Simon and Schuster, 1975.

Buhrich, Neil and Neil McConaghy. "Three Clinically Discrete Categories of Fetishistic Transvestism," *Archives of Sexual Behavior*. 1979.

Buhrich, Neil and Neil McConaghy. "Parental Relationships During Childhood in Homosexuality Transvestism and Transsexualism," *Australian and New Zealand Journal of Psychiatry*, 1978, June, XII (2), 103–108.

Burgess, Ann W., et al. *Sexual Assault with Children and Adolescents.* Toronto: Lexington Books, 1978.

Cauldwell, D. O. "Psychopathia Transsexualism," *Sexology*. 1967, XVI, 274–280.

Cauldwell, David O. *Transvestism: Men in Female Dress.* New York: Sexology Corp., 1958.

Chesser, E. *Strange Loves: The Human Aspect of Sexual Deviation*. New York: William Morrow, 1971.

Churchill, Wainwright. *Homosexual Behavior among Males: A Cross-Cultural and Cross-Species Investigation*. New York: Hawthorn, 1967.

Clinard, M. B. and R. Quinney. *Criminal Behavior Systems* (2nd ed.). New York: Holt, Rinehart & Winston, 1973.

Cohen, Albert K. "The Sociology of the Deviant Act: Aromie Theory and Beyond," *American Sociological Review*, Feb–Mar, 1965, pp 5–14.

Cohen, M., R. Garafalo, R. Boucher, and T. Seghorn. *The Psychology of Rapists. Seminars in Psychiatry*, 1971, 3, 307–327.

Cohen, M., T. Seghorn, and W. Calmas. "Sociometric Study of the Sex Offender," *Journal of Abnormal Psychology*. 1969, pp. 74, 249–255.

Comfort, A. *The Joy of Sex: A Gourmet Guide to Lovemaking*. New York: Crown Publishers, 1972.

Commission on Obscenity and Pornography (1970). *The Report of the Commission on Obscenity and Pornography*. New York: Bantam Books, 1970.

Cortes, J. B. and F. M. Gatti. *Delinquency and Crime: A Biophysical Approach*. New York: Seminar Press, 1972.

Coser, Lewis A. and Bernard Rosenberg. *Sociological Theory: A Book of Readings* (4th ed.). New York: Macmillan, 1976, p. 458–464.

Craft, M. "The Meanings of the Term 'Psychopath'." In M. Craft (ed.), *Psychopathic Disorders and Their Assessment.* Oxford: Pergamon Press, 1966.

Culliton, B. J. "Grave-robbing: The Charge Against Four from Boston City Hospital." *Science*, 186:420–423., 1974.

Dale, M. W. "Barriers to the rehabilitation of ex-offenders." *Crime and Delinquency*, 1976, 22, 322–337.

DeRiver, J. Paul. *The Sexual Criminal: A Psychoanalytic Study*. Springfield: Charles C Thomas, 1950.

East, Norwood. *Sexual Offenders*. London: Delisle, 1955.

Egen, Frederick W. *Plainclothesman: A Handbook of Vice and Gambling Investigation*. New York: Greenberg, 1952.

Ellis, Albert. *The Folklore of Sex*. New York: Charles Boni, 1951.

Ellis, Albert and Ralph Brancale. *The Psychology of Sex Offenders*. Springfield: Charles C Thomas, 1965.

Ellis, Albert. "The Sex Offender and His Treatment." In *Legal and Criminal Psychology*, edited by Hans Toch, pp. 400–416. New York: Holt, Rinehart, 1961.

Evans, D. "Exhibitionism." In C. G. Costello (ed.), *Symptoms of Psychopathology: A Handbook*. New York: John Wiley, 1970. 560–573.

Eysenck, H. J. "Obscenity—officially speaking." *Penthouse*, 1972, Nov., 95–102.

Fong, R. "Dangerous Deviations." *Nursing Times*, 74:1062–1063.

Ford, Clellan S. and Frank A. Beach. *Patterns of Sexual Behavior*. New York: Harper, 1951.

Fox, Vernon. *Introduction to Criminology*. Englewood Cliffs: Prentice Hall, 1976.

Gagnon, J. and W. Simon. *Sexual Conduct: The Social Sources of Human Sexuality*. Chicago: Aldine Publishing Co., 1973.

Gagnon, John H. and William Simon (eds.). *The Sexual Scene*. Chicago: Aldine, 1970.

Gebhard, Paul H., John H. Gagnon, Wardell B. Pomeroy, and Cornelia V. Christenson. *Sex Offenders: An Analysis of Types*. New York: Harper and Row, 1965.

Gebhard, Paul, John H. Gagnon, Wardell B. Pomeroy, and Cornelia V. Christenson. *Sex Offenders*. New York: Harper and Row, 1965.

Gebhard, P. H., J. H. Gagnon, W. B. Pomeroy, and C. V. Christenson. *Sex Offenders: An Analysis of Types*. Harper-Hoeber, New York, 1965.

Giarretto, H. "Humanistic Treatment of Father-Daughter Incest." in *Child Abuse and Neglect: The Family and the Community*. Cambridge, Mass.: Ballinger Publishing Co., 1976., pp. 143–158.

Gibbons, D. *Society, Crime and Criminal Behavior* (4th ed.). Englewood Cliffs, NJ: Prentice Hall, 1982.

Gibbons, Don. *Society, Crime and Criminal Careers*. Englewood Cliffs, NJ: Prentice Hall,·1976, p. 130–131.

Gigeroff, Alex, K. *Sexual Deviations in the Criminal Law: Homosexual, Exhibitionistic, and Pedophilic Offences in Canada*. Toronto: University of Toronto Press, 1968.

Glueck, S. and E. Glueck. *Unraveling Juvenile Delinquency*. New York: Harper and Row, 1950.

Gold, L. H. "Psychiatric profile of the firesetter." *Journal of Forensic Sciences*, 1962, 7, 404–417.

Goldenson, Robert M. *The Encyclopedia of Human Behavior: Psychology, Psychiatry and Mental Health*. New York: Doubleday & Co., 1970.

Goode, E. and R. Troiden. *Sexual Deviance and Sexual Deviants*. New York: William Morrow and Co., Inc., 1974.

Goring, C. *The English Convict*. Montclair: Smith, 1972.

Gosselin. "The Transvestite 'Double Image': A Preliminary Report." *Personality and Individual Differences*, 1980, I (2), p 172–173.

Greenwald, H. *The Call Girl*. New York: Ballantine Books, 1958.

Guyon, Rene. *Sexual Freedom*. New York: Knopf, 1950.

Guttmacher, S. *The Mind of the Murderer*. New York: Farras, Straus and Cudahy, 1960.

Halleck, S. *Psychiatry and the Dilemma of Crime*. New York: Harper and Row.

Hawke, C. C. "Castration and sex crimes." *American Journal of Mental Deficiency*. 1950, pp. 55, 220–226.

Heston, L. L. and J. Shields. "Homosexuality in Twins: A Family Study and a Registry Study." *Archives of General Psychiatry*. 18:149–160. 1968.

Hirschfeld, M. *Sexual Anomalies and Perversions*. London: Francis Adlor, 1944.

Hite, S. *The Hite Report. A Nationwide Study on Female Sexuality*. New York: Macmillan Publishing Co., Inc., 1976.

Hodgson, J. E., R. Smith, and D. Milstein. "Menstrual Extraction: Putting It and All Its Synonyms into Proper Perspectives as Pseudonyms." *Journal of the American Medical Association*, 228:849–850. 1974.

Hoffman, M. "Homosexuality." In *Human Sexuality in Four Perspectives*, F. A. Beach (ed.). Baltimore: Johns Hopkins University Press, 1977.

Hollender, M., W. Brown, and H. Roback. "Genital Exhibitionism in Women." *American Journal of Psychiatry*, 134:4. 1977.

Karlen, A. *Sexuality and Homosexuality: A New View*. New York: W. W. Norton and Co., Inc., 1971.

Katz, D. and R. L. Kahn. *The Social Psychology of Organizations*. New York: Wiley Publishers, 1978.

Keller, Ursula. "Feasibility of a Dynamic Psychiatric Treatment Strategy for Archaic Ego Illnesses with the Example of a Sexually Perverse Reaction," *Dyna misch Pschiatrie*, 1978, II (2–3), 191–211.

Kennedy, R. E. Behavior modification in prisons. In W. Craighead, A. Kasdin, & M. Mahoney (eds.), *Behavior modification: Principles, issues, and applications*. Boston: Houghton-Mifflin, 1976.

Kinsey, A. C., W. B. Pomeroy, and C. E. Martin. *Sexual Behavior in the Human Male*. Philadelphia: W. B. Saunders Co., 1948.

Kinsey, A. C., W. B. Pomeroy, C. E. Martin, and P. H. Gebhard. *Sexual Behavior in the Human Female*. Philadelphia: W. B. Saunders Co., 1953.

Kopp, S. B. "The character structure of sex offenders." *American Journal of Psychotherapy*, 1962, 16, 64–70.

Krafft-Ebing, Richard von. *Psychopathia Sexualis*. Brooklyn: Physicians and Surgeons Book Co., 1926.

Kruger. "Symptom Passing in the Transvestite Father and Three Sons," *American Journal of Psychiatry*, 1978, CXXXV (6), 739–742.

Lee, M., P. G. Zimbardo, and M. Bertholf. "Shy murderers." *Psychology Today*, November 1977, pp. 68–70, 148.

Lillyquist, M. *Understanding and Changing Criminal Behavior*. Englewood Cliffs, NJ: Prentice Hall, 1980.

Lloyd, Robin. *For Money or Love: Boy Prostitution in America*. New York: Vanguard, 1976.

Longford, Earl of. *Pornography: The Longford Report*. London: Hodder, 1972.

London, Louis S. *Sexual Deviations in the Male: Fourteen Detailed Case Studies*. 2 vols. New York: Julian, 1937, 1957.

Lunde, D. T. *Murder and Madness*. San Francisco: San Francisco Book Co., 1976.

McDonald, J. M. *Rape: Offenders and Their Victims*. Springfield: Charles C Thomas, 1971.

McDonald, J. M. *The Murderer and His Victim*. Springfield: Charles C Thomas, 1961.

Maisch, Herbert. *Incest*. New York: Stein & Day, 1972.

Marcus, Steven. *The Other Victorians: A Study of Sexuality and Pornography*. New York: Basic Books, 1966.

Marshall, Clinard. *Sociology of Deviant Behavior.* New York; Holt, Rinehart and Winston, 1975.

Meyer, J. K. "Individual Psychotherapy of Sexual Disorders," in Kaplan, H. I., B. J. Sadock and A. M. Freedman (eds.). *The Sexual Experience.* Baltimore, Maryland: The Williams and Wilkins Co., 1976.

Mohr, Johan W., R. Edward Turner, and M. B. Jerry. *Pedophilia and Exhibitionism.* Toronto: University of Toronto Press, 1964.

Money, John. *Sex Errors of the Body: Dilemmas, Education, Counselling.* Baltimore: Johns Hopkins Press, 1968.

Morneau, Robert H. and Robert Rockwell. *Sex, Motivation and the Criminal Offender.* Springfield: Charles C Thomas Co., 1980.

O'Leary, K. Daniel and G. Terence Wilson. *Behavior Therapy.* Englewood Cliffs, N.J.: Prentice-Hall Publishing Co., 1975.

Perkins, Michael. "Sick Fuckers," in *Screw Magazine.* Milkyway Productions. New York: January 12, 1981.

Palmer, S. *Psychology of Murder.* New York: Thomas Y. Crowell, 1960.

Person, Ethel and Lionel Ovesey. "Transvestism: New Perspectives," *The American Academy of Psychoanalysis,* 1978, July, VI (3), 301–323.

Pomeroy, W. "Some Aspects of Prostitution," *Journal of Sex Research,* Vol 5, pp. 177–187, 1965.

Portillo, Alfredo. "Sexuality and Delinquency," *Revista De Estudios Penitencianos,* 1970, XXVI (190), 691–701.

Prince, V. and P. M. Bentler. "Survey of 504 Cases of Transvestism," *Psychological Reports,* 1972, Vol 31, 903–917.

Qualls, C. B. "The Prevention of Sexual Disorders: An Overview," in *The Prevention of Sexual Disorders: Issues and Approaches.* New York: Plenum Press, 1978.

Queen's Bench Foundation. *The Rapist and His Crime.* New York: John Wiley, 1978.

Rada, R. T. "Alcoholism and Forcible Rape," *American Journal of Psychiatry.* 1975, Vol 32: 444–446.

Rachman, S. J. "Sexual Fetishism: An Experimental Analogue," *Psychological Record.* 1966, Vol 16: 293–296.

Radzinowicz, Leon. *Sexual Offences.* London: Macmillan, 1957.

Reich, Wilhelm. *The Sexual Revolution: Toward A Self-Regulating Character Structure.* New York: Simon & Schuster, 1974.

Rosengard, I. Stuart. "Mate-swapping—Why Is It So Popular?" *Sexology,* 1971, June, pp. 17–20.

Roche, P. *The Love of Sappho.* New York: Mentor Books, 1966.

Rogers, Carl. *Client-Centered Therapy.* New York: Houghton-Mifflin, 1951.

Rooth, G. "Exhibitionism Around the World." *Human Behavior,* 1974, Vol. 3, p. 61.

Ross, Michael W., Leslie J. Rogers, and Helen McCoullough. "Stigma, Sex and Society: New Look at Gender Identification and Sexual Variation." *Homosexuality,* 1978, III (4), pp. 315–330.

Russell, D. E. H. *The Politics of Rape: The Victim's Perspective.* New York: Stein and Day, 1975.

Sadoff, R. L. *The Sexual Experience.* Baltimore: The Williams and Wilkins Co., 1976.

Savitz, L. D. Introduction in Ferrero and Lombroso. *The Criminal Man*. Montclair, NJ: Smith, 1972.

Schacter, S. *Emotion, Obesity and Crime*. New York: Academic Press, 1971.

Sheldon, N. H. *Varieties of Delinquent Youth: An Introduction to Constitutional Psychology*. New York: Harper and Row, 1949.

Simon, W. and J. H. Gagnon. *Homosexuality: A Formulation of a Sociological Perspective in the Same Sex*. Philadelphia: Pilgrim Press. 1969.

Slovenko, Ralph. *Sexual Behavior and the Law*. Springfield: Charles C Thomas, 1965.

Small, I. F. and J. G. Small. "Sexual Behavior and Mental Illness," in B. J. Sadock, H. I. Kaplan, and A. M. Freedman, (eds.). *The Sexual Experience*. Baltimore: The Williams and Wilkins Co., 1976.

Smith, R. Spencer. "Voyeurism: A Review of the Literature," *Archives of Sexual Behavior*, V (6), 585–608, 1976.

Socarides, Charles W. *The Overt Homosexual*. New York: Grune & Stratton, 1968.

Spencer, C. "A Typology of Violent Offenders." Administrative Abstract No. 23, California Department of Corrections, September, 1966.

Steiner, Betty W., John Satterberg, and Craig F. Muir. "Flight Into Femininity: The Male Menopause," *The Canadian Psychiatric Journal*. 1978 October, XXIII (6), 405–410.

Stoller, R. J. *Sex and Gender: On The Development of Masculinity and Femininity*. New York: Science House, 1968.

Student, V. and S. Drvota. "Types of Sadists." *Ceskoslovenska Psychiatrie*, 1978, April, Vol. 74 (2), 91–94.

Sussman, N. "Sex and Sexuality in History," in B. J. Sadock, H. I. Kaplan, and A. M. Freedman (eds.). *The Sexual Experience*. Baltimore: The Williams and Wilkins Co., 1976.

Szasz, Thomas S. *The Myth of Mental Illness*. New York: Harper & Row, 1974.

Tappan, Paul W. "The Habitual Sex Offender." Report and Recommendations of the Commission on the Habitual Sex Offender. Trenton: State of New Jersey, 1950.

Traini, Robert. *Murder for Sex*. London: William Kimber, 1960.

Van Kammen, Daniel P. and John Money. "Erotic Imagery and Self-Castration in Transvestism and Transsexualism: A Case Report." *The Journal of Homosexuality*, 1977, II (4), 359–366.

Velarde, A. J. "Become Prostituted." *British Journal of Criminology*, 1975, Vol 15, 251–263.

Virkkunen, M. "Victim-Precipitated Pedophilia Offenses." *British Journal of Criminology*, 1975, Vol 15, 175–180.

Weinberg, S. K. *Incest Behavior*. New York: Citadel, 1955.

West, Donald. *Homosexuality*. Chicago: Aldine Press. 1968.

Wise, Thomas, Carol Dupkin, and Jon Meyer. "Partners of Distressed Transvestites." *American Journal of Psychiatry*. 1980 September, CXXXVIII (9), 1221–1224.

Wolfenden, John et al. "Report of the Departmental Committee on Homosexual Offenses and Prostitution." London: Her Majesty's Stationery Office, 1956.

ANNOTATED BIBLIOGRAPHY ON SEX CRIMES AGAINST CHILDREN

Ackerman, A. Bernard; Goldfaden, Gary; Cosmides, James C. "Acquired syphilis in early childhood." *Arch Dermatol*, 106(1): 92–93, July, 1972.

Documents three cases in which young children contacted syphilis through sexual abuse of adults. Infection results from intimate skin-to-skin contact with diseased adults, and clinical characteristics of the disease are the same in children as in adults. Genital chancres were found to be more common in older children while extragenital chancres were more common in infants. In all three cases, the disease waned after injections of penicillin G benzathine.

Alstrom, Carl-Henry. "A study of incest with special regard to the Swedish penal code." *Acta Psychiatrica Scandinavica*, 1977 (Nov), Vol. 56(5), 357–372.

Presents a historical review of incest penalties in Sweden, with particular emphasis on the special incest section of the current Swedish Penal Code. It is argued that there is no logical justification for retaining the incest paragraph in the Code. Neither genetic nor sociopsychological reasons for doing so have been found. The French Penal Code for almost two centuries has contained no regulations regarding sexual relations between adult relatives. The incest taboo has deep psychological roots, and penal sanctions appear to be rationalizations without preventive significance. A series of studies in Sweden reveals that the general trend has been that legal action should be avoided as far as possible, since it may lead to harmful effects on the minors concerned.

Anderson, Lorna M.; Shafer, Gretchen. "The character-disordered family: A community treatment model for family sexual abuse." *American Journal of Orthopsychiatry*, 1979(Jul), Vol. 49(3), 436–445.

Presents a collaborative approach to treating sexually abusive families, in which such families are viewed as analogous to "character-disordered" individuals. This model, unlike traditional voluntary treatment models, assumes that effective intervention requires authoritative control and careful coordination of all professional activity. Phases of treatment are outlined and a case history is presented.

Andrew, June. "Sexual exploitation of children: Hearings before the Subcommittee on Select Education of the Committee on Education and Labor." Washington, DC: US GPO, 1977, p. 451.

Contains documents and testimony related to the problem of sexual abuse of young children, both for the sale and making of pornographic material and for the exploitation of children within other settings, including the family. The hearings were held before the Subcommittee on Select Education of the Committee on Education and Labor of the House of Representatives, 95th

Congress, and were intended to clarify the need for, and scope of, corrective legislation.

Armentrout, James A.; Hauer, Allen L. "MMPIs of rapists of adults, rapists of children, and non-rapist sex offenders." *Journal of Clinical Psychology*, 1978(Apr), Vol 34(2), 330–332.
Compared MMPI group mean profiles of 13 rapists of adults, 21 rapists of children, and 17 nonrapist sex offenders. Mean age of the 51 male Ss was 30.5 years. Though there was marked heterogeneity in the 2-point codes within groups, the group results support the notion that while all 3 types of sex offenders are impulsive and self-centered with poor social intelligence, rapists of adults are more hostile, resentful, and interpersonally alienated than are rapists of children, and both types of rapists show those hostile and resentful characteristics more than do nonrapist sex offenders.

Asnes, Russell S.; Grebin, Burton. "Gonnococcal infection in children: Letter to editor." *Journal of Pediatricians* 81: 192–93, July, 1972.
Briefly discusses the examination procedure followed to ascertain whether a gonococcal infection in a child has been transmitted through sexual molestation.

Barnes, Josephine. "Rape and other sexual offenses." *Behavior Medical Journal*, 2(5547): 293–95, April, 1967.
Describes the physical examination which a physician should conduct on the victims of various alleged sexual offenses, including rape, incest, and sodomy. Emphasis is placed on the particular need for a thorough medical examination when the victims are children and may be unable to give adequate verbal testimony.

Becker, Judith V. "Evaluating social skills of sexual aggressives." *Criminal Justice & Behavior*, 1978(Dec), Vol 5(4), 357–368.
Reviews current means of assessing social skills and applying skills training treatment in one skills area does not generalize into other skills areas. That is, specific skills deficits must be resolved by treatment to improve that very deficit, since generalization from other skills areas is minimal. Finally, the interrelationship between various social skills deficits and rape behavior has to be worked out. Self-report measures confirm that in some rapists and child molesters, a close correlation exists between failures in the social skills area and increased urges to rape or molest, but this relationship is far from absolutely clear.

Bender, Lauretta; Blau, Abram. "The reaction of children to sexual relations with adults." *American Journal of Orthopsychiatry*, 7(4): 500–518, October, 1937.
Discusses the effects of sexual relations with adults on 16 children, aged 5–12 years. The children evidenced less trauma and anxiety over the experience than was anticipated. In fact, their personalities and emotional calm indicated that perhaps they had a part in initiating the experience and had derived some pleasure from it. Guilt appeared only after they had been separated from the sex object and were under the influence of authorities. Effects noted were (1) in the infantile stage, a tendency toward regressive behavior; (2) in early latency, a decreased educability and social adaptation; and (3) in prepuberty, problems in adolescent adjustment. Treatment focused on discusion of affectionate relationships with adults. Implications for theories of

childhood sexuality are discussed and a survey of varying cultural norms is included.

Berlinger, Lucy; Stevens, Doris. "Advocating for Sexually Abused Children in the Criminal Justice System." *RESPONSE: to Intrafamily Violence and Sexual Assault*, Vol. I(2), December 1976.
Discusses the fact that the community at large is outraged by the crime of child molesting. The legal system has failed to develop mechanisms which support and encourage successful prosecution when the victim/witness is a child. If criminal prosecution is the avenue society chooses to deal with this problem, then society has an obligation to adjust the requirements of the legal system to conform to the special needs and abilities of children. These changes would necessitate specialized training for all official figures involved with the investigation and prosecution, as well as development of new and flexible procedures. Legislation should be explored to provide the legal foundation for special protection of the child witness.

Bethscheider, J. L.; Young, J. P.; Morris, P. "A study of father-daughter incest in the Jarris County Child Welfare Unit." *Criminal Justice Monogram*, 4(4): 1–131, 1973.
Presents case reports of thirty families in which incest occurred, along with those of seventy families judged to be negligent. Outside of the crowded conditions in which both groups typically lived, the incestuous families had little in common with the negligent families; the negligent families generally being less educated and poorer than the families in which incest occurred.

Blumberg, Marvin L. "Child sexual abuse: Ultimate in maltreatment syndrome." *New York State Journal of Medicine*, Vol. 78(4), 612–616.
Discusses sexual abuse of children in today's permissive society. A number of psychological reasons motivate the offender and induce the child victim to submit even when physical force is not employed. Sexual abuse of children has various manifestations, including digital manipulation, masturbation, fellatio, sodomy, and intercourse. Using children for pornography is a particularly degrading form of abuse. Immediate emotional trauma is usually evidenced in the misused child. Persistent psychological effects can produce future sexual maladjustments and marital problems in adulthood. Except in cases of violent crime, offenders and their victims should both be handled by a multidisciplinary rehabilitative approach.

Boekelheide, Priscilla D. "Incest and the family physician." *Journal of Family Practice*, 1978(Jan), Vol 6(1), 87–90.
Reviews incest from epidemiologic, familial, and individual points of view. The incest taboo has characterized almost every culture and society throughout the ages. Respect for the incest barrier is a cultural demand made by society and is not a physiological or biological imperative. Overt incest occurs in a dysfunctional family through tension-reducing "acting out." The family physician is in a unique position to observe and understand the family dynamics which both help maintain defenses against the incestuous wishes as well as, in some families, contribute to the practice of incest.

Brant, Renee S.; Tesza Veronica B. "The sexually misused child." *American Journal Orthopsychiatry*, 47(1): 80–90, January, 1977.

Discusses the plight of the sexually misused child, stressing that sexual misconduct with children too often goes undetected. After carefully reviewing hospital emergency room and pediatric gynecology clinical records at the Children's Hospital Medical Center in Boston, a group of child psychiatrists concludes that physicians must learn to consider a diagnosis of sexual misuse when children are treated for genital injury, irritation, and infection. The group also stresses that sexual misuse is a symptom of family pathology and denounces the current tendency to call the adult participant the "abuser" and the child the "victim." Guidelines for acute case management of sexual misuse focusing on the advantages and disadvantages of taking legal action are included.

Brongersma, Edward. "The Meaning of Indecency with Respect to Moral Offenses Involving Children." *Britian Journal of Criminology*, Vol. 20, No. I, January 1980.

Since the late 1960s there has been increasing dissatisfaction in both houses of the Dutch Parliament with those sections of the Penal Code which deal with moral offences. Discusses a liberation of the code especially in reference to the areas involving children. Concludes that the term "indecent" can no longer be used to include sexual behavior which arises through love, tenderness, or affection and which is not carried out against the will of the child. As long as there is no revision of the legislation, the judge must be just, and it is not just to throw a citizen in jail for behavior that is born of a positive inclination and is positively valued.

Brown, Wenzell. "Murder rooted in incest." *Patterns of Incest*, New York: Julian Press, 1963. 301–27.

Describes the case of a young boy who murdered his mother following years of incestuous relations with her. The mother's rejection of her husband, along with her seductive treatment of her son, led to sexual relations between them. Filled with guilt, the mother withdrew from the boy, abandoning him to his confused feelings. Gradually, he also withdrew into himself, developing fetishist behaviors and obsessively spying on his mother's activities. Impotent with other women and ashamed of his activities, he became angry with his mother and finally killed her.

Burch, Genevieve; Mohr, Vicki. "Evaluating a Child Abuse Intervention Program." *Social Casework: The Journal of Contemporary Social Work*, November 1980, p. 90–99.

Abusing parents who became part of an educational-developmental treatment program, Positive Parenting, were compared with a control group of abusers in a pre- and posttesting evaluation process. Significant and positive change in the treatment group demonstrated the effectiveness of this intervention model.

Butler, Sandra. *Conspiracy of Silence: The Trauma of Incest*. San Fransisco: New Glide Publications, 1978.

The roots of incestuous assault go beyond the psychological problems of adults who impose their sexual desires upon their children in a futile attempt to overcome feelings of anger or frustration or to satisfy unmet emotional needs. Calls into question some of society's most basic attitudes about sex, the sanctity of the nuclear family unit, male/female role expectations and, above all, the rights of children over their own minds and bodies.

Caruso, Phillip A. "Pelvic inflammatory disease: Rare sequela of battered child syndrome." *New York State Journal of Medicine*, 75(13): 2405–6, 2415, November, 1975.

Cites a case report of an eighteen-year-old girl who had been sexually abused. The child presented with symptoms of nonspecific vulvovaginitis. Although these symptoms are more commonly caused by such problems as poor perineal hygiene or intestinal parasites, they can also be an indication of deliberate sexual molestation. Physicians must maintain a high index of suspicion in such cases and not hesitate to report suspected sexual abuse.

Chaneles, S. "Child victims of sexual offenses." *Federal Probation*, 31(2): 52–56, June, 1967.

Surveys the results of the Child Victim Sutdy of the American Humane Society. The study focused on the sexual abuse of children and found that sexually molested children generally sustained deep psychic damage as a result of their experience—damage which was often exacerbated by the prosecution of the molester. Most sex offenses against children, especially incest and homosexual assaults on boys, are not reported. Several characteristic traits of the adult sex offender are offered, along with a recommendation calling for special agencies to help victimized children.

Cliffe, Michael J.; Parry, Stephen J. "Matching to reinforcer value: Human concurrent variable-interval performance." *Quarterly Journal of Experimental Psychology*, 1980 (Nov), Vol 32(4), 557–570.

A 36-yr-old male pedophile offender chose between pairs of sexual stimulus classes in a 2-operandum procedure with reinforcement arranged according to concurrent VI-VI schedules. Condition 1 involved choice between slides of women and slides of men; Condition 2, slides of men vs. slides of children; and Condition 3, slides of women vs. slides of children. Estimates were obtained from the data in Conditions 1 and 2 of the values of slides of women and of children relative to slides of men. Results support the use of matching based scaling of reinforcer values in the prediction of choice between qualitatively different reinforcers and extend the application to a human S, the 2-operandum precedure, and sexual stimuli.

Conger, Rand D.; Burgess, Robert L.; Barrett, Carol. "Child Abuse Related to Life Change and Perceptions of Illness: Some Preliminary Findings." *The Family Coordinator*, Vol 28, No. 1, January, 1979.

A total of 40 parents from child abuse and matched control families were examined for variation on life change scores, perceptions of physical and emotional health and punitiveness of their own parents. Abusive parents had higher life change scores, more numerous perceptions of emotional physical ill health, and a more punitive childhood than their matched controls. Abusive parents were far more likely to experience both rapid life change and a history of punitive childrearing. The data are shown to be consistent with a social learning explanation of child abuse.

Conran, Michael B. "Incestuous failure: Studies of transference phenomena with young psychotic patients and their mothers." *International Journal of Psycho-Analysis*, 1976, Vol 57(4), 477–481.

Reports observations of 20 disorganized psychotic boys in a hospital ward. A strategy of treatment is described that involved the patient-nurse relationship and work with the parents. It is suggested that a significant factor in the development of schizophrenia is a failure of the early mother-son incestuous relationship. This relationship is part of the early normal attachment experience and makes later incestuous acts or anxiety in adolescence less necessary.

Cormier, Bruno M.; Kennedy, Miriam: Sangowicz, Jadwiga. "Psychodynamics of father daughter incest." *Deviancy and the Family*, 1973, p. 97–116.

Describes the psychodynamics of father-daughter incest in terms of the psychopathology of the non-deviant and non-criminal father. In a disintegrating marriage, the father turns to the daughter as the symbol of the young girl he courted and married. In doing so, his own roles are confused between husband and father, and he returns to his self as a young man. He then places the wife in the position of the disapproving mother, and he views the daughter as the nurturing mother he lost as a child. Prevention is difficult unless a family member suspects and reports the possibility. Once incest is disclosed, recidivism is rare. The deep impact of each family member prevents the denial which occurred previously, and the cycle is broken.

Courtois, Christine A. "Victims of rape and incest." *Counseling Psychologist*, 1979, Vol 8(1), 38–40.

Discusses the counseling of victims of rape or incest. Research indicates that the incidence of these crimes is increasing. At the same time, attitudes toward victims are changing. Counselors may become involved with rape or incest victims during the crisis stage immediately following the assault or during the reorganization period that follows, during which the victim recovers from the experience. Treatment is predicated on the personal situation and characteristics of the individual client.

de Saint-Basile, Elisabeth; Levy, Ghyslain. "Perversion in the theory of sexuality: Concerning pedophilia." *Etudes Psychotherapiques*, 1977(Jun), Vol 8(2), 126–132.

Reports data from a questionnaire answered by 129 male pedophiles. Most Ss chose boys as partners, but many also had sex with adult males or with young girls. Few were married. Their typical sex partner was a young adolescent, and mutual masturbation was the most common activity. Though most Ss were dissatisfied with their sex lives, few sought therapy. The authors view pedophiles as revolutionaries, people who can experience pleasurable closeness in a relationship against which society has erected a strong prohibition.

Devine, Raylene A. "Incest: A Review of the Literature." *Psychoanalytic Quarterly*, 27: 485–500, 1978.

Discusses how incest remains the most emotionally charged and socially intolerable form of sexual abuse, the most difficult to understand and accept. An understanding of the people involved and the dynamics of the incest relationship will improve the ability to work with these children and their families. Unfortunately, incest, by its very nature, tends to remain a family secret. Families in which incest occurs require long-term support by social and legal agencies. These supportive services must be made available, for they can make a difference in the lives of all family members and allow the family to again function as a healthy unit.

Devine, Raylene A. "Sexual Abuse of Children: An Overview of the Problem." *Medicine, Science, and Law*, 4: 245–53, 1975.
Children have been described as "polymorphous perverse," meaning that they can be led into a variety of sexual activities. Occasionally, these sexual activities involve an adult, often an adult the child knows, trusts, and views as a dominant figure. This sexual involvement between child and adult has a harmful potential that far outweighs what may have been innocent, playful beginnings. Whatever the child's needs, it is the adult who must exercise control. Although children sometimes find the moment pleasurable, the attention gratifying, they cannot and should not be blamed for the sexual activity. This responsibility clearly rests with the adult.

Devine, Raylene A. "The Sexually Abused Child in the Emergency Room." *Pediatric Clinics of North America*, 19: 717–25, 1972.
The impact of a sexual assault on a child and many of its damaging effects can result less from the abusive incident itself than from adult reactions to and management of the incident. It is possible to prevent much of the damage caused by childhood sexual abuse, even after the actual assault has occurred. Prevention can begin as soon as the child and family arrive in the hospital emergency room. Trained and sensitive professionals can provide the basic supports needed by parents and child to help them return to a normal life by integrating the sexual assault into their life experience with as little permanent damage as possible.

Dietz, Christine; Craft, John L. "Family Dynamics of Incest: A New Perspective." *Social Casework: The Journal of Contemporary Social Work*, 1980, p. 602–609.
A study of protective workers was designed to explore their perceptions of the relationship between incest and other forms of familial abuse and the role of the mother in an incestuous relationship. Overall, the workers believe that there is a lack of literature on and available training for work with incest cases.

Dixon, Katherine N.; Arnold Eugene; Calestro, Kenneth. "Father-son incest: Underreported psychiatric problem?" *American Journal of Psychiatry*, 1978(Jul), Vol 135(7), 835–838.
Describes 6 families in which 10 sons were involved incestuously with a natural father or stepfather. Four fathers were known to be violent and physically abusive toward the children and had a history of poor judgment and impulse control. All fathers had histories of alcoholism or sociopathy or both. There appeared to be a high degree of complicity on the part of the mothers. Father-son incest appears to be a more frequent clinical entity than was thought previously.

Elonen, Anna S.; Zwarensteyn, Sara B. "Sexual trauma in young blind children." *New Outlook Blind*, 69(10): 440–42, December, 1975.
Cases of blind children who were sexually assaulted are described, along with measures parents and professionals should take to prevent such occurrences.

Finkelhor, David. "Psychological, cultural and family factors in incest and family sexual abuse." *Journal of Marriage & Family Counseling*, 1978(Oct), Vol 4(4), 41–49.
Reviews clinical experience and research evidence about father-daughter incest and family sexual abuse and suggests 6 factors important in its etiology:

(1) the personal characteristics of the offender, (2) the role of the mother, (3) a milieu of abandonment, (4) subcultural isolation, (5) poor family sexual boundaries, and (6) opportunity factors.

Fisher, Gordon; Howell, L. M. "Psychological needs of homosexual pedophiliacs." *Dis Nervous System*, 31(1): 623–35, September, 1970.
The histories of fifty men convicted of homosexual pedophilia link them more strongly to heterosexual pedophiles than to homosexuals. Most of the subjects were middle-aged, white, unmarried, of average intelligence, unorganized, and guilt ridden.

Gagnon, John H. "Female child victims of sex offenses." *Social Problems*, 13(2): 176–92, Fall, 1965.
Examines the literature dealing with the female victim of sex offenses against children, focusing particularly on the single study which followed the victims' progress through adulthood. It is suggested that it may be erroneous to assume that the offense will do permanent psychological damage to the victim.

Gentry, Charles E. "Incestuous abuse of children: The need for an objective view." *Child Welfare*, 1978(Jun), Vol 57(6), 355–364.
Discusses the need for more data on incestuous abuse of children and examines the victim's the abuser's and the family's response to the incestuous behavior. It is argued that family life education, screening of high risk families, public education regarding the dependency of abusers, involvement of caring volunteers, and better coordination and accessibility of resources and support systems for families in need are required to prevent and/or reduce the prevalence of all types of child abuse, including incestuous.

Gibbens, T. C.; Soothill, K. L.; Way, C. K. "Sibling and Parent-Child Incest Offenders." *Britain Journal of Criminology*, Vol 18, No 1, January 1978.
The majority of cases of incest coming before the Court concern offences committed by a father against his daughter or daughters, usually in their early teens. In all cases involving parents the court takes a stern view of the offence, and sentences in the region of six years imprisonment are common. Some cases of brother-sister incest have attracted interest but the recent interest has been due to cases on which the law seemed to press exceptionally hard—a half brother and his sister had a daughter of 10 months and were expecting another child and were told by a judge to part forever. Today the judiciary is likely to take a comparatively lenient view in sentencing brother-sister liaisons where there is obvious consent by both parties.

Gordon, Lillian. "Incest as revenge against the pre-Oedipal mother." *Psychoanalytical Review*, 42(3): 284–92, July, 1955.
Documents a case study of a young women's incestuous activity used as a defense against her pre-Oedipal attachment to her mother. What appears to be an Oedipal fixation on the father is, in fact, a defense which takes the form of masochistic revenge on the pre-Oedipal mother.

Goodwin, Jean; Simms, Mary; Bergman, Robert. "Hysterical seizures: A sequel to incest." *American Journal of Orthopsychiatry*, 1979 (Oct), Vol 49(4), 698–703.
Describes 6 cases in which hysterical seizures developed after psychotherapeutic exploration of the incestuous experience. Patients were adolescents referred for seizures, suicide attempts, sexual problems, and running away. It is

suggested that Navajo and Galenic folk beliefs connecting epilepsy with incest may derive from observations of this symptom pattern in incest victims.

Gross, Meir. "Incestuous rape: A cause for hysterical seizures in four girls." *American Journal of Orthopsychiatry*, 1979 (Oct), Vol 49(4), 704–708.
Presents 4 cases of hysterical seizures in adolescent girls as a consequence of forced incestuous relationships with their natural father, stepfather, or mother's live-in boyfriend. It is suggested that for all girls with symptoms of hysterical seizures a detailed history be taken that will include information about the family dynamics, with particular attention to the possibility of incest.

Groth, Nicholas A.; Birnbaum, Jean H. "Adult sexual orientation and attraction to underage persons." *Archives of Sexual Behavior*, 1978 (May), Vol 7(3), 1750181.
Screened 175 males convicted of sexual assault against children with reference to their adult sexual orientation and the sex of their victims. The Ss divided fairly evenly into 2 groups based on whether they were sexually fixated exclusively on children or had regressed from peer relationships. There were no examples of regression to child victims among peer-oriented, homosexual males. The possibility emerges that homosexuality and homosexual pedophilia may be mutually exclusive and that the adult heterosexual male constitutes a greater risk to the underage child than does the adult homosexual male.

Gutheil, Thomas G.; Avery, Nicholas C. "Multiple overt incest as family defense against loss." *Family Process*, 105–16.
Considers a case in which father-daughter incest represented a defensive stratagem against the departure of the mother. The mother, conforming to the expected pattern, had been rejected by her mother and had abdicated her own role to her daughters. The family was bound together by an incestuous tie between father and daughter.

Guttmacher, Manfred S. *Sex offenses: The problem, causes and prevention*. New York: W. W. Norton, 1951.
A study of 172 sex offenders, seventy-nine of whom had had sexual relations (including fondling, exhibitionism, and intercourse) with children. It was found that pedophiles were on the average older and more seriously defective mentally than other sex criminals. Clinical statistics denoting the age, physical abnormalities, school and work history, religious affiliation, and parent-child relationship of the sex offenders are presented. Laws dictating the handling of sex offenses in various states are examined, and recommendations for early detection and treatment of potential sex offenders discussed.

Halperin, Sandra L. "Abused and Non-abused Children's Perceptions of their Mothers, Fathers and Siblings: Implications for a Comprehensive Family Treatment Plan." *Family Relations*, Vol 30, No. 1, January 1981.
Utilizing the findings of a research project identifying family perceptions of abused children and their siblings, the author proposes a comprehensive treatment model for abusive families. Because the abuse affects all of the members of an abusive family, it is argued that the entire family system must be assessed and treated. A three-phase comprehensive assessment and treatment model is proposed that includes not only individual, marital, and sibling dynamics, but also family dynamics.

Hartley, Albert I.; Ginn, Robert. "Reporting child abuse." *Texas Medical*, 71(3): 84–86, February, 1975.
Evaluates procedures used in handling 22 cases of sexual abuse to children during a period of 6 years at the University of Texas Medical Branch Hospitals. One purpose of the evaluation was to determine the impact of the reporting laws on physicians involved in the cases. A suggested form for reporting abuse is offered.

Hayman, Charles R.; Lanza, Charlene; Fuentes, Roberto. "Rape in the District of Columbia." *American Journal Obstetrics Gynecology*, 113(1): 91–97, May, 1972.
Summarizes statistics of 1,200 female rape victims, many under the age of 18, and describes the Department of Public Health's assistance and follow-up.

Hayman, Charles R. "Sexual assault on women and girls in the District of Columbia." *Southern Medical Journal*, 62(10): 1227–31, October, 1969.
Reports procedured and statistics for 3,000 sexual assault victims, including children, between September 15, 1965 and June 30, 1968 in D.C. Some 1,000 referrals for reexamination are described. It is recommended that initial examinations in emergency areas by residents in gynecology or pediatrics be eliminated.

Heim, Nikolaus. "Sexual behavior of castrated sex offenders." *Archives of Sexual Behavior*, 1981(Feb), Vol 10(1), 11–19.
Reports data on the sexual behavior of 39 released sex offenders who agreed voluntarily to surgical castration while imprisoned. Findings indicate sexual desire and sexual arousability were perceived by Ss as having been considerably impaired by castration. In comparison with other studies, it was shown that male sexual capacity was not extinguished soon after castration. Particularly noteworthy is that 11 of 35 castrated were still able to engage in sexual intercourse. Rapists proved to be sexually more active after castration than homosexuals or pedophiliacs, There seemed to be a strong effect on sexual behavior only if castration were performed between the ages of 46 and 59 years. In general, the findings do not justify recommending surgical castration as a reliable treatment for incarcerated sex offenders.

Henderson James D. "Incest: a synthesis of data." *Canadian Psychiatric Association Journal*, 17(4): 299–313, August, 1972.
Theories attempting to account for the universality of the incest taboo are discussed, along with studies of actual cases of father-daughter incest, their common features, and the possibility for treatment. The incest taboo is regarded as arising from several different human needs; the protection of the family unit and the promotion of endogamous sexuality in order to prevent the weakening of the race are the principal bases suggested.

Horwitz, Elinor L. "A grieving mother fights back." *McCalls*, 101(2): 40, March 1974.
Tells of one mother's fight for legislation making molestation of children a federal offense with harsh penalties. Her efforts followed the brutal slaying of her own daughter.

Jaffe, Arthur C.; Gershon, Anne A. "Sexual abuse and herpetic genital infection in children: letters." *Journal of Pediatrics*, 89(2): 338, August, 1976.
A case of a child with genital herpes. Because genital infections in children can signal sexual abuse, the examination should include a family history.

James, Jennifer; Womack, William M. "Physician reporting of sexual abuse of children." *Journal of the American Medical Association*, 1978(Sep), Vol 240(11), 1145–46.

Anonymous mail survey of 300 general practitioners and pediatricians to assess the extent of physician contact with sexually abused children and to evaluate the frequency of reporting. 51 of 96 respondents reported seeing at least one identifiable sexually abused child annually. The most common type of abuse was intercourse or molestation with a daughter. Only 32% of the physicians indicated that they urged the family to report the incident. Two thirds believed either that reporting would be harmful to the family or that the problem could be handled more easily privately, and one third were dissatisfied with the manner in which state agencies handled such cases.

James, Jeffifer; Meyerding, Jane. "Early sexual experience as a factor in prostitution." *Archives of Sexual Behavior*, 1978(Jan), Vol 7(1), 31–42.

Examined the pattern of early sexual experience among prostitutes and how it differs from that common to nonprostitute women. Significant differences were found between the samples of prostitutes and the samples of "normal" women. Prostitute samples, on the whole (1) learned less about sex from parents and more from personal experiences, (2) as children experienced more sexual advances by elders, (3) were more victimized by incest, (4) generally initiated sexual activity at a younger age, (5) more often had no further relationship with their 1st coital partner, and (6) experienced a higher incidence of rape. The analysis of these data on early sexual history concentrates on abusive sexual experiences such as incest and rape. It is concluded that an abusive sexual self-identity relates to the development of an adult female pattern of occupational deviance such as prostitution.

Kaplan, Stuart L.; Poznanki, Elva. "Child psychiatric patients who share a bed with a parent." *Journal of American Child Psychiatry*, 13(2): 344–56, Spring, 1974.

Presents a retrospective clinical study by chart review of child psychiatric patients and their parents who sleep in the same bed. Data is given on the sleeping arrangements of 100 societies.

Katan, Anny. "Children who were raped." *Psychoanalytical Study Child*, 28: 208–24, 1973.

Attempts to record the impact on adults of undetected and untreated sexual trauma suffered during childhood. The subjects had been raped in all 6 cases. All had experienced similar traumas of forced sexual overstimulation at a very early age and each was left with an extremely low self-esteem. The subjects were found to be fixated at the phallic development stage and experienced tremendous excitement in conjunction with phallic fantasies. Much more serious disturbances emerged as a result of childhood rape, namely, aggression and masochism. While greatly encouraged by warmth the fusion of libido and aggressive drives becomes extremely difficult when direct, aggressive sexual stimulation is experienced instead. Such a furion was completely disrupted in these women, who at an early age had experienced more aggressive sexual stimulation than affection.

Keltner, Alfred A. "The control of penile tumescence with biofeedback in two

cases of pedophilia." *Corrective & Social Psychiatry & Journal of Behavior Technology, Methods & Therapy*, 1977, Vol 23(4), 117–121.
Describes the treatment of 2 mixed pedophiles with response-contingent rather than stimulus-contingent conditioning. Verbal instructions and differential reinforcement were made contingent on auditory feedback which signaled the reduction in penile tumescence in response to pedophilic sexual stimuli. One patient completed all 12 biofeedback sessions, while the other opted for chemical castration and terminated during the 5th session. Both patients showed a reduction in sexual arousal to inappropriate pedophilic stimuli, but the partial treatment case showed neither the degree nor consistency observed in the complete case. It is not possible, to determine whether the improvement in the hormone-treated patient is attributable to behavioral or medical treatment.

Kremsdorf, Ross B. "Orgasmic reconditioning without deviant imagery: A case report with a pedophile." *Behavior Research & Therapy*, 1980, Vol 18(3), 203–207.
Treatment of a male pedophile did not utilize deviant imagery. Treatment consisted of having S masturbate to ejaculation while speaking fantasies concerning adult females aloud. Results show an increase in response to slides of female adults and a decline in response to slides of female children. Follow-up measurement sessions indicated that treatment gains were maintained 2 months following treatment. Results suggest that in some cases the use of deviant imagery during orgasmic reconditioning is not necessary to facilitate treatment. It is also suggested that a comprehensive change in sexual orientation is more than a conditioning process and requires a modification of an individual's self-perception of his/her sexual identity.

Laws, D. R. "Treatment of bisexual pedophilia by a biofeedback-assisted self-control procedure." *Behavior Research & Therapy*, 1980, Vol 18(3), 207–211.
Reports successful treatment of a male pedophile. When told to develop a strategy of self-control using biofeedback, S's response to young boys and girls was treated sequentially in a multiple baseline design. His concurrent response to boys, girls, and adult males was evaluated in separate generalization sessions. Treatment was successful in suppressing deviant response while maintaining nondeviant response in strength. Debriefing revealed that he had used a self-developed technique of covert sensitization to suppress deviant response and had used the biofeedback to confirm and validate this self-control strategy.

Laws, D. R. "Sexual response faking by pedophiles." *Criminal Justice & Behavior*, 1978(Dec), Vol 5(4), 343–356.
The issue of faking erection responses to erotic stimuli is examined by looking at various methods used by a client as he attempted to fake in the laboratory. It is clear that Ss have the capability of generating erection responses to stimuli to which they normally are highly aroused. Steps that the therapist can take so that faking will be minimized are listed.

Leaman, Karen M. "Sexual Abuse: The Reactions of Child and Family." *Child Welfare*, 52: 147–57, 1973.
The sexual abuse or assault of a child can create a crisis for the entire family. Ways in which the child and family react to this crisis and the kind of professional intervention provided them during the crisis have important

implications for the child's welfare—both immediate and long-term. The child's age, emotional maturity, and capacity for intellectual understanding of the episode will greatly influence his or her reactions. The reactions of parents will depend on their perceptions of and emotional responses to the incident. By gaining an understanding of the factors involved in these reactions, it is possible for the professional to anticipate and respond with sensitivity to the needs of all concerned.

Leaman, Karen M. "Sexual Acts Against Children: Medical-Legal Aspects." *Child Today*, 5(4): 2–5, 34–35, July, 1976.

The sexual abuse or assault of a child is a crime. Those who work with child victims and their families cannot ignore the impact of the legal system. Laws concerning sexual acts against children vary from jurisdiction to jurisdiction throughout the country. Stresses the need for physicians, nurses, social workers, police officers, and all other helping persons who work with children to be thoroughly familiar with their obligations under the laws of their own jurisdictions. Draws some inferences about laws dealing with sexual offenses against children and to consider some implications of these laws for the children they are designed to protect.

Lewis, Melvin; Sarrel, Philip M. "Some psychological aspects of seduction, incest, and rape in childhood." *Journal of the American Academy of Child Psychiatry*, 4(4): 606–19, October, 1969.

Sexual abuse of children and adolescents potentially ranges from mild sexual excitement to malicious physical attack. Several case studies illustrate the acute and long-term psychological effects which may result from sexual assault. The family dynamics leading to sexual abuse of children are discussed from a psychoanalytic point of view.

Lukianowicz, Narcyz. "Incest: Paternal." *Britian Journal Psychiatry*, 120(556): 301–13, March, 1972.

Incest was studied within the context of another culture which does not view incest as sexually deviant behavior, but rather as the unfortunate but inevitable result of such conditions as crowded housing, isolation, or libidinous excess. Fifty-four cases of incest in a county in Northern Ireland are reviewed. Over half of these involve father-daughter relationships, generally found to produce the most harmful lasting effects. Character disorders and frigidity resulted in 16 of the 26 girls, while 6 showed no apparent ill effects.

Macdonald, G. J.; Di Furia, G. "A guided self-help approach to the treatment of the habitual offender." *Hospital Community Psychiatry*, 22(10): 310–13, October, 1971.

Examines a program at Western State Hospital for the rehabilitation of sex offenders. A number of the offenses had been committed against children. The program involved at least ninety days observation of the patient by a psychiatrist; the treatment seemed relatively successful, since its rate of recidivism compared favorably with that of state correctional institutions.

McCaghy, Charles H. "Child molesting." *Sex Behavior*, 1:16–24, August, 1971.

A survey of 1,800 college students indicated that one-third of them had childhood experiences with sexual deviants, about half of them involving family members. The experiences are categorized and six types of molesters are described. It was found that the child's response to the experience, and its subsequent effect on him, are greatly influenced by the parent's reaction to the incident.

McCaghy, Charles H. "Drinking and deviance disavowal: the case of child molesters." *Social Problems*, 16(1): 43–49, Summer, 1968.
Reports the results of interviews with 158 men convicted of child molestation. The study represented an investigation of the hypothesis that those molesters who claim that their assaults had been the result of excessive drinking actually disavow their offenses as much as do those who overtly deny committing them. The hypothesis was borne out by the results of the study, which suggested that drinkers who have received a certain amount of rehabilitative therapy are more ready to assume full responsibility for their actions.

McIntyre, Kevin. "Role of mothers in father-daughter incest: a feminist analysis." *Social Work*, Vol 26, No 6, November, 1981, p. 462–466.
Much of the current theory of incest and approaches to treatment ignore the impact of a patriarchal society and culture in promoting and encouraging incestuous assault. Examines sexist assumptions about the roles of family members, on which basis the mother—instead of the actual offender—is usually blamed for the assault. Presents an analysis of incest that seeks to help professionals empower the victims of male violence.

Milner, Alan. "Indecency With Children Act, 1960." *British Journal of Criminology*, 2(3): 282–91, January, 1962.
Considers a British law which allows the conviction of a person who induces a child under 14 to engage in indecent behavior without the use of threats or force. Coupled with harsher penalties for existing sex crimes against children, the Indecency With Children Act is an attempt to encourage more severe punishment of child molesters.

Mitchell, Giles; Wright, Eugene. "Duke Ferdinand's lycanthropy as a disguise motive in Webster's *The Duchess of Malfi*." *Literature & Psychology*, 1975, Vol 25(3), 117–123.
Explores the relationship of incestuous feelings to lycanthropy and to necrophilia, psychoses which afflict Duke Ferdinand in *The Duchess of Malfi*. Necrophilia and lycanthropy are examined in psychoanalytical terms and defined as fundamentally incestuous in nature. It is concluded that modern psychoanalytical studies of the relationship of incest to lycanthropy and necrophilia indicate that Webster's understanding of the matter, whether intuitive or conceptual, is clinically precise.

Mohr, J. W.; Turner R. E. *Pedophilia and Exhibitionism*. Canada: University of Toronto Press, 1964.
Explores the nature of pedophilia and exhibitionism which represent the majority of sex offenses that are coming to the attention of the courts. The prognosis for sex offenders is generally good but it is better for some categories of offenders than others. The heterosexual pedophile who is a first offender is not likely to repeat; the outlook for the homosexual pedophile with a criminal record is much less favorable. The sex offender is usually not mentally ill except with regard to his sexual deviation. Psychotic pedophiles

are rare; they are a bad risk and should not be treated outside an institution. The prediction cannot be made about sex offenders generally because the recidivism rate varies with such factors as the type of offense, the nature of the act, and previous criminal record.

Mokran, A. "Incest and incestuous behavior in forensic practice." *Ceskoslovenska Psychiatrie*, 1976 (Oct), Vol 72(5), 320–323.

Describes 14 cases of confirmed incest, most of which involved sexual intercourse between fathers and daughters. Most of the male incest perpetrators were aggressive, dominant, and alcoholic but not mentally retarded. The average age of the girls was 12.9 yrs. In most cases, they resisted the sexual abuse and confided in their mothers.

Newton, David E. "Homosexual behavior and child molestation: A review of the evidence." *Adolescence*, 1978(Spr), Vol 13(49), 29–43.

Notes that male homosexuality and child molestation tend to be associated with each other in the minds of a large percentage of the general public. Designing a research study to test this hypothesis presents a number of methodological problems which are not easily resolved. Existing studies that contain data on this general question provide no reason to believe that anything other than a random connection exists between homosexual behavior and child molestation.

Panton, James H. "Personality differences appearing between rapists of adults, rapists of children and non-violent sexual molesters of female children." *Research Communications in Psychology, Psychiatry & Behavior*, 1978, Vol 3(4), 385–393.

Analysis of MMPI test results of 30 adult rapists, 20 child rapists, and 28 nonviolent child molesters revealed no significant mean scale differences between the 2 rapist samples but considerable mean scale differences between the rapist and child molester samples. The coded mean profiles of the 2 rapist groups implied aggravated hostility, resentfulness, social alienation, self-centeredness, and impulsive seeking of immediate gratification. In contrast, the mean coded profile of the child molesters implied self-alienation, low self-esteem, self-doubt, anxiety, inhibition of aggression, aversion to violence, need for reinforcement from others, and feelings of inadequacy, insecurity, and fear of heterosexual failure. The motivation of the 2 rapist groups appeared to be more assaultive than sexual, whereas the motivation of the molester group appeared to be the satisfying of sexual needs at an immature level of sexual development.

Paulson, Morris J. "Incest and sexual molestation: Clinical and legal issues." *Journal of Clinical Child Psychology*, 1978(Fall), Vol 7(3), 177–180.

Presents an overview of the coinidal and legal issues surrounding incest and sexual abuse of children and discusses a history of child abuse intervention, which reflects a number of developing stages. Early articles focused on incidence studies, clues for the early identification and treatment of abusive parents, and reporting laws specific to the maltreatment of abusive parents, and reporting laws specific to the maltreatment of children. Needs of the abused and neglected child received attention, with child advocates focusing on the treatment needs of the child and the child's right to same quality of care as that given to its abusing parents. Rights issues in child abuse intervention are discussed, as well as general legal issues that arise in child abuse cases.

Pinta, Emil R. "Treatment of obsessive homosexual pedophilic fantasies with medroxyprogesterone acetate." *Biological Psychiatry*, 1978(Jun), Vol 13(3), 369–373.
Describes a 31-year-old male patient with obsessive homosexual pedophilic fantasies who was treated with psychotherapy and medroxyprogesterone acetate, a progestin with antiandrogen activity. Long-acting MPA, administered for a 2-month period, caused a prompt reduction in fantasies and in accompanying anxiety and depression. MPA was observed to have psychological benefits that outlived its physiological activity.

Rada, Richard T. "Legal aspects in treating rapist." *Criminal Justice & Behavior*, 1978(Dec), Vol 5(4), 369–378.
Outlines various legal and ethical problems involved in dealing with rapists and child molesters. A critical element is to have a detailed understanding of their history, current behavior, response to treatment, and current ability to control behavior. The very act of obtaining such information generates issues of confidentiality and privileged communication normally not dealt with by the average therapist. The issues of confidentiality, privileged communication, and informed consent are explored to illustrate the potential problems incurred while working with such clients.

Regestein, Quentin R.; Reich, Peter. "Pedophilia occurring after onset of cognitive impairment." *Journal of Nervous & Mental Disease*, 1978(Nov), Vol 166(11), 794–798.
Reports the cases of 4 married male patients who first manifested pedophilia and other signs of disinhibition after sustaining illnesses that lead to cognitive impairments. It as argued that although pedophilia may often be related to a longstanding inadequacy of sexual functioning, the onset of pedophilia in an individual without a previous history of sexual perversion may indicate the presence of recently sustained cognitive impairments.

Ringrose, A. C. "Medical assessment of the sexually assaulted female." *Medical Trial Technology Quarterly*, 15:245–47, 1969.
Reports statistics of 100 rape cases occurring in Edmonton, Canada, between July, 1965 and January, 1967. Proper examining and documenting procedures are suggested. It is noted that most cases of child molestation occurred in the summer.

Rosenfeld, Alvin A. "Sexual Misuse and the Family." *Psychiatric Theories*, VIII, No 8 (1978).
Traced the evolution of psychiatric ideas about incest. Incest has been conceptualized as a symptom of family dysfunction rather than as etiologic of certain disorders. It is important to realize that incest and the sexual misuse of children are extreme ends of a spectrum that includes normal sexual life in the family. Different cultures and families express and incorporate sexuality into the family in varying ways. When sexuality is well-integrated into family life, it supports healthy growth and gives a child a heightened sense of worth and security.

Rosenfeld, Alvin A. "Sexual abuse of children." *Journal of the American Medical Association*, 1978 (Jul), Vol 240(1), 43.

Discusses the psychological origins of sexual abuse of children, emphasizing that the situation is more complex than its ordinary characterization as violent acts done by an adult perpetrator to a child victim. Aberrant family functioning is seen as the primary factor in such cases. The need for greater supportive services for these families, interventions that will both end the abuse and provide an adequate atmosphere for childrearing, is discussed.

Sandes, Gladys M. "Sexual assaults on children." *British Journal of Clinical Practice*, 17(3): 143–44, March, 1973.

Outlines medical and legal procedures to follow in cases of sexually assaulted children. A specific format for the medical examination is included. It is advised that the child be seen as soon as possible by a female medical specialist in the presence of a policewoman. The physician's part in obtaining medical evidence in cases of incest and homosexuality is explained.

Schmitt, Barton; Gray, Jane; Kempe, Henry C. "Incest and other family related sexual abuse cases: Physician's guildlines to management." *National Center for the Prevention and Treatment of Child Abuse and Neglect*, Colorado: Nov. 1977.

Sexual abuse of children by parents or caretakers includes incest, sodomy, oral genital contact, and molestation. Most of these incidents occur without force. By contrast, rape usually is defined as sexual intercourse, forced by violence or threats of harm, and with a stranger as the offender. All family-related cases of incest and all molestation cases should be evaluated by the pediatric house staff. Rape cases should also receive a brief workup by the pediatric house staff before requesting gyn-consultation. They should be seen promptly, since the family usually looks upon the situation as an emergency. Guidelines are recommended for the pediatrician.

Schultz, LeRoy G. "The sexual abuse of children and minors: A bibliography." *Child Welfare*, 1979(Mar), Vol 58(3), 147–163.

Presents a bibliography of works that examine the history of sexual abuse of children, normal sexual development of children and minors, forms of sexual abuse, treatment and prevention of sexual abuse, and the state of treatment of the problem.

Schultz, LeRoy G. "The child sex victim: social, psychological and legal perspectives." *Child Welfare*, 52(3): 147–57, March, 1973.

Offers social work techniques for eliminating or at least lessening the trauma suffered by child sex offense victims. Studies indicate that trauma is caused more by the parents' overreaction to the assault and by poorly managed legal proceedings than by the actual sexual offense. If the family decides to prosecute, the social worker must work toward reducing the trauma of testifying. In general, a child's personality development is not damaged by the sexual assault itself, but by events following the assault.

Scott, Edward M. "The sexual offender." *International Journal of Offender Therapy & Comparative Criminology*, 1977, Vol 21(3), 255–263.

Discusses various types of sexual offenses: exhibitionism, child molestation, incest, and rape. Several illustrative case histories are presented, and a clinical profile of the typical offender is described. A theory that a rapist's power over his victim is often violent and threatening is discussed.

Sgroi, Suzanne M. "Sexual molestation of children: The last frontier in child abuse." *Child Today*, 4(3): 18–21, 44, May–June, 1975.
Presents case histories of suspected sexual molestation in children age two months through four years. Three obstacles to identifying the sexually abused child include (1) a lack of willingness to recognize the condition; (2) failure to obtain immediate medical collaboration – including physical and psychological examinations; and (3) a reluctance to report suspected cases to protective services. The reasons for these obstacles and ways to overcome them are discussed.

Sierra, Sali. "Rx to check child molesting." *Illustrated Medical Journal*, 135(6)L, 731–32, 735, 750, June, 1979.
Examines the problems, prevention, and treatment of child molestation. If a child is molested despite self-protection, the hysterical reactions of his parents or the trauma of courtroom procedures may have a more damaging effect on the child than the actual assault. The physician can be particularly helpful at this time in calming the parents and reassuring the child. A discussion of corrective measures for offenders suggests a combination of confinement and treatment. General characteristics of offenders and victims are offered.

Spodak, Michael K. "The hormonal treatment of paraphiliacs with Depo-Provera." *Criminal Justice & Behavior*, 1978(Dec), Vol 5(4), 304–314.
Reviews a newer and more reversible form of castration: chemical castration by use of the female hormone medroxyprogesterone acetate (Depo-Provera®) and the new antiandrogen, cytroterone acetate. These drugs decrease the functioning of the male hormone, testosterone, which decreases overall sexual drive and allows the rapist or child molester to gain control of aggressive sexual urges. Seven paraphiliac cases are briefly described. When coupled with psychotherapy, these drugs are viewed as a valuable adjunct to the therapist's armamentarium.

Summit, Roland. "Sexual Abuse of Children: A Clinical Spectrum." *Canada Psychiatry Association*, 7: 203–217, 1972.
Household sex education, sexualized play, incest, child molestation, and ritual sexual exploitation are all aspects of an interest of adults in the sexuality of children. The objective distinctions between loving support and lustful intrusion are disquietingly subtle. Sexual abuse is the most concealed, most distressing, and most controversial form of child abuse. It deserves the same quality of enlightenment and helping resources that have revolutionized the approach to the forms of abuse.

Swift, Carolyn. "The prevention of sexual child abuse: Focus on the perpetrator." *Journal of Clinical Child Psychology*, 1979(Sum), Vol 8(2), 133–136.
In contrast to conventional approaches to the prevention of sexual assault, which focus on the victim, this paper presents 2 hypotheses relating to the development of the behavior of sexual child abuse in males, reviews empirical evidence supporting these hypotheses, and projects approaches to the prevention of sexual child abuse based on these hypotheses. The hypotheses are that a large proportion of males who abuse children sexually (1) have been sexually abused themselves as children and (2) are sexually ignorant and socially immature.

Terrell, Mary E. "Identifying the sexually abused child in a medical setting." *Health and Social Work*, 1977(Nov), Vol 2(4), 112–130.
Presents findings from a 4 month study of 40 children treated for gonorrhea in a pediatric emergency clinic to explore the problem of sexual abuse of children. A method for identifying sexually abused children in the medical setting is described, and the role of the social worker in these cases is discussed.

Tsai, Mavis. "Therapy groups for women sexually molested as children." *Archives of Sexual Behavior*, 1978(Sep), Vol 7(5), 417–427.
Describes therapy groups composed solely of women who were sexually abused in their childhood. The goals of these groups are the alleviation of sexual guilt and shame and the clarification of emotional and behavioral consequences of molestation. Treatment consisted of a 4-session format: (1) each group participant described her molestation in detail; (2) and (3) focused on how these experiences have affected the women; and (4) dealt with individual stages of recovery and further treatment plans. Clinical findings included feelings of guilt and depression, negative self-image, and problems in interpersonal relationships associated with an underlying mistrust of men. Identification and emotional closeness instilled by a warm and supportive environment where a common bond was shared were results of the groups.

Tsai, Mavis; Edgar, Margaret. "Childhood molestation: Variables related to differential impacts on psychosexual functioning in adult women." *Journal of Abnormal Psychology*, 1979(Aug), Vol 88(4), 407–417.
Three groups of 30 women were recruited to participate: (1) a clinical group consisting of women seeking therapy for problems associated with childhood molestation, (2) a nonclinical group of women molested as children who had never sought therapy and considered themselves to be well adjusted, and (3) a control group. The clinical group was significantly less well adjusted than either the nonclinical or control group on measures of psychosexual functioning and the MMPI. It is proposed that differences in adult adjustment may be mediated by emotional responses evoked at the time of the incident(s), which in turn can be linked to the frequency and duration of molestation and to developmental factors associated with the age of last molestation.

VanDeventer, A. D. "Orgasmic reconditioning to redirect sexual arousal in pedophiles." *Behavior Therapy*, 1978(Nov), Vol 9(5), 748–765.
Pretreatment assessment of sexual arousal indicated high responsiveness to stimuli of young boys, while response to adults was considerably lower or absent. Treatment consisted of having S masturbate to ejaculation while speaking his fantasy aloud. Weeks wherein he masturbated to deviant themes (boys) were alternated with weeks where the theme was nondeviant (women). Each S underwent a measurement session in which his response to 3 deviant and 3 nondeviant slides was evaluated and attitude measures administered. Results for 1 S indicated that sexual response to both stimulus categories declined: he continued to responed as a pedophile. Results for the 2nd S showed considerable increases in response to adults and decline in response to children: shift away from boys to women. Follow-up measurement sessions with this S indicated that treatment gains were maintained 2 months following the end of treatment.

Voight, Jorgen. "Sexual offences in Copenhagen: A medicolegal study." *Forensic Science*, 1(1): 67–76, April, 1972.

The medical and personal data regarding some 710 victims of sexual assault over a ten-year period in Denmark are analyzed. The greatest number of offenses consisted of indecent interference with young girls. Most of the victims belonged to the lower class, and two-thirds of the perpetrators were either acquaintances or strangers.

Weber, Ellen. "Sexual abuse begins at home." *Ms*, 5(10): 64–67, April, 1977.

Explores the emotional and psychological conflicts experienced by victims of incest. The average age of victims is 11, although most girls are trapped in the incestuous relationship for months or even years. At the onset, many naive victims try to please their assailants and maintain secrecy. Teenage victims are more apt to rebel against the forced relationship and confide in a responsible adult or run away from home. As adults, childhood victims of incest suffer numerous sexual problems. The treatment program at the Santa Clara Child Sexual Abuse Treatment Program is described.

Wells, Lloyd A. "Family pathology and father-daughter incest: Restricted psychopathy." *Journal of Clinical Psychiatry*, 1981(May), Vol 42(5), 197–202.

Presents 3 cases of father-daughter incest, each of which illustrates a primary pattern of dysfunction: sociopathy, restricted psychopathy, and family chaos. A family perspective is used that also considers the role of the siblings, mother, and grandparents. Treatment considerations and the ramifications of restricted psychopathy are discussed.

Williams, J. E. "The neglect of incest: a criminologist's view." *Medical Science Law*, 14(1): 64–67, January, 1974.

Studies 68 cases of reported incest considered for parole. Most had previous convictions for crimes; in many cases marital difficulties were noted. The victim was usually the offender's child. In most cases, the offender was not released to his home. The issue of punishment for the crime of incest is discussed, as is the need for research on the role of the victim. The environmental and social problems which often prompt incestuous relationships should be defined and remedied.

Wilson, Jim L. "The dynamics of incest: Presentation of one family in acute crisis." *Journal of Family Practice*, 1978 (Aug), Vol 7(2), 363–367.

Presents a grand rounds discussion of a case of father-step-daughter incest and a general discussion of incest. The incidence and cultural and legal aspects of incest, as well as its dynamics, are reviewed. Participants include a psychiatrist, a 3rd year family practice resident, a marriage and family counselor, and a family physician who is professor and head of a department of family practice.

Yorukoglu, A. "Children not severely damaged by incest with a parent." *Journal of Child Psychology*, 5: 111–24, 1976.

Two separate cases of incest between a parent and a child in early puberty are detailed. In both cases, the children suffered no apparent psychological damage.

INDEX

S

T

U

V

W

X

Y

Z